AVIATION SAFETY PROGRAMS —
A MANAGEMENT HANDBOOK

By Richard H. Wood

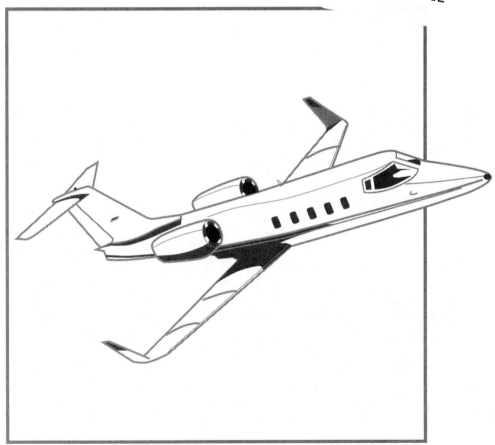

Library of Congress Cataloging-in-publication number: **91-199507**

Jeppesen Sanderson Inc.
55 Inverness Dr. East
Englewood, Colorado 80112-5498
ISBN 0-88487-236-X

JS312627D

AUTHOR _____

Richard Wood has been in the aviation safety business for over 30 years. He is a professional pilot, a Safety Engineer (California) and a Certified Safety Professional (CSP). He was Chief of Safety Policy and Programs for the United States Air Force, a Professor of Safety Science at the University of Southern California and President of Southern California Safety Institute. He has taught aviation safety subjects all over the world and is the author of numerous books, articles, and papers on aviation safety. He is co-author (with Robert W. Sweginnis) of *Aircraft Accident Investigation*; the current definitive text on that subject.

He lives (and writes) in Snohomish, Washington where he is an aviation safety consultant. He can be reached via e-mail at woodrh@ix.netcom.com.

To my wife, Priscilla.

A lady of infinite patience and understanding.

ACKNOWLEDGEMENTS ————————

This edition benefited from a technical review by people who have used the first edition as a teaching text. They are all experienced in the field of aviation safety and very familiar with the shortcomings of the first edition. Their comments and suggestions on the manuscript were invaluable.

The technical reviewers were: **Terry S. Bowman, Ph.D.**, Associate Professor, Aviation Management and Flight, Southern Illinois University at Carbondale; **Olof Fritsch**, former Chief AIG of the International Civil Aviation Organization and Course Director for the Swedavia Institute of Aviation Safety in Stockholm, Sweden; **Don Hunt**, Associate Professor, Embry-Riddle Aeronautical University; **William Martin**, Professor of Aeronautical Science, Embry-Riddle Aeronautical University; **Jim Page**, Aviation Safety Consultant and former Director of Ground Safety, United States Air Force; **Michael J. Polay**, Associate Professor, Embry-Riddle Aeronautical University; **John Richardson**, Director of Operations, Southern California Safety Institute; **Lemuel C. Shattuck**, Assistant Professor, Central Missouri State University; **Bob Sweginnis**, Associate Professor, Embry-Riddle Aeronautical University; and **David W. Thomson**, CHCM, Safety Consultant and Director of Program Development, Southern California Safety Institute.

Also appreciated were the ideas and comments from my good friend and colleague **Jerome Lederer**, President Emeritus, Flight Safety Foundation and retired Director of Safety of NASA.

The drudgery of proof-reading was done superbly by **Valerie Radle**. At Jeppesen, **Dale Hurst**, Editor, made it all look like a book; a skill largely unappreciated outside of the writing world.

Thank you all.

PREFACE
TO THE SECOND EDITION _____

In the six years since printing the first edition of this book, our industry has seen many changes involving safety. In the United States, FAR Part 121 operators are now required to have a Director of Safety. By inference, you would think that they are also required to have an aviation safety program. That's not exactly what the Federal Aviation Regulation says, but we are going to assume that is the intent.

Also, the United States embarked on an initiative to reduce air transport accidents to zero. That deserves expanded comment as does potential problems involving contractors.

Two new chapters have been added; one on Flight Line Safety and the other on Environmental Safety. New material has been added to all other chapters. All references have been moved to the annotated bibliography in the back of the book. This is meant not only as a list of references, but a source of additional help.

Since the book is widely used as a text, discussion questions have been added to most chapters.

As I said in the first edition, you build an aviation safety program to suit the needs of your organization. You do not need everything in this book. Also, there are still no magic answers to all aviation safety problems. There are choices. The correct choice is always the one that will work in your organization based on your resources, time available, and company objectives.

It is still true that aviation safety is very much a "people" problem as opposed to an equipment problem. We must consider not only the crewmembers and maintenance technicians who are exposed to the risks of aviation, but the managers who are in a position to act (or not act) on managing those risks.

On the whole, aviation safety is a growth industry. Read and grow with it.

RHW

TABLE OF CONTENTS

SECTION 1

SECTION 2

SECTION 3

SECTION 4

INTRODUCTION TO SECTION I

THE BASICS

Most of the theory and philosophy about aviation safety is in the first six chapters. Here, we try to put aviation safety into perspective and show where it fits in an organization and what it can contribute. We also cover some aviation safety concepts and define many of the terms we are going to use.

The chapter on prevention methods lists ideas that are fundamental to any safety program. Finally, there is a chapter on risk management concepts. This is for managers who already realize that aviation safety is a management problem.

THE ECONOMICS OF AVIATION SAFETY

CHAPTER 1

INTRODUCTION

I started out in this business on the wrong foot. I assumed that the Director of Safety carried a fairly big stick and that all he had to do was point out a safety problem and people would drop whatever they were doing and correct it.

Wrong! Not only did they not stop, they didn't even pause in what they were doing to tell me they weren't going to correct it.

To make matters worse, I discovered that other managers who couldn't get one of their problems solved would claim that it was a safety problem in order to get a higher priority. Up at the top, where priorities were set, I found that my legitimate safety problems were lost in a sea of fake safety problems.

It took me a year or so to figure out what was wrong. Believe me, it was a tough lesson. If you'll stick with me here, I think I can save you some time.

Let's forget the emotional aspects of safety and look at some cold hard facts. Safety is not a moral problem or an ethical problem or a pain and suffering problem. It is an economic problem. Safety, by itself, generates a lot of sympathy, but very little action. Only the economics of safety generate action. In the entire history of safety, nothing good ever happened unless it was either economically beneficial or mandated by the government. Granted, we are sometimes forced to act on a safety problem for moral or ethical reasons. When that happens, though, it is frequently because we are confronted with a financial penalty if we do not act. Failure to anticipate that situation is usually the result of myopic vision on the part of management or, possibly, failure on the part of the Safety Director to adequately explain this to management. Sorry, but that's the way the system works. I have been there, done that (as the saying goes) and there is no need for you to repeat those mistakes. This is one of those things that you don't have to like, but you do have to understand. Money talks. Sympathy doesn't.

As an example, consider how we got into the safety business in the first place. In the 1800s, the industrial revolution was in progress and there was no organized effort to reduce accidents or injuries. The worker injured on the job suddenly had no income and large medical expenses. In many cases he became an instant pauper. If the accident was the fault of the company and he wanted compensation, he had to hire a lawyer and take the company to court; which almost never worked. The company could simply outlast him.

In the late 1800s, an idea, called workers compensation began brewing in Europe. Basically, it said that the employer should be responsible for on-the-job injuries and the injured worker should receive medical treatment and be compensated for loss of income until he was able to work again. This idea migrated to the United States and by 1930 all states had workers compensation laws on the books. The costs of the program were paid by the employer through a mandatory insurance scheme where the employer's premiums were based on his accident record. Suddenly it became clear to the employer that it was a lot cheaper to not have the accident in the first place than it was to pay for the results. That economic incentive was the basis for the entire industrial safety movement. Prior to that, there was no incentive. All an accident cost the employer was some sympathy and perhaps a bouquet of flowers for the funeral.

Another example. A major automobile manufacturer got in trouble several years ago based on their calculation that it would cost more to correct a safety problem than it would to pay for the expected accidents. That news hit the street during litigation over some accidents and, as it turned out, the manufacturer seriously underestimated how a jury would react to that line of reasoning. That miscalculation cost the manufacturer a lot of money.

Nevertheless, there is nothing wrong with the manufacturer's logic. If a dollar spent on safety does not prevent at least a dollar's worth of accidents, he should spend his dollar somewhere else. That makes sense and that's exactly how many executives view aviation safety. "I have more things I could spend money for than I have money. If you want me to spend money on a safety project, you better show me why that's a better use of my money than any other project."

In other words, our entire industry is driven by economic forces; mainly money. Like it or not, you must put safety in those terms or nothing will happen.

Fair enough. Let's start with some basic business concepts.

COST OF RISK

In the business world, we pay others to assume certain risks for us. We call this "insurance" and we do it by either paying premiums to an insurance company who can spread the risk around a little or by being self-insured (government agencies, for example) and setting aside funds to be used to cover risk. Either way, risk has a cost and we are paying for it.

If we never have an aircraft accident, then our cost of risk is the minimum insurance premium that we can get. It never gets any lower and it is a fixed cost of doing business.

If, on the other hand, we do have an aircraft accident, then our cost of risk is the minimum insurance premium plus the excess premium (bad record, you know) plus uninsured costs or losses.

UNINSURED COSTS

The term "uninsured costs" deserves an explanation. Think of it this way. When you have a "fender-bender" in your automobile, you may eventually get it fixed and paid for by someone else's insurance company, but you'll never recover the costs of the time, inconvenience, and aggravation of doing so. Your time has some value, as does your inability to use your car while it is in the shop. Also, if the accident turns out to be your fault and your insurance company pays, you can expect to pay higher premiums next year. Those are uninsured costs and in the case of an aircraft accident, they can get really big.

Any textbook on safety will talk at some length about the uninsured costs of accidents. The reason is that uninsured costs are generally double or triple the insured costs. In the case of aircraft accidents, that may be conservative. One example is the situation where an airline executive discovered that the real cost of some minor ground damage to an aircraft was not the damage itself. It was the cost of aircraft downtime (loss of revenue) and system rescheduling costs which were nearly 70 times the damage costs. A ratio of 70 to 1 is probably a little high, but it can certainly happen.

To give you some idea of the numbers involved, typical insurance payouts for a major accident (1995) were $120-200 million U.S. dollars for hull loss and an average liability of $2.8 million per passenger. One specific example involving a B737 resulted in $35 million for the hull and total liability of $375 million. Because of those costs, that particular airline's insurance premiums are about twice the average for the industry. That ought to be an incentive! (It should be noted that accidents generate insurance premium increases for the entire industry; although the companies having the accidents have by far the largest increases.)

On the other end of the scale, ground damage to aircraft (or "hangar rash" as it is sometimes called) is incredibly expensive. This type of damage is rarely classified as an aircraft accident and, unless someone was injured, it doesn't get reported as a ground accident either. Thus the numbers are not precisely accurate, but best estimates are that the airline industry in the United States pays about $850 million a year for this type of damage. You would think there would be some incentive there, too.

An understanding of these uninsured or indirect costs is fundamental to an understanding of the economics of aviation safety. Let's examine some basic ideas about costs.

We insure our airplanes for hull and liability. For our own employees, we are already paying workers compensation premiums and we are covered for their injuries. When it is time to report the cost of the accident, we add up all those insurance payments and use that number. We almost never consider the uninsured costs because they are difficult to calculate and they do not necessarily occur with every accident. Furthermore, they are hidden to the extent that we cover them out of some other budgetary pocket and we don't really notice them. If we are going to correctly assess the cost of accidents, though, we have to understand them. Here are some typical uninsured costs of an aircraft accident.

- **INSURANCE DEDUCTIBLES**. The insurance policy on your car requires you to pay the first $300 or $500 (whatever) of any accident. That's called the "deductible." In the aviation business, our insurance deductible tends to be quite high. This is money directly out of our pocket and it is not recoverable. In the airline business, a deductible of about one million on the hull is not unusual.

- **LOST TIME AND OVERTIME**. When an aircraft accident occurs, the flying operation generally comes to an abrupt halt — at least until the dust settles and we are able to get back in business. During this time, though, we are still going to pay everybody who happens to be on duty. In industry, this cost is called "stand-around costs." The production line has stopped and everybody is just standing around — and getting paid for it. Furthermore, the accident is going to generate a lot of work for many of our managers and employees. We are either going to do this work at the expense of whatever we're supposed to be doing, or we are going to pay a lot of people overtime to get the job done. One corporate operator estimated that the aftermath of an aircraft accident consumed two full man-years each for two of their executives. That's an uninsured cost.

- **COST OF INVESTIGATION**. This can get expensive. We are going to assign one or more of our employees full time to the investigation and we are going to pick up all of their travel and living expenses plus salary. We are going to use our copying machines (and time) to furnish any and all documents requested by the investigative team. We may provide some facilities for the investigators to lay out the wreckage or office space for them — all at a cost. If the wreckage is inaccessible, the costs really go up. The National Transportation Safety Board may pay for some of the recovery, but rarely all of it.

- **COST OF HIRING AND TRAINING REPLACEMENTS PERSONNEL**. If our employees have been injured or killed and we intend to stay in business, we are going to have to hire and train replacements. There is a cost to this. Ask any personnel director.

- **LOSS OF PRODUCTIVITY OF INJURED PERSONNEL**. Let's suppose that we are a Fixed Base Operator (FBO) offering charter services and one of our pilots is injured in an aircraft accident. That pilot's services had some economic value to us and we lose the value of those services until we can find a replacement. Maybe the replacement will start as a copilot and not be upgraded to captain for several months. Then, we also lose the difference in the value of the services of the copilot and the captain. Another example. Suppose we injure one of our aircraft maintenance technicians and we only had ten of them to begin with. Our choices are to do less maintenance, work the other nine longer hours or hire temporary help. None of those are particularly attractive and there are some uninsured costs there.

Those are fairly simple examples of the hidden costs of injuries. What if we are a corporate operator and one (or several) of our passengers are senior officers in the corporation? Does their injury or loss represent an uninsured cost to the company? You bet!

- **COST OF CLEANUP AND RESTORATION OF ORDER**. Someone has to clean up the mess. Let's suppose that during the aircraft accident, residual fuel was spilled and soaked into the ground. Cleaning that up is usually an uninsured cost. Within that same subject, suppose we have had fatalities among our passengers. We are probably going to provide travel and lodging for relatives and assist with funeral arrangements. How do we account for those costs?

- **LOSS OF USE OF EQUIPMENT**. This is a big one. If we have four airplanes and we break one — that's 25% of our revenue producing capability. Airlines have discovered that cost of damage is sometimes minor compared to loss of revenue. Actually, this category is almost a hidden problem within the industry. Ground damage to our aircraft costs us revenue in terms of aircraft down time, but we tend to ignore that loss if the damage does not qualify as an accident. See Chapter 23 on Flight Line Safety.

- **COST OF RENTAL OR LEASE OF REPLACEMENT EQUIPMENT.** We may need to lease equipment just to stay in business.

- **INCREASED OPERATING COSTS ON REMAINING EQUIPMENT.** Suppose we have four airplanes and we break one. Initially, we may try to maintain the same flying schedule with three planes instead of four. This is going to result in some unexpected maintenance and inspection costs on those planes. In addition, we may pick up some night and overtime maintenance costs.

- **LOSS OF SPARES OR SPECIALIZED EQUIPMENT.** If we destroy a one-of-a-kind airplane, which is not unusual in this business, we also lose our stock of spare parts and specialized equipment for that airplane — minus, of course, the resale value of the parts.

- **FINES AND CITATIONS.** It happens. The FAA, the Occupational Safety and Health Administration (OSHA) and the Environmental Protection Administration (EPA) are all empowered to impose financial penalties as a result of an accident. Also, as we now know, the FAA can shut an airline down if it feels that it is unsafe.

- **LEGAL FEES RESULTING FROM THE ACCIDENT.** When an aircraft accident occurs, your legal counsel starts the meter running. Protecting your interests is likely to get expensive.

- **INCREASED INSURANCE PREMIUMS.** They always go up after an accident.

- **LIABILITY CLAIMS IN EXCESS OF INSURANCE.** The final settlement may exceed your insurance. Because of that possibility, you may have to put money into escrow now.

- **LOSS OF BUSINESS AND DAMAGE TO REPUTATION.** What did this accident really cost you in terms of your business? It's hard to say. Some major oil companies will not charter aircraft from an operator with a bad accident record. Some passengers will absolutely not fly on certain airlines.

- **COST OF CORRECTIVE ACTION.** This is hard to calculate as an uninsured cost. It is not unusual, though, to be in a situation where you previously had an opportunity to correct a problem at a reasonable cost. Now that you have had an accident, you are forced to take the same action at any cost. Prices are probably higher now and you are in no position to shop around or bargain. The loss is the difference between what you could have paid and what you are going to pay.

These are just a few of the uninsured and hidden costs that result from an aircraft accident. Calculating them is difficult, but it is worth doing occasionally, because it reminds management of what an accident really costs. An awareness of this concept of uninsured costs is essential to understanding the next step.

ACCOUNTING FOR ACCIDENT COSTS

On the company's profit and loss statement, profit is the difference between gross income and costs. In a deregulated or free enterprise system, income is generally determined by the marketplace and the biggest profits go to the organization that can operate at the lowest cost. To a large degree, modern management is an exercise in controlling costs.

We deal with two types of costs — fixed and variable. Fixed costs are those that we must pay just to stay in business. We can't do anything about them. In aviation, these include the costs of fuel, spare parts, landing fees, licenses, debt payments and so on. Included as a fixed cost is the minimum cost of risk — no accidents. This is our minimum insurance premium. Our variable costs are those we can do something about. These include personnel costs, training, safety, advertising, public relations, and so on. Included here are our excess insurance premiums and our uninsured costs (cost of risk with accidents.)

As a general rule, there is about an 80/20 split between fixed and variable costs. Eighty percent of our costs are fixed and we can't do anything about them. Twenty percent are variable and here is where managers manage. In the aviation industry, the cost of excess premiums and uninsured losses runs about five percent of total costs — not an unmanageable amount. As a percent of variable costs, though, they may be perhaps twenty to twenty-five percent of those costs. That's a lot and should get the attention of most managers. When we talk aircraft accident prevention and aviation safety, we are talking about something that may represent a large portion of our variable costs. It deserves, therefore, an equally large portion of our interest, time, and energy. That's what we mean when we say safety is an economic issue.

If you are sold on that idea, then one of the ways you could define safety is that it is a means of controlling costs. Not only does it eliminate the cost of doing something wrong; it eliminates the cost of doing something twice when it could have been done correctly in the first place. That idea works out nicely with some ideas presented in later chapters about where safety fits in our company. Beyond economics, there are some other good reasons for having an aviation safety program.

LITIGATION

These days, having an aviation safety program won't necessarily keep you out of court, although it ought to help. If you do get involved in litigation, consider that at some point the opposing attorney is going to ask about your company's attitude toward safety. You, naturally, are going to testify that safety has a high priority in your organization and that you are absolutely dedicated to a safe operation. OK so far, but how are you going to handle the next question? "Would you please show the jury exactly what your safety program is and how it is managed?" If you don't really have a safety program, that's a tough question.

PUBLIC RELATIONS

The existence of an aviation safety program ought to be marketable. Some companies are reluctant to mention the word "safety" for fear of scaring the passengers, but they are wrong. Thanks to our friends in the news media, the public already has a strong suspicion that airplanes are dangerous and they are naturally suspicious of any organization that tries to pretend that they aren't. The fact that you have a strong safety program and are genuinely concerned about your customers ought to get you more business; not less.

If an accident does occur, you can expect your safety program to be put under a microscope; not only by the news media, but by the regulators and investigators.

MISSION

Maybe you are operating aircraft for a government agency and don't have to worry much about profit or litigation or customers. Try this.

During World War II, we (the United States) geared up our production capabilities and we manufactured airplanes at a rate that is unbelievable even today. We could build an airplane much faster and cheaper than we could train a pilot to fly it. Consequently, the loss of an airplane meant very little to us. There were plenty more where they came from and we had more of them than we could actually use in any theater of operations. Our ability to complete the mission seldom suffered from a lack of airplanes.

This attitude prevailed well into the 1950s and 60s and it is still alive and well today in many government organizations. The truth is that there is no bottomless barrel of airplanes and there hasn't been for some time. You were given X number of airplanes to perform a particular mission and if you destroy one, you are expected to perform the same mission with one less airplane. We only bought so many planes and there are no spares. If you break enough of them, you are out of business, because you can no longer perform your mission. In this respect, inability to perform the mission ought to have about the same effect that inability to produce revenue has on the commercial operator. The results are the same.

SO WHAT DO WE DO?

There are really only two choices. We either need an aviation safety program or we don't.

WE DON'T NEED AN AVIATION SAFETY PROGRAM. This used to be a common reaction, since aviation safety programs were not mandatory. One airline, for example, decided not to have a formal aviation safety program because, "In this airline, aviation safety is a fundamental part of everyone's job." To prove that, they changed all of the titles of their executives. Now we have the Vice President for Operations and Safety; the Vice President for Maintenance and Safety; the Vice President for Passenger Services and Safety; and so on. It was, to put it bluntly, all lip service. The airline's real interest in safety didn't go much beyond the titles on the offices and the stationery. Everyone may have been involved, but no one was responsible. The Vice President for Ops and Safety, for example, didn't mind having safety as part of his title, but he had no plans for committing any portion of his workday to it. He had plenty of operations problems to keep him busy.

That's probably an extreme example, but it is easy to spot an organization that does not have a safety program. There is no internal reporting system; no deliberate selection of standards; no investigation or resolution of incidents or hazards; and (worst of all) no knowledge on the part of top management as to whether things are safe or unsafe. Since they haven't had any accidents recently, they assume that things are safe and they don't really need a safety program. As we shall see, that is not a good way to measure safety. If they do have an accident, it is not unusual for them to rush out and hire someone (frequently a retired military officer) to become an instant vice president for safety. This doesn't hurt and might even help; but it's a little late.

The actual requirement for an aviation safety program in the United States is not well defined. If you are operating under FAR Part 121, you are required to have a Director of Safety (FAR Part 119.65), but it does not specifically say that you must also have an aviation safety program. Obviously, that is not the intent of the requirement and that is certain to change. In any case, the argument that you are not required to have an aviation safety program may be technically correct, but it is not going to be well-received as an explanation of why you don't have one.

WE DO NEED AN AVIATION SAFETY PROGRAM. Good. You're convinced. That's probably why you are reading this book, so let's approach this logically.

HOW BIG A PROGRAM DO WE NEED? That depends on how big we are. How many planes do we have? How many different types? Do we operate out of one central location like a corporate flying operation or are we dispersed like a helicopter operator with several hospital EMS contracts? Do we fly locally, regionally, nationally, or internationally? There are some fundamentals that go with any program, but there are some program elements that we may be able to do without. Remember, we are going to build our program to meet the needs of our organization.

WHERE ARE WE GOING TO PUT IT? Interesting question. Good people can make any organizational structure work. Poor people will fail in the best of organizations. Some organizations, however, will work better than others and we are going to discuss that.

WHAT WILL IT DO? Another good question. We don't need an aviation safety program just for the sake of having one. That could be worse than no program at all. We ought to have some expectations, goals, or objectives for it. If we don't know where the program is supposed to go, how will we know when it gets there?

WHO WILL RUN IT? Do we need to go out and hire a full time Director of Safety? Maybe. If we are operating under FAR Part 121, that's exactly what we need. The rest of us are going to assign one of our pilots or maintenance supervisors to handle aviation safety as an additional or collateral duty. Does that work? Yes, it can work quite well. We'll discuss that. Can the program be combined with some other program such as security or workers compensation? This is discussed at some length in Chapter 4. The short answer is that safety does not combine well with ongoing activities that are likely to take precedence over it. If, for example, you were suddenly handed the job of Safety and Personnel Administration, which part of that do you think would consume most of your time?

HOW DO WE GET STARTED? Easy. Here's our first list of things to do.

1. Decide who's in charge. Where do we place responsibility and authority?

2. Determine the scope of our program. How big a program do we need? What will it include?

3. Agree on program policy, goals, and objectives.

4. Get organized. Assign responsibility. Decide where in our organization we are going to fit the aviation safety program and who is going to run it.

5. Pick the elements that will make up our aviation safety program. Describe how the program elements will work. Write all this down and publish it as the company aviation safety program.

6. Determine how we are going to measure the success (or failure) of our program. How will we know if it is working?

Does all this sound like an exercise in management? It should, because it is. Good aviation safety programs are managed the same way any other successful business activities are managed. That's what the rest of this book is all about.

DISCUSSION QUESTIONS

1. Let's suppose that one of our airliners is parked at the gate and being serviced. The flight crew and passengers are not on board. The catering truck is mis-positioned and, as it is elevated, it damages the fuselage skin near the right rear door. There are no injuries, but the damage requires sheet metal repair. Technically, this is not an aircraft accident (See Chapter 3) because there was no one on board intending to fly. It isn't even an industrial accident (OSHA) because there were no injuries. Suppose, though, that you are the Director of Safety for this airline.

   • What, if anything, are you going to call this event?

   • Will it be reported? Investigated? By who?

   • What are the direct (insured) costs of this event?

   • What are the possible indirect (uninsured) costs of this event?

2. You are the Director of Safety for an airline and you are recommending installation of a new piece of safety equipment on all of your aircraft. The FAA will probably not make it mandatory; at least not for several years. What arguments will you use in your recommendation?

3. The president of your organization has decided that there will be a full time Director of Safety and you're it! The president has not decided (or doesn't know) what a Director of Safety is supposed to do, so you have the opportunity to define your job for him. What are you going to tell him?

AVIATION SAFETY CONCEPTS

SAFETY FIRST

The slogan "Safety First" has been around a long time and is probably the result of some long-forgotten safety manager's efforts to bring emphasis to the safety program. It sounds good, but, unfortunately, it isn't true and never has been. Belief in it has led many a safety manager down the wrong path. It implies that the mere mention of safety will make everyone drop what they are doing and focus exclusively on safety. Some managers who can't achieve an objective by any other means have been known to add the word "safety" to the objective in the hope of getting a little more attention. For the reasons stated in Chapter 1, it doesn't work that way.

All flying organizations were formed to achieve some goal or objective — and it wasn't safety. Perhaps we have a mission to perform, or maybe we're hauling passengers or cargo and trying to make money for our stockholders. Whatever we're doing, our primary objective is not to just be safe. If it were, the obvious way to achieve that objective would be to chain the airplanes to the ramp and not let anyone fly them.

Safety certainly fits into our objectives somewhere, but its role is that of supporting the primary mission or objective and helping to get the job done — safely, but done! The old time industrial safety inspector (who really believed that safety was first) is often pictured running around with a handful of red tags and padlocks. By shutting down operations and taking equipment out of service, he was actively helping to not get the job done and he was at least partially responsible for the reputation safety people have among some managers.

In the aviation business, that approach just won't work. The first thing we have to do is to put safety in perspective and decide exactly where it fits in our organization and what level of safety we need. It clearly belongs somewhere above the lip service level where we have no intention of letting safety influence operations, but below the number one objective level where we let safety drive the operation.

Safety is actually a method of controlling costs (See Chapter 1). It allows us to do whatever we're doing repetitively with minimum damage to our equipment or injury to our personnel. It assists management by developing the most efficient method of accomplishing a mission with the least risk. The aviation safety manager is in the business of actively helping to achieve the organization's objectives.

SAFETY VERSUS MISSION

Isn't there an inherent contradiction between aviation safety and a military combat mission?

It would certainly seem so and we have certainly treated it as a contradiction in the past. In World War II and Korea we literally threw away the safety manual with the attitude that, "This is combat. We don't have to be safe anymore." And we weren't. Our accidental losses exceeded our combat losses and not by just a little bit. In World War II we lost more pilots in training accidents in the United States than we did in combat in all theaters of operation. Many of us think that it was even worse. Combat losses were somewhat expected and acceptable while accidents generated a lot of unpleasant paperwork. There was a definite tendency to mis-classify accidents as combat losses.

Along came Vietnam and this type of thinking started to change. It became obvious that we could not afford that volume of accidental losses and still have anything left to fight with. The war in Vietnam included a fairly strong aviation safety program which didn't cure the problem by any means, but it took a pretty good cut at it. It did keep the accidents within the same general range as the combat losses. One lesson learned from that era is that whatever safety standards we impose upon ourselves in peacetime ought to work equally well in combat. If they don't, they will be ignored.

The war in the Persian Gulf was a significant improvement. United States aircraft accidents (non-operational losses) were less than the combat or operational losses — which were very few indeed. That is a remarkable achievement and one that contributed significantly to the outcome. If our aircraft accident rate had been anywhere near that of WWII, we would have been out of business in a few days and there is some doubt whether the American public would have supported continued involvement. It is clear that aviation safety was taken very seriously in the Persian Gulf.

This brings up a point that is applicable to any flying operation, military or civil. Many of our operations and maintenance standards are really safety standards. They were developed as a result of some safety problem or resulted from the recommendations of a safety manager. Regardless of what we call them, they have to be practical or they'll be ignored in favor of getting the job done.

BLOOD PRIORITY

This term has been around for a long time in the aviation safety business and it is sometimes called "Tombstone Safety." It is still used and it is still generally true. It refers to the idea that it is a lot easier to get something corrected if you have just had an accident that has killed someone — there is literally blood on the accident report. The corollary to this is that it is difficult to get something corrected if it has not caused an accident. This is the, "If it ain't broke, don't fix it" mentality. That's a cute saying, but we can't operate airplanes without maintaining them. We do a lot of aircraft maintenance that is purely preventive; not corrective. Likewise, we can't pretend that we have an accident prevention program if we are unwilling to correct hazardous situations that haven't (yet) produced an accident. To quote an old safety adage, "If you need an accident to prove that you have a problem, then you are part of the problem."

KNOWN PRECEDENT

This is another term that has been around a long time. This is the idea that there aren't too many new causes of accidents. There are new technologies, to be sure. Composite structures don't fail in the same manner as metal structures, for example. The root causes of the failures (overstress, maybe) tend to remain pretty much the same. Part of the aviation safety manager's stock in trade is in knowing, generally, what has caused accidents in the past. This provides the answer to the question, "Why correct it? It hasn't caused an accident yet." Answer: "Yes it has. It just hasn't caused one here — yet."

THE RANDOMNESS OF DAMAGE AND INJURY

When a hazardous situation occurs, we have no way of predicting the results of that situation. Take an engine failure. Maybe the fuel pump fails and the engine just quits. What happens next is strictly random and depends entirely on what we happen to be doing at the time, and how badly we need that engine. The results can vary from a major aircraft accident with fatalities, to a mere nuisance if it occurs while we're taxiing. Keep in mind, now, that this is the same engine and in all cases it fails for the same reason. Question: Which failure was most important and deserves a full scale investigation and correction? Answer: What difference does it make? One failure did result in serious damage and injuries, but the other one certainly could have had the same result. Does the fact that it didn't mean that we don't have to worry about it? Of course not. Any engine failure should be treated seriously as it obviously could have had disastrous consequences under different circumstances. As an example, engine failures on landing roll-out may not be taken seriously — until someone needs that engine for a go-around. It doesn't make much sense to wait until the failure kills someone before we investigate it and correct it.

But isn't that exactly what we do? Our investigation and correction activities tend to be based on the amount of damage and injury — which is random. We don't really have prevention programs; we have accident correction programs.

The basic problem is that all of our definitions of an accident (Chapter 3) include some degree of damage or injury. If the event doesn't involve damage or injury, it may get some attention, but it most likely will not. Thus, our efforts tend to be focused on the results (which are random) instead of on the event itself.

There are some strong feelings among aviation safety professionals that we should change that; and perhaps we will. Because of the excellent safety record, aviation, as an industry, could probably make this change more easily than any other industry.

Until that happens, though, the best approach is for aviation organizations to build strong incident and hazard reporting programs. That will work and those techniques are covered elsewhere in this book.

Let's summarize by making a few points about our present focus on damage and injury.

- There is very little correlation between any particular event (or hazard, if you prefer) and any resulting damage or injury. In aviation, as a matter of fact, an accident involving damage or injury is the least likely result of any event.

- Concentrating our investigation and correction resources on a random and unlikely result is bound to be inefficient. In some cases, we are going to spend our money foolishly trying to correct something that has a very low probability of ever happening again. Consider a Military KC-135 which had what should have been a very minor taxi accident involving a wing tip hitting the tower supporting a set of parking ramp lights. Unfortunately, the tower began swaying and, due to its design and the weight of the lights, it collapsed on top of the KC-135 doing an immense amount of damage. Because of the damage, the accident generated a large investigation and a thick report. Regardless of the amount of damage, it was still nothing more than a taxi accident and it should not have taken very long to figure out what happened and how to prevent it. In other cases, of course, we are going to miss the opportunity to fix something because we are generally unwilling to spend much of our time on things that don't produce damage or injury. In the case of the KC-135, we obviously could have straightened out our taxi procedures without waiting for the plane to hit something.

- In theory, any particular event has a certain built-in probability for disaster. In aviation, this probability is usually low, but it certainly exists. If we were able to calculate these probabilities with any accuracy, we should apply our preventive efforts to those with the highest likelihood of disaster regardless of whether that disaster has ever occurred. On the other hand, we should not waste our money trying to prevent something of very low probability even though we realize that a disaster is still technically possible. The pole could still fall on the airplane, but how often do we think that's going to happen?

- Aviation safety needs to be "event oriented" and not "result oriented." Aircraft accident investigations are a part, but only a small part, of the broader field of aviation safety.

ZERO ACCIDENT RATE

Is it possible to achieve a zero aircraft accident rate? Sure — theoretically. If each accident is individually preventable, then they are all collectively preventable. There are no (or almost no) accidents that can be truly termed, "Acts of God." Therefore, a zero accident rate is achievable. It's a good goal. In 1995, the Secretary of Transportation for the United States established that as a goal for commercial air transport.

In practice, though, there are two factors that we ought to recognize and accept. First, the risk in any operation is never zero. It may be very low, but it is always a positive number. Since the risk never goes to zero, neither does the accident rate. It just gets very low.

This would seem to argue that we could never achieve a zero accident rate. What actually happens is that we drive the rate down to such a low number that the mathematicians refer to it as "a number so small as to be indistinguishable from zero." Translated, that means that it should never happen.

Can we do that with all aircraft accidents? Not yet. We can probably do it with certain types of accidents and we should. We could, for example, drive runway incursion accidents down to one of those numbers "indistinguishable from zero." When we have a runway incursion accident, we seldom learn anything we didn't already know. Other types of accidents, controlled flight into terrain (CFIT) accidents, for instance, will require more work. That shouldn't stop us from trying.

The second factor affecting a zero accident rate involves economics. Preventing accidents involves some expense and the costs go up as the rate goes down. It takes money, time, and effort to just maintain a good rate. It takes even more to lower it. At some point, an additional dollar spent on prevention does not prevent a dollar's worth of damage or injury.

At that point, an organization's enthusiasm for spending money on prevention starts to drop off. We should mention that no organization has reached that point yet. A dollar well spent on prevention is still one of the best investments a company can make.

THE CONCEPT OF CHANGE

If we want to prevent accidents from happening, we are going to have to change something. Prevention requires change. If what we are presently doing is producing more accidents or incidents than we want, we are going to have to do it differently, with different equipment, or whatever. If we don't change something, we are going to continue to have those same accidents and incidents. To quote one anonymous bit of wisdom, "If you continue to do what you did, you are going to continue to get what you got!"

Now, that would seem self-evident; maybe even a little simplistic. It can't be too simplistic, though, because there are a lot of people out there who either don't understand it or don't believe it. That disbelief is what makes the whole science of accident prediction or accident rate projection work. It is very easy to take last year's accident rate and next year's projected flying hours and predict next year's accidents. This can be very accurate providing we are confident that nothing is going to change between now and the end of next year. That is usually a very good bet and we will look very smart.

We do things the way we are doing them because that's the way we've always done them and we like it that way. Aviation is full of activities that make no particular sense, but are extremely difficult to change. Consider, for example, the 360 degree overhead approach favored by military pilots. This approach was developed during World War II for safety reasons. The reciprocating engine was not particularly reliable (compared to today's jet engines) and we invented the 360 overhead to get the plane safely on the runway with or without the engine. Now, with high performance jets, we still fly the pattern, but we have forgotten why. We fly it because it looks good and we've always done it that way. Even though it is not a particularly efficient pattern for either weather or fuel conservation and it no longer serves any emergency purpose, we have no intention of changing.

AUTHOR'S NOTE:

This still generates argument among the gray-haired pilots of my vintage. It is generally true that the 360 overhead is the most efficient way to recover a flight of aircraft in good weather if fuel is not a problem. Otherwise, the most efficient way to recover them is to have approach control split them up at altitude and bring them straight down the chute to the runway. That uses the least fuel and works in any weather. This controversy points out a problem common to the safety business. People who are emotionally attached to a procedure can always defeat someone who is merely armed with the facts.

Making predictions and identifying what must or should be changed is easy. Getting people to actually do things differently is difficult. Even good changes that benefit everyone and make life easier will be resisted. People like the way things are and they really don't want to change.

If you don't believe this, think back on how computers and word processing systems were finally accepted in your organization. If yours was typical, it took a lot of time and nagging to get people to use the new technology. Even today, there are probably some managers in your organization who adamantly refuse to have anything to do with computers. They've always scribbled out their correspondence on a yellow pad or dictated it to a secretary and they like it that way.

Taking this idea one step further, if prevention requires change, the person responsible for prevention must be someone who can make changes. This answers the classic question of who is responsible for accident prevention in an organization. It is someone with line authority who can make changes. It is not someone with staff authority who cannot.

This concept should set the tone of the relationship between the aviation safety manager, who is a staff person, and any of the line managers. Here's how it goes.

- If the accident/incident situation within your organization is not acceptable to you (the line manager), then you are going to have to make some changes. Prevention always requires change. As a specialist in aviation safety, I am here to recommend what changes should be made and how they should be made, but the change orders have to come from you. This is your organization and your aviation safety program and prevention (change) is your responsibility. You always have the options of accepting my advice; modifying it; rejecting it and making some other change; or rejecting it completely and doing nothing. It's your call and whatever changes are made are going to involve your assets. Whatever happens, you are going to get the credit or the blame for the success or failure of the program, because you are the only one in a position to act — or not act.

There. That's a little blunt, but it is absolutely true. If you can get all of your line managers to nod their heads and agree with that, you have made monumental progress. You have established the basic idea of whose program this is and who is responsible for it. You have also established the idea that you are here to help them with their program and objectives; not the other way around. It is the only really satisfactory relationship a staff safety specialist can have with line management.

SAFETY AND MANAGEMENT

Early in the aviation safety business, we spent about a third of our time exhorting and cajoling people to be safe; another third wandering around with a clipboard trying to catch them not being safe; and the other third investigating accidents. That kept us busy, but we didn't seem to be making a lot of progress. Eventually, we realized that safety was very much a function of management and it was time to start treating it that way. Current thinking holds that accidents are indications of a failure somewhere in the management system.

If you agree that accident prevention requires change, then you must agree that the key player is not the aviation safety manager. It is some other manager with the power and authority to direct change. This is absolutely true and it puts the burden of accident prevention right where it belongs; in the line manager's office; not the safety office. Once we get by that hurdle, it is easy to see that safety programs can be managed just like any other program. Basic management principles work just fine.

ACCIDENT CAUSES

Here is a useful definition of accident causes.

- Causes are those factors, events, acts, or conditions which singly or in combination with other causes resulted in the damage or injury that occurred and, if corrected, eliminated, or avoided, would likely have prevented or reduced the damage or injury.

Any cause of an accident should be able to pass what lawyers refer to as the "but for" test. "But for this event, omission, action, or whatever, this accident would not have occurred." In other words, that cause was essential to the accident. It had to be there or we wouldn't have had an accident.

Any cause should also have some element of correctability in it. It does absolutely no good to talk about causes that are uncorrectable. "Pilot Error" is an uncorrectable cause. On the other hand, "Pilot Error Due to Lack of — Training" is correctable. We can do something about that. Another way to look at it is to consider "proximate" and "root" causes. Pilot error is a proximate cause. You get to the root cause by continually asking "Why?" When that question can no longer be asked, you have arrived at the root cause.

Causes may be categorized as either unsafe acts or unsafe conditions. These categorizations go back to the 1930s and they still work. An unsafe condition refers to the equipment. An unsafe act refers to the way we use the equipment. Anyone who has been in aviation for a while would agree that the equipment we fly really isn't that bad. It's the way we fly it that gets us in trouble. Best estimates are that between eighty and ninety per-cent of all accident causes are unsafe acts; not unsafe conditions. If you agree with that, then you must agree that aviation safety is more of a "people" problem than a "thing" problem.

We should point out that this idea of human error being involved in a large percentage of our accidents is not new; nor is it unique to aviation. William Heinrich (see bibliography) figured that out back in 1931 when he wrote his classic book on industrial accident prevention.

MULTIPLE CAUSE VERSUS SINGLE CAUSE

Back in the 1930s, safety theory held that each accident had one and only one cause. That was the single cause theory and it has taken us a long time to abandon it. Some haven't abandoned it yet and will go to their grave arguing about "PRIMARY CAUSE" or some such terminology.

Actually, there are very few accidents that have just a single cause. This is particularly true in aviation where we have built a system that is supposed to tolerate the single failure or single mistake. As it turns out, almost all aircraft accidents are composed of several causal factors each of which had to occur or the accident wouldn't have happened. Remember the "but for" test. Each cause has to be essential to the accident. If that is true, then each cause is infinitely important. There is no such thing as "primary," "main," or "most important" cause. The inevitable result of attempting to make those categorizations is that the "minor" causes (which are still essential) are ignored. They do not get the attention they deserve and, therefore, are not corrected. Today, safety professionals are solidly in agreement with the theory of multiple causation. This theory holds that all accidents result from multiple factors combined together in random fashion. If we fail to identify all of those factors as causes, we miss the opportunity to correct them.

The evidence is overwhelming. Attempting to explain an aircraft accident with only a single cause is an exercise in futility.

Looking ahead, there are some theorists in the aviation safety business who argue that causes serve no purpose. All that counts are the factors sig-nificant to the accident and the recommendations to prevent it. They are probably right. Australia has been doing it that way for several years. In the United States, though, it will be a while before we give up causes.

DISCUSSION QUESTIONS

1. Consider the following accident sequence.

   A. Single engine aircraft.

   B. Engine fails on takeoff.

   C. High speed abort (RTO).

   D. Heavy braking.

   E. Tire fails on main landing gear.

   F. Aircraft departs runway.

   G. Aircraft hits cement base of runway marker.

   H. Landing gear is sheared — substantial damage.

How many causes are there in that sequence? Which is the primary cause? What additional information do you want before you make recommendations?

2. Which of the following would you categorize as "Act of God" accidents? Why? Why not?

   A. Birdstrike. Substantial damage.

   B. Lightning Strike. Aircraft destroyed.

   C. Windshear encounter. Aircraft destroyed.

   D. Flight through volcanic ash. Substantial damage.

3. What is the role of safety within an organization?

4. Discuss two methods by which safety controls costs.

5. What is the relationship between safety and the every day practicality of getting the job done?

6. Discuss the concept that, "An accident involving damage or injury is the least likely result of any event."

7. Discuss the concept that, "Aviation safety needs to be event oriented and not result oriented."

AVIATION SAFETY TERMS DEFINED

The title of this chapter may be a little optimistic. It implies that I have some magic insight that allows me to wipe away all controversy and give you the firm and final definitions of all safety terms. Wrong. I can give you the choices and suggest areas where you might want to develop your own definitions to suit your organization.

As an example, the word "accident" can generate a lot of discussion. Technically, it is an unplanned and unwanted event that results in damage or injury caused by unknown and totally random factors. There is an implication that it was "accidental" and, therefore, easily forgiven and of little importance. It was, after all, only an "accident."

That, obviously, is not the way we use the term. Granted, an accident is an unplanned and unwanted event, but it is certainly not caused by unknown or random factors. It could have been prevented if we had been smart enough to do so. That is the basis for all safety programs.

The definitions in ICAO 13, "Aircraft Accident and Incident Investigation," (see bibliography) are accepted by the vast majority of the members, or "contracting states" as they are called, of ICAO. At the time of this writing, only three of the 188 contracting states have informed ICAO that their definitions differ to some extent from those in the Eighth Edition of ICAO Annex 13.

Thus, if we want to make sure that we all mean the same thing when we talk about safety, we should agree to use the ICAO definitions for Accident, Serious Injury, Incident, and Serious Incident. These are presented below with comments where appropriate. For comparison, United States definitions are included and identified as such.

We should note that in some contracting states, the wording or editorial presentation differs somewhat from that of ICAO, but the substance remains the same. This, as we will see, is true of the United States.

AIRCRAFT ACCIDENT (ICAO)

An occurrence associated with the operation of an aircraft, which takes place between the time any person boards the aircraft with the intention of flight until such time as all such persons have disembarked, in which:

a. a person is fatally or seriously injured as a result of:
   • being in the aircraft, or
   • direct contact with any part of the aircraft, including parts which have become detached from the aircraft, or
   • direct exposure to jet blast,
   • EXCEPT when the injuries are from natural causes, self-inflicted, or inflicted by other persons, or when the injuries are to stowaways hiding outside the areas normally available to the passengers and crew; or

b. the aircraft sustains damage or structural failure which:
   • adversely affects the structural strength, performance or flight characteristics of the aircraft and
   • would normally require major repair or replacement of the affected component,
   • EXCEPT for engine failure or damage, when the damage is limited to the engine, its cowlings or accessories; or for damage limited to propellers, wing tips, antennas, tires, brakes, fairings, small dents or puncture holes in the aircraft skin; or

c. the aircraft is missing or is completely inaccessible.
   NOTE. A fatal injury is an injury resulting in death within thirty days of the date of the accident.

SERIOUS INJURY (ICAO)

An injury sustained by a person in an accident and which:

a. requires hospitalization for more than 48 hours, commencing within seven days from the date the injury was received; or

b. results in a fracture of any bone (except simple fractures of fingers, toes, or nose); or

c. involves lacerations which cause severe hemorrhage, nerve, muscle, or tendon damage; or

d. involves injury to any internal organ; or

e. involves second or third degree burns, or any burns affecting more than five percent of the body surface.

AUTHOR'S NOTE:

The definition used by the National Transportation Safety Board is essentially the same as the ICAO definition. (See 49 CFR 830.)

AIRCRAFT ACCIDENT (NTSB) means an occurrence associated with the operation of an aircraft which takes place between the time any person boards the aircraft with the intention of flight and all such persons have disembarked, and in which any person suffers death or serious injury, or in which the aircraft receives substantial damage.

In 1997, the NTSB developed accident sub-categories based on severity. These are primarily for analysis and do not affect the basic definition of an aircraft accident or its reportability. The NTSB accident categories are listed below.

MAJOR ACCIDENT. One that results in the destruction of an aircraft operated under FAR Part 121, or in which there were multiple fatalities, or that an aircraft operated under Part 121 is substantially damaged and at least one fatality occurs.

SEVERE ACCIDENT. One that results in only one fatality and an aircraft operated under Part 121 is not substantially damaged, or there was at least one serious injury and the aircraft was substantially damaged.

INJURY ACCIDENT. A non-fatal accident having at least one serious injury but without substantial damage to an aircraft.

DAMAGE ACCIDENT. An accident in which there are no fatalities or serious injuries, but an aircraft is substantially damaged.

FATAL INJURY (NTSB)

Fatal injury means any injury which results in death within 30 days of the accident.

SERIOUS INJURY (NTSB)

Serious injury means an injury which:

  a. requires hospitalization for more than 48 hours, commencing within seven days from the date the injury was received;

  b. results in a fracture of any bone (except simple fractures of fingers, toes, or nose);

  c. causes severe hemorrhages, nerve, muscle, or tendon damage;

  d. involves any internal organ; or

  e. involves second or third degree burns, or any burns affecting more than five percent of the body surface.

AUTHOR'S NOTE:

This definition, which keeps the United States in conformance with the ICAO definition, is slightly at variance with the injury definitions established by the Department of Labor under the Occupational Safety and Health Act (OSHA). In some situations, either definition could apply.

SUBSTANTIAL DAMAGE (NTSB)

Substantial damage means damage or failure which adversely affects the structural strength, performance, or flight characteristics of the aircraft, and which would normally require major repair or replacement of the affected component. Engine failure or damage limited to an engine if only one engine fails or is damaged, bent fairings or cowling, dented skin, small punctured holes in the skin or fabric, ground damage to rotor or propeller blades, and damage to landing gear, wheels, tires, flaps, engine accessories, brakes, or wingtips are not considered "substantial damage."

AIRCRAFT MISHAP

This is a term used primarily by the United States military services to describe any safety-related reportable occurrence involving aircraft. The military definition of injury (fatal, permanent total, permanent partial) follows those established by the Department of Labor and OSHA.

Whereas the ICAO and NTSB definitions of damage are somewhat subjective, the military classifies damage in terms of dollar costs. This has some advantages in that it is fairly simple to establish the accident (mishap) classification and the use of dollar amounts provides an index of mishap severity by requiring calculation of the direct costs of the mishap. Its disadvantages are that the dollar amounts need to be regularly adjusted for inflation and there is no way to accurately determine the real value or cost of a destroyed military aircraft. The figure reported for a destroyed aircraft is acquisition cost, which is convenient and consistent, but is probably low in terms of the aircraft's actual value.

The U.S. Military also defines "aircraft operation" slightly differently. Where the ICAO definition involves people on or off the airplane, the military definition runs from start of takeoff roll until the aircraft has cleared the runway after landing. The military has other mishap categories to cover other times the aircraft is in operation.

Outside of the military, the term "mishap" is not defined. It is perhaps a convenient way to describe both accidents and incidents, but it is not widely used. ICAO and many of its contracting states, use the term "occurrence," although you will occasionally catch them using "condition," or "circumstance." Personally, I have trouble spelling "occurrence" and I like the word "event" to describe a happening that we have not yet categorized. It could be anything. Throughout this book, you'll find that the words, mishap, occurrence, and event all have about the same thing meaning.

INCIDENT (ICAO)

An occurrence, other than an accident, associated with the operation of an aircraft which affects or could affect the safety of operation.

SERIOUS INCIDENT (ICAO)

An incident involving circumstances indicating that an accident nearly occurred. Note: The difference between an accident and a serious incident lies only in the result. (Examples of ICAO Serious Incidents are listed in Chapter 11.)

AUTHOR'S NOTE:

Why distinguish between an "Incident" and a "Serious Incident?" Some background may help. The 1992 ICAO Investigation Divisional Meeting laid the foundation for the current (Eighth) edition of Annex 13. A main concern of the meeting was to find ways to get more prevention activity from the incidents that were obviously occurring. With tens of thousands of incidents occurring every year, some priorities needed to be set. Thus the "everyday" incidents would be recorded in the various data collection systems of the world while the serious ones would be investigated as if they had been accidents.

This was a major step forward for the ICAO contracting states. Previous editions of Annex 13 carried a note: "Nothing in this Annex is intended to impose an obligation on States to conduct an investigation into an incident." Now, Annex 13 recommends that Serious Incidents be investigated wherever they occur in the world. That may not seem like a big deal in the United States, but it represents real progress.

INCIDENT (NTSB)

The NTSB definition of an incident is identical to the ICAO definition. The NTSB does not use the term, "Serious Incident." Events that the NTSB considers to be reportable incidents are listed in Chapter 11.

The United States military does not use the term "Incident" and the closest analogy would be a "Class C Mishap." A list of these (for the United States Air Force) is included in Chapter 11.

HAZARD

This term is not defined in ICAO 13, although the ICAO Accident Prevention Manual defines a hazard as, "Any condition, event, or circumstance which could induce an accident." There is clearly an overlap with the term "Incident." Some would define a hazard as an event not involving damage or injury, but with the potential for damage or injury to occur. This is convenient and it can be argued that a hazard must exist in order for an accident or incident to occur. We could say that all accidents and incidents involve hazards, but not all hazards result in accidents or incidents.

One way to keep hazards and incidents separate is to think of "incident" as a defined event that requires a report. A hazard, on the other hand, is an undefined event that is reported only at the discretion of the person noticing or encountering it. See also Chapter 11.

In the United States, OSHA has pretty much taken over the term "hazard" and requires employers to maintain a hazard reporting program wherein employees can bring hazards to the attention of management. The USAF has a program called the Hazardous Air Traffic Report (HATR) where narrowly defined hazards including Near Mid Air Collisions (NMAC) can be reported and investigated. The U.S. Navy's "Anymouse" program is probably one of the oldest and most successful hazard reporting systems. Many countries have initiated anonymous reporting programs which are essentially hazard reporting systems. These include the Aviation Safety Reporting System (ASRS, United States) and several similar systems throughout the world.

SAFETY

There are many definitions of safety — some too long and involved to quote here. The simplest one is that safety is freedom from hazard; the absence of risk. Another is that safety is the preservation of resources; people, material, money, and time. A similar one was suggested in Chapter 1. Safety is a method of controlling costs.

One very workable definition is based on the acceptability of risk. If a particular risk is acceptable, then we consider that thing or operation to be safe. Conversely, when we say something is unsafe, we are really saying that its risks are unacceptable. This is consistent with the idea that there is no such thing as absolute safety, because there is no such thing as zero risk. It also suggests that the Safety Director is primarily in the business of identifying and determining the magnitude of the risks.

RISK

Risk is simply the probability that an event will occur. For our purposes, we usually modify our risk calculations by the number of times we expose ourselves to that event and the severity of the event if it does occur. Correctly measured, there are varying degrees of risk and the task confronting us is to weigh those risks against the potential benefits of taking them (risk-benefit analysis) and deciding whether the risks are acceptable or not. In this manner, we also decide whether something is safe or unsafe. This is consistent with the last definition of "safety" stated above.

The question of who is in charge of identifying risk and determining its acceptability deserves comment. This was discussed in Chapter 2. Basically, the Safety Director is in the business of identifying risks and providing some guidance as to their magnitude. The decision to accept or not accept them is always a management decision.

It is sometimes useful to sub-define risk in four categories:

1. INFORMED RISK. This is the risk correctly identified and assessed as described above.

2. UNINFORMED RISK. This is the risk we don't know we are taking. We have either not identified it or we have incorrectly measured it.

3. POINTLESS RISK. This is the risk we take without reason. There is no possible benefit. This describes the pilot who flies under the bridge or does an aileron roll on takeoff.

4. BENEFIT-DRIVEN RISK. This is the risk we take because the perceived benefits are so great that it is worth any risk. If, for example, we put a pilot in a position where he must (or thinks he must) accept a particular risk or lose his job, we have created a benefit-driven risk. Not all benefit-driven risks are necessarily bad. Sometimes, we have a choice and the benefit-driven risk may be the best one.

Obviously, we would like all our risks to be "informed risks".

PUBLIC AND CIVIL AIRCRAFT

These definitions are peculiar to the United States and are included because the use of the aircraft determines which FARs apply and who has investigative authority if there is an accident.

In our skies, there are only two types of aircraft; public or civil. Although everyone (including the FAA and the NTSB) uses the term "military aircraft" it is not defined anywhere. Technically, a military aircraft is a public aircraft.

In general, public aircraft need only comply with Subpart B of FAR Part 91, which are the traffic rules of the air. The NTSB investigates civil aircraft accidents and has no authority to investigate public aircraft accidents unless there is some pre-existing agreement with the agency operating the aircraft.

This mess goes all the way back to 1926 and the first serious attempt to straighten it out didn't come until 1995. That removed many aircraft from the "public" category, but it muddied the water somewhat. Now, any aircraft (except military or intelligence aircraft) could be a "public aircraft" depending on how it is being operated at the time. Thus Safety Directors of companies who occasionally do business with the Federal Government, states, counties or cities need a working knowledge of the definition or at least knowledge of where to find it in a hurry. If you are not in that situation, you might want to skip the rest of this chapter.

- **PUBLIC AIRCRAFT** (49 CFR 830) means an aircraft used only for the United States Government, or an aircraft owned and operated (except for commercial purposes) or exclusively leased for at least 90 continuous days by a government other than the United States Government, including a state, the District of Columbia, a territory or possession of the United States, or a political subdivision of that government. "Public Aircraft" does not include a government-owned aircraft transporting property for commercial purposes and does not include a government-owned aircraft transporting passengers other than: transporting (for other than commercial purposes) crewmembers, or other persons aboard the aircraft whose presence is required to perform, or is associated with the performance of a governmental function such as firefighting, search and rescue, law enforcement, aeronautical research, or biological or geological resource management; or transporting (for other than commercial purposes) persons aboard the aircraft if the aircraft is operated by the Armed Forces or an intelligence agency of the United States. Notwithstanding any limitation relating to use of the aircraft for commercial purposes, an aircraft shall be considered to be a public aircraft without regard to whether it is operated by a unit of government on behalf of another unit of government pursuant to a cost reimbursement agreement, if the unit of government on whose behalf the operation is conducted certifies to the Administrator of the Federal Aviation Administration that the operation was necessary to respond to a significant and imminent threat to life or property (including natural resources) and that no service by a private operator was reasonably available to meet the threat.

- **CIVIL AIRCRAFT** means any aircraft other than a public aircraft.

AUTHOR'S NOTE:

That sounds like a facetious definition, but that's exactly what the law says. This subject is discussed further in Chapter 17.

SUMMARY

All definitions of an aircraft accident require some degree of damage or injury and they all differentiate between an airplane that was acting like an airplane and one that was just an aluminum structure sitting in a hangar. If there was no damage or injury, or if the plane was not acting like a plane, it may have been a serious event, but it wasn't an aircraft accident.

All aircraft accidents (as defined by whatever system you are using) are reportable. That does not mean that within your own organization you cannot define some other event as an aircraft accident. Of course you can. If it suits the needs of your safety program, you should.

Incidents are fairly serious events, but they are not well defined. Hazards exist in all accidents and incidents, but they can also exist by themselves. As a practical matter, an incident is reportable and (therefore) should be defined. The decision to report a hazard is generally left to the person who notices it and determines that it is, in fact, a hazard. Reporting systems are discussed in Chapter 11.

Safety is really a function of risk acceptability. That will be discussed in several chapters.

DISCUSSION QUESTIONS

1. Construct scenarios where the same identical event could be an aircraft accident (ICAO or NTSB), a lost-time accident (OSHA), or a "nothing" depending on the results and the people involved.

2. Inflight, a compressor blade of a turbine engine fails, severely damaging the engine and requiring shutdown. The blade itself penetrated the compressor case and cowling and punctures the aircraft fuselage. There is no other damage and no injury. Would you classify this as an aircraft accident? Why?

3. Construct accident scenarios in which the risk was: informed, uninformed, pointless, and benefit-driven.

BUILDING AN AVIATION SAFETY PROGRAM

CHAPTER 4

Some of you already have an aviation safety program, but many of you are going to start from scratch and build one. How do you do that?

Here, we'll discuss five basic steps.

1. Decide who's in charge.

2. Determine the scope of the program.

3. Agree on program goals and objectives.

4. Get organized.

5. Begin developing the program.

These steps match those listed in Chapter 1. The sixth step, measuring the success of the program, is addressed in Chapter 14.

STEP 1. DECIDE WHO'S IN CHARGE

Let's start by agreeing on a few definitions. Authority is the right or power to command or make decisions. Responsibility is an assigned function or duty that a person is expected to accomplish. Accountability is frequently assumed to mean the same thing as responsibility. Accountability is a somewhat stronger term and implies that the results of the assigned function or duty will be measured. In this book, I will stick with responsibility and assume that persons responsible are also accountable.

Deciding who is in charge is a critical step. Responsibility and authority have to exist somewhere. There is a tendency to confuse responsibility for managing the program with responsibility for its results. This is a mistake. Consider the comments made earlier about prevention and change. If we are going to prevent something, we are going to have to change something. The authority to commit resources, spend money, and bring about change is an inherent part of line management. Unless we are prepared to give our aviation safety managers that authority, it is hardly fair to hold them responsible for correcting something they cannot change. As a practical matter, accepting responsibility (or accountability) for something without the equivalent authority is never a good idea in any management situation.

Let's make sure we understand the difference between "line" and "staff" as used in basic management.

The head of an organization (President, Chief Executive Officer, Commander) has the authority necessary to direct the activities of the organization. The CEO delegates to the Chief of Flight Operations (for example) the authority necessary to operate the aircraft and to the Chief of Maintenance the authority necessary to maintain them. This authority delegation trickles down even to the captain in the cockpit of the airplane who has the necessary authority to operate the aircraft. This is called "line" authority and the line manager is responsible for both the proper use of authority and the results of it. The line manager gets the credit for good results and the blame for bad results.

At almost every management level, we provide the line manager with specialists to help in specific areas. These specialists are called "staff" and they act in an advisory mode. They may actually manage a program, but they lack the authority to commit resources or make changes. (Within their own staff office, of course, they do have line authority; but that's not what we're talking about.) As an example, the personnel director is usually "staff." The personnel director doesn't decide who will be hired or fired, but the director does manage the program in terms of how people will be hired and fired. Likewise, the budget director doesn't spend the money. The budget director does determine how it will be budgeted and accounted for.

In almost all cases, the aviation safety manager (or Director of Safety) is "staff." Responsibility for accidents (and their prevention) belongs to the line manager and so does the accident prevention program. If that is true, then the Director of Safety cannot logically be a line manager. The aviation safety manager is there as a specialist to run the program for the line manager and advise on what changes should be made. If the aviation safety manager is positioned correctly, direct access to top management and the ability to operate across other line functions takes full advantage of the concept of "staff."

Based on this, we can make a general statement that would be true for any aviation organization.

- Aircraft accident prevention is a responsibility shared by each line manager at each level within the aviation organization. Since each line manager has prevention responsibility, each needs access to and assistance from a staff aviation safety specialist.

Now, we can answer the question, "Who's in charge?" At any level, it is the line manager. It's the line manager's program and responsibility. When building an aviation safety program, it is essential that everyone understand and agree on this. If senior management feels that accident prevention is the responsibility of the Director of Safety, my advice is to look for another job. You're not going to succeed in that one.

STEP 2. DETERMINE THE SCOPE OF THE PROGRAM

If we establish a Director of Safety position, does that mean that person is in charge of all safety or just aviation safety? Can safety be combined with some other activity or must it be separate?

There are no absolute rules. A company has considerable latitude on how it organizes itself. This is a book on aviation safety, but it was not written in ignorance of other safety activities. As mentioned in Chapter 2, the line drawn between flight safety and ground safety is a thin one. There are many events that could fit in either category and there is clearly a need for interaction between flight and ground safety no matter how you are organized.

My personal preference is to combine all safety activities under a single safety director, but it doesn't have to be done that way. There are, in fact, some drawbacks. Ground safety or, more properly, occupational safety and health, is heavily regulated. From the point of view of the safety manager, just complying with the regulations requires a disproportionate amount of time. Correspondingly, less time is available to spend on proactive safety activities. Aviation safety is not heavily regulated; at least not yet. The standards used aren't really safety standards; they are operations and maintenance standards. Consequently, the development and compliance process is largely a function of line management; not the safety department. That possibly explains why the safety record in aviation is so much better than in almost any other industry.

Nevertheless, I still believe it is essential to bring maintenance safety or ground safety or whatever you want to call it into the overall company safety program. My experience with separate programs is that they tend to develop an attitude that if it doesn't involve flight, it is not a flight safety problem. I don't believe that.

That explains why this book contains chapters on aircraft maintenance safety, flight line safety, and even one on airports. If you are going to be the Director of Safety, you may need them.

A word about consolidating the safety program with other activities. A lot of combinations have been tried. Some work, some don't. A few of the possibilities are:

- Safety and Security

- Safety and Certification

- Safety and Training

- Safety and Compliance

- Safety and Human Relations (Workers Compensation)

- Safety and Certificate Actions

- Safety and Disaster Control or accident preparedness

In general, it is not a good idea to combine safety with a function that clearly belongs to some other manager. Pilot certificate actions, for example, belong somewhere in operations; possibly with the Chief Pilot. Workers compensation is a personnel function. Putting those activities in the safety department in effect transfers some line authority to a staff function.

It is also not a good idea to combine a line activity with a staff activity. Security, for example, is a line activity and demands constant oversight. Offices of Safety and Security tend to be mostly security, which cannot be ignored. Safety, as we all know, can be ignored.

Of the combinations listed above, the only one that consistently works well is the one involving disaster control or accident preparedness. Planning for this is a staff function and it is not the unique responsibility of any other manager. It involves the entire organization. In small companies, this is frequently assumed to be a part of the aviation safety manager's responsibilities.

Most of this book assumes that the aviation safety program stands alone. Clearly, that's not the way it has to be.

STEP 3. AGREE ON PROGRAM GOALS AND OBJECTIVES

If we really want an aviation safety program, there ought to be something we want from it. It must be of some benefit to us or we probably don't need it. Ideally, its benefits ought to be measurable so we'll know whether the program is worth its costs.

In the safety business it is difficult to set measurable objectives because we are really trying to measure a negative — no accidents. How do you take credit for something that didn't happen? This is particularly difficult in aviation, because we have so few accidents in the first place. Who's to say that we wouldn't have exactly the same record if we had no safety program at all? You can try something like, "This year, we didn't have two accidents and next year, we are not going to have five accidents. That's progress." If you can slip that one by them without getting laughed at, you've got a good thing going for you.

We'll deal with the question of measuring the effectiveness of the program in a later chapter. For now, let's pick some reasonable goals and objectives and try to keep them as realistic as possible. Keep in mind, that your list of goals and objectives should be based on the mission of your organization. Here's a list of goals and objectives that have been used in other programs. Some of these should fit your organization.

1.   Provide a safe and healthful working environment for all our employees.

2.   Prevent aircraft and industrial accidents.

3.   Minimize damage and severity of injury resulting from accidents that do occur.

4.   Prevent damage and injury to non-company property and personnel as a result of our aircraft operations.

5.   Incorporate aviation safety planning into all operational activities.

6.   Provide an aviation safety review of all proposed new equipment, facilities, operations, or procedures.

7.   Reduce insurance costs.

8.   Reduce operating costs and increase operational capability by reducing damage to company aircraft and equipment.

9.   Assist in developing standards for safe operation of company aircraft and equipment.

10.   Provide aviation safety training for all aviation personnel.

11.   Identify hazardous conditions. Assess the associated risk, and propose risk mitigation actions. (A safety staff function.)

12.   Allocate resources to eliminate or mitigate hazardous conditions. (A line management function).

13.   Provide an analysis program to identify potentially hazardous events or conditions.

14.   Provide for the reporting and investigation of hazardous events.

15. Incorporate aviation safety into all aircraft maintenance activities

16. Maintain an active hazardous materials control program.

17. Participate in national and international aviation safety forums.

18. Provide for compliance with all laws and regulations applicable to aviation safety.

Once you have developed your objectives (and obtained line management agreement), the best thing to do is to condense them into a policy statement to be signed by the Chief Executive Officer. This makes it official and it becomes the aviation safety director's license to begin developing the program to meet those objectives. It also provides a written commitment on the part of senior management on what they expect from the aviation safety program.

There are many ways to write an aviation safety policy statement. One sample policy statement has been incorporated into the sample aviation safety program in Chapter 20. Shown in Figure 4-1 is the current (as of 1996) safety policy statement of United Airlines. While this doesn't cover many of the objectives listed above, it certainly leaves no doubt as to the commitment of UAL senior management. Keep in mind that this policy statement goes well beyond just aviation safety.

United in Safety

Our Commitment

Safety is our corporate value because we care deeply about the health and safety of our fellow employees and customers.

We believe that each one of us – from senior managers to front-line employees – has a responsibility to make our workplaces safer for everyone.

We support the open sharing of information on all safety issues and encourage all employees to report significant safety hazards or concerns.

We pledge that no disciplinary action will be taken against any employee for reporting a safety hazard or concern to United Airlines management

Signed:	*Signed:*
President	Chairman

(Printed with permission of United Airlines)

Figure 4-1. United Airlines Policy Statement

STEP 4. GET ORGANIZED

Where are we going to put the aviation safety department? How many of them are there going to be? Who do they report to? Are they full time or part time?

Stop! Let's answer some other questions first.

1. How big is our organization?

    - How many people?

    - How many aircraft?

    - Do we deal with outside contractors?

    - What are our resources?

2. Is it consolidated at one location or dispersed at many locations?

3. How complicated is it?

    - Single mission or multi-mission?

    - One type of aircraft or several types?

    - One type of support equipment or several types?

4. Does it operate regionally, nationally, or internationally?

5. How hazardous is it?

    - Relatively low, such as transport or charter operations?

    - Relatively high, such as military tactical operations, law enforcement, search and rescue, aerial fire suppression, etc.?

6. What is our accident experience and the general industry accident experience in this type of flying?

7. What safety resources are already available within our company?

The answers to these questions should provide a clue as to the size of the aviation safety effort. Consider a point made earlier. A line manager with accident prevention responsibilities needs either an assigned aviation safety specialist or direct access to one. Consider also that aircraft accidents seldom occur at the company headquarters. They occur down at the bottom of the organization where we have airplanes, pilots, maintainers, and support people. That is also the place where the most direct prevention opportunities occur. This means that appointing a single aviation safety manager (or Director of Safety) at the corporate level will only work in very small organizations. In most cases, the problems are occurring several levels down and the aviation safety manager can't possibly provide specialized advice to all the flight managers and station managers who need it.

The solution to this is to build an aviation safety infrastructure throughout the organization. Wherever you have a definable aviation activity in terms of organization or location, designate an aviation safety specialist (probably as an additional or collateral duty) to handle the aviation safety problems at that level or location and provide specialized advice and assistance to that line manager. This aviation safety specialist works for and reports to the line manager of that activity. The specialist stays in close contact with the corporate Director of Safety or company aviation safety manager and gets all the help available. That's why we keep referring to the top aviation safety person as a manager. The aviation safety manager gets the job done primarily by working with and through all of these part time aviation safety specialists who are actually doing the day-to-day work. This is a very common management situation and it is found in almost every managerial activity in every large company.

Thus, the answer to the questions posed above determines the size of your safety staff. You need one person (full or part time) for each identifiable aviation activity plus one more to manage the program. If you are operating under Part 121 of the Federal Aviation Regulations, your Director of Safety must be full time.

One point before we move on. When a line manager selects someone within the organization to be an additional duty aviation safety specialist, the most important criteria is to select someone who wants the job. Appointing someone who doesn't want it will guarantee a poor program.

Another point about organization. Who should the aviation safety manager report to? Under FAR Part 119, you are not given much choice. The Director of Safety reports directly to the company CEO for Part 121 operators. Is this a good idea? Yes, providing, as suggested above, there is an infrastructure of safety specialists down at the airplane and pilot level where the problems are.

At any level, the aviation safety manager (or aviation safety specialist) should report to the line manager at that level. Interposing an extra level between the safety department and the boss (such as having the safety department work for the staff director of personnel) creates difficulties. It denies the boss direct advice in a technical area (which was what we wanted in the first place) and it dilutes the ability of the safety staff to influence change among the other line managers. It may, in fact, erect a barrier between the aviation safety manager and the line manager who needs the information and can make the required change.

Having said that, it should be pointed out that the actual organizational structure is not as important as the people involved or the company policies. Good people can make a bad organization work and a good organization won't help a company with bad people or bad policies. They will defeat it somehow.

As a case in point, consider the fairly common airline practice of placing the aviation safety function under the Chief of Flight Operations. This is still technically possible, as FAR Part 119 calls for a Director of Safety at the top; not necessarily a Director of Flight Safety. From a pure management point of view, this is not the ideal location, mainly because it gives the flight safety department very little clout in aircraft maintenance, passenger services, station management, engineering, etc. There is a risk that these departments (who have a definite role in aviation safety) will be left out of the program. In some airlines, this works quite well. The Aviation Safety Manager (who works in Flight Ops) has no trouble working directly with the Chief of Aircraft Maintenance. They both understand the problem and the needs of the organization.

It would be wrong to imply that the aviation safety manager operates completely without any authority. That's not true. In addition to the classic staff "rights" (to question, advise, and warn) the aviation safety manager usually accumulates other types of authority, such as:

- **DELEGATED AUTHORITY**. This is a small slice of the boss's authority conferred upon the aviation safety manager. The safety manager could, for example, be given the authority to initiate certain types of investigations or to assign hazardous situations to line managers for resolution.

- **POSITIONAL AUTHORITY**. This is sometimes called "implied authority." This type of authority comes with the job. If the aviation safety manager reports directly to the Chief Executive Officer, then the aviation safety manager is perceived as carrying a little bit of the CEO's authority. This type of authority can be used — or misused.

- **AUTHORITY DERIVED FROM LAWS AND REGULATIONS**. It is generally assumed that the aviation safety manager has the authority to direct compliance applicable aviation safety laws and regulations.

- **AUTHORITY BASED ON EDUCATION REPUTATION**. If the aviation safety manager is the most knowledgeable person on aviation safety and has consistently provided sound advice and acted in support of the organization's objectives, then people tend to pay attention to the aviation safety manager's recommendations. This is a form of authority.

STEP 5. BEGIN DEVELOPING THE PROGRAM

There are literally hundreds of different aviation safety elements, methods, and techniques. There is no one-size-fits-all aviation safety program that you can plug in and start using. Chapter 20 contains a sample program, but, at best, that can merely help you develop your own. Before you turn to Chapter 20, let's list some requirements that are fairly basic to any aviation safety program. Then we can take a look at the different ways to meet those requirements.

1. We need a method of collecting information about what's going on (with respect to aviation safety) within our organization and our industry. We can't sit in our ivory tower and react to what we think is going on. Somehow, we have to have some facts.

2. We need one or more methods of distributing the information that we collect to someone who can benefit by knowing about it or who can act on it. Remember. We're not going to issue too many orders from the safety office. The information that we collect isn't going to do much good if it never gets out of our office.

3. We need to participate in the selection and development of standards and procedures for our organization. Most of the standards are going to emerge as operations or maintenance standards. We are probably not going to go into the standards publishing business ourselves. We don't have the authority to do that and we can't enforce them anyway. Nevertheless, if our method of collecting information works well, then we are the office most likely to notice the need for a changed standard or procedure.

4. We need one or more methods of ensuring that our company safety standards are being met. Our boss is entitled to know. While we're at it, we would like to be able to tell him that his aviation safety objectives and polices are also being met and that the safety program is doing what he wants it to do.

5. We need one or more methods of achieving action to correct identified problems. Remember, we are not personally going to correct them. That authority belongs to someone who can authorize change.

6. If an aircraft accident occurs, we need to be able to react to it promptly and correctly and either conduct or participate in the investigation and development of corrective actions.

7. We need a training program that will indoctrinate new employees into our aviation safety program as soon as possible and provide for recurrent training where appropriate.

8. We need an analysis program that will enable us to chart our progress and help us identify our problem areas.

That about covers it. If we can come up with ways to handle all those items, we'll have plenty to keep us busy. The remaining chapters up through 19 are designed to do that. Chapter 20 summarizes all that in the form of a sample aviation safety program.

SUMMARY

Safety programs have been around a long time and once something becomes part of the program, it tends to be part of it forever; or at least long after it is needed. One reason is because it is difficult to prove that it is no longer needed — so we keep doing it. Another reason is that we tend to copy other safety programs on the theory that if it works for them, it will probably work for us. Actually, we don't know whether it works for them or not, and they may not know either!

Also, consider that our industry is fairly dynamic. We regularly change equipment, mission, environment, and procedures. Why don't we continually adjust the safety program to meet those changes?

I firmly believe that safety programs should be dynamic; not static. Whatever we do should satisfy some purpose and have some value to us. If it doesn't, we should either change it or stop doing it. Any program needs constant review and revision. That philosophy explains the repetitive comments in this book about not copying the sample program in Chapter 20 and expecting it to work for you. It's your organization and you can do better than that.

DISCUSSION QUESTIONS

1. The official Director of Safety for the United States Government heads the Office of Occupational Safety and Health for federal agencies. This is a branch of the Occupational Safety and Health Administration which is in the Department of Labor. Do you see any problems with this organization?

2. The Author stated that "Positional Authority" can be either used or misused. Cite some examples of the use and misuse of positional authority.

3. Assume an organization consisting of a president, vice presidents for operations, personnel, finance, and aircraft maintenance; a comptroller, corporate counsel, and a director of safety. Construct a chart or organizational diagram showing how these functions might be related. Show where additional duty safety specialists should be located.

4. Using the diagram created above, show line authority and staff relationships.

5. Review United Airlines statement of safety policy (Figure 4-1) and suggest improvements.

6. What is the difference between an objective and a goal?

PREVENTION METHODOLOGY

CHAPTER

5

In the introduction to this part of the book, we said that basic accident prevention was neither difficult nor complicated. In any particular segment of safety (aviation, industrial, vehicle, construction, etc.) the technology changes, but the techniques of prevention stay pretty much the same. There are, after all, only a few basic ways to prevent accidents and they can be applied to almost any situation. Basically, you decide how you are going to do things; make sure you do them that way; identify hazardous situations and correct them.

That's fairly simple and plugging away consistently at those four ideas is bound to give you a sound safety program. Alternatively, if you don't do those things it is unlikely that you will have an effective safety program.

Looking at this from the point of view of the safety manager, let's take those four ideas one at a time.

STEP 1. SET YOUR STANDARDS. (Decide how you are going to do things).

It would be hard to overemphasize the importance of this step. You are never going to be any better than your operations and maintenance standards. The standards established by the FARs are, in almost all cases, minimums. You must meet them just to stay in business. If they are also your maximums, you don't really have a very good operation. You have no intention of getting any better and you are not allowed to get any worse. You may have a safety program, but it's not going to do much. It can't!

Let's talk about standards. How are you going to operate? What rules and procedures are you going to follow in flying your aircraft? Some of these are contained in the laws and regulations of your country. ICAO develops and publishes standards that are generally followed by all countries. (Any ICAO Contracting State may notify ICAO of differences between their national regulations and ICAO Standards and Recommended Practices. Many, including the United States, do file notices of differences.) In the

United States, the Federal Aviation Administration establishes minimum standards to regulate civil aviation. The U.S. military (because its aircraft are operated as "public aircraft") establishes its own standards. In addition, many of the standards established under OSHA apply directly to how we maintain and service our aircraft. The Environmental Protection Agency (EPA) establishes standards on how hazardous materials which we use in aircraft maintenance) will be managed.

As already mentioned, these government standards are minimums. The process of setting the standards almost ensures that they will be set at the minimum level. There is nothing, however, that says you can't operate to a higher standard and, in most cases, you should. As an example, a pilot with as few as 1500 hours total flying time can legally serve as pilot in command of an air transport operating under FAR Part 121. Few airlines will even hire copilots or flight engineers with that little experience. They obviously set their standards higher than that.

Another example. Most corporate flying operations in the United States can and do operate under FAR Part 91, which is the least restrictive of all the operating standards. They can do this because they are not operating their aircraft commercially even though they may be flying something as big as a B727, and flying it just like an airline. Realistically, their standards should be at a level commensurate with the type of flying they are actually doing.

The point is that minimal compliance with the FARs means a minimal operation; not necessarily a safe one. The process of developing internal operating standards is an important one and is the real basis for the aviation safety program.

This standards-setting business isn't difficult. The chances are good that someone has already figured out the best way to operate your type of aircraft on your type of mission. The standards are already available. It's just a matter of finding them and picking those that suit your operation. Here is a list of common sources of standards.

1. Federal Aviation Regulations. Not only those that apply to your operation, but those that apply to the next higher level of operation.

2. FAA Advisory Circulars. These are usually not mandatory, but many of them contain some excellent information and advice.

3. Professional societies or trade associations such as:

    • American Association of Airport Executives

    • Air Transport Association

- Association of Air Medical Services
- Flight Safety Foundation
- Helicopter Association International
- International Air Transport Association
- International Civil Aviation Organization
- National Business Aircraft Association
- National Fire Protection Association
- National Safety Council
- Professional Aviation Maintenance Association
- Society of Automotive Engineers
- Airborne Law Enforcement Association
- American Society of Safety Engineers

4. Other organizations flying similar aircraft or missions. In this business, we are pretty good about exchanging safety information with each other. A simple thing like offering to swap copies of operations manuals or pre-accident plans can lead to some valuable ideas.

Beyond these, you will still run into some situations where nothing applies and you are going to have to develop your own standard. Let's suppose that you are flying a mission where you obviously need more fuel reserve than that suggested in any available standard. Who should decide what the reserve should be? You, the Director of Safety?

No, that's not really your job. You are the one most likely to notice the need for the standard, but setting it is really the job of the Chief Pilot or Director of Flight Operations. This relates back to the idea of change as a requirement of prevention and the idea that the authority to change things belongs to line management.

One solution is to assemble a group of senior pilots and ask them what they think the fuel reserve should be. As professionals, they are almost certain to come up with a good answer. This is the idea of "participation" mentioned earlier. If they participate, it becomes their standard; not your standard. Any group will tend to accept the restrictions they place on themselves, but they will tend to resist restrictions imposed on them. Thus you have partially solved your next problem, which is getting them to comply with the new standard on fuel reserve.

For that reason alone, getting the people involved who must live with the standard is very effective.

ISO 9000 AND ISO 14000 STANDARDS.

This would be a good place to address the impact of ISO 9000 and 14000 standards on aviation safety. ISO 9000 is primarily a quality management system developed by the International Organization for Standards in Switzerland. They have been adopted by over 100 countries including the United States. Following a quality audit, individual companies may become ISO-registered. ISO 14000 is newer and provides standards for environmental management. There are several advantages to registration; particularly in the international business arena.

While the ISO Standards are more oriented to quality management, part of that includes a company's safety, health, and environmental practices. If the company operates aircraft, their aviation safety standards would almost certainly be included.

At the present time (1997), the International Organization for Standards (ISO) has proposed developing a standard for occupational safety and health management systems. In the United States, safety and health professionals are divided over whether this standard is needed or even whether it would be a good idea. The consensus seems to be that it is not needed at this time. If developed, this standard would certainly impact aviation safety programs. Stay tuned.

Even if the company does not seek ISO 9000 registration, the Director of Safety should understand the ISO 9000 processes. They contain a lot of excellent ideas for development and maintenance of standards. See Bibliography.

STEP 2. COMPLY WITH THE STANDARDS.

Once you've picked your standards, the next problem is to comply with them. If you did not get line management participation in selecting the standards, you definitely need it here, because you personally cannot compel compliance. That takes the authority of a line manager.

It would seem that just agreeing on the standard and publishing it in the Ops Manual ought to be good enough, but it isn't. Our manuals are full of rules that we are not following. We call these "eyewash" or "lipservice" rules. They look good on paper, and (possibly) impress the inspectors, but nobody is actually doing it that way. In some cases, we would never get anything done if we did. There have been occasions when a union has brought a company to a standstill by merely following the company's standards exactly. That might be a clue that something's wrong. In other cases, we consider them unnecessary, or we don't like them, or they are not enforced so who cares. In the long run, it does no good to have worthless rules on the books. We should either enforce them, change them, or get rid of them.

While we're on this subject, let's talk about FAA determination of compliance and enforcement. When the FAA inspectors show up, they can only measure your compliance against their standards; not your standards. Since we've already established that their standards are minimums, a passing grade from the FAA means only that you are meeting their minimums; not your minimums. Thus, it is wrong to assume that because the FAA found nothing wrong, you, therefore, have a safe operation. Maybe you do — but maybe you don't!

In any case, the problem of enforcing the standard and knowing on a day-to-day basis whether it is being complied with or not belongs to the line manager. In the fuel reserve example we have been using, the Chief Pilot ought to be the one most interested in knowing. If the pilots are not meeting the fuel reserve standard, it should come to the Chief Pilot's attention before it comes to yours. It's really the Chief Pilot's standard and the Chief Pilot can correct any deviations without your help. If we wait for you to discover the deviation, we're doing it wrong.

Wherever possible, set up a system where knowledge of lack of compliance automatically goes to the person who can act on it. This way, you are not trying to do the line manager's job; you are helping the line manager to do it better.

As said before, setting high standards and meeting them is the basis for any accident prevention program.

STEP 3. IDENTIFY HAZARDS

These are situations which crop up regularly in any flying operation and are not covered by steps 1 and 2 above. There are several ways to approach this, and two of them have already been mentioned:

1. Have a strong internal incident reporting program (Chapter 11).

2. Have a strong hazard reporting program (Chapter 11).

There are other ways:

1. Maintain a regular organizational inspection or audit program (Chapter 14). Sometimes, you just have to go out and see what's going on for yourself. There is no other way.

2. Develop an analysis program that will track significant events and note unexplained changes (Chapter 18).

3. Keep track of what hazards are occurring in your segment of the industry that might apply to your organization. You do this through trade associations, personal contacts, and a constant review of aviation safety-related literature.

4. Hire a consultant to come in and tell you what your hazards are. Sometimes this is valuable as a good consultant can bring a fresh pair of eyes and a considerable amount of experience with similar flying operations. On the other hand, the consultant only sees what exists at the time. A consultant can augment an internal safety audit program, but never replace it.

Regardless of how the hazards are identified, it is well to apply some pri-oritizing method (Chapter 11) so that you are concentrating your resources on your worst problems. It is bad enough to waste your time on something that will probably never hurt you. It is even worse to miss the opportunity to work on a really serious hazard because you are over-loaded with the insignificant problems.

STEP 4. ACT TO RESOLVE THE HAZARDS

Assuming that the hazard is worth resolving, there is a fairly standard approach to deciding what to do about it. These are ranked in the order of effectiveness.

1. Engineering Solution. This is the one that corrects the hazard and eliminates it so it doesn't bother us anymore. We fill the hole in the taxiway or cut down the tree that is obstructing our approach. We re-engine our helicopter for more power and better reliability. This is always the most desirable solution, but it is also likely to be the most expensive and the most time-consuming. Sometimes the engi-neering solution just isn't practical. You can't take that action and still get the job done. Sometimes the engineering solution creates a bigger problem than it solves. I'm thinking of a situation many years ago when an engine manufacturer had an unwanted vibration in the center section of the engine. The solution was to physically restrain that part of the engine so it couldn't vibrate; an engineer-ing solution. As some engineers predicted, this merely changed the vibration mode of the engine. Now the center stayed still, but both ends vibrated.

2. Control Solution. This is where we leave the hazard as it is, but put a guard on it or somehow change our procedures so that we are less exposed to it. Instead of cutting down the tree on the approach, for example, we displace the runway threshold. The tree is still there, but we have reduced the probability that we will hit it. Instead of

buying new engines for our helicopter, we impose operating limitations on the one we have and we inspect it more often. All of us are probably operating aircraft that have one or more limitations imposed on them for safety reasons. This solution is less effective than the engineering solution, but sometimes it is the most practical.

3. Personnel Solution. This is where we can't get rid of the hazard or control it; so we warn people about it. "Watch out for the tree on the approach to runway 25." We put that out as a NOTAM, we cover it in our briefings and so on. This is obviously less effective than either of the other two solutions, but sometimes that's all we can do.

4. Protective Equipment Solution. This does not correct the hazard, but only reduces its effects. It is primarily a solution to industrial safety problems and seldom applies to aviation safety. In essence, it says that a particular hazard is unavoidable. By wearing this piece of protective equipment, it won't hurt as much when you run into it. From a professional safety point of view, this is the least effective solution to a safety problem.

As an example, let's suppose we discover a pothole on our aircraft parking ramp. It's not exactly on the taxi line, but it is big enough to do some damage if a plane runs into it.

The engineering solution is, obviously, to fill the pothole. That gets rid of the hazard. For some reason, though, we can't do that; at least not immediately. For control solutions, we might be able to rearrange our taxi pattern (reduction of probability) or put a metal plate over the hole (reduction of severity.) If neither of those are practical, we are down to personnel solutions. Here, we mark the hole with paint and lights; post signs and brief all the pilots. Those are our choices. As you can see, there is no practical "protective equipment" solution which is usually the case when dealing with aviation safety.

The point of all this is that you should always start with the engineering solution and work your way down as far as you have to go to resolve the hazard. Sometimes, you just can't do what you would like to do and you have to accept what can be done within the available time and resources.

There. Those four steps (set your standards, comply with them, identify hazards, resolve them) describe basic accident prevention methods. There are many other things you could do, but if you do these well, you should have a pretty good program.

DISCUSSION QUESTIONS

1. One of your aircraft parking positions is partially obstructed by a maintenance line shack. List as many solutions to this as you can and organize them as engineering, control, or personnel solutions.

2. One of the examples used in this chapter involved the development of a new or different standard on fuel reserve. Develop a method that the Chief Pilot could use to determine if the fuel reserve standard was being met.

3. Assume you have been appointed as the Director of Safety for a new FAR Part 141 Flight Training School. Where would you look for references concerning appropriate safety standards?

CHAPTER 6

RISK MANAGEMENT

Risk management has a lot in common with basic accident prevention methodology. They both involve an assessment of the types of hazards, the risks the hazards generate, and a logical approach to deciding what to do about them. The chapter on prevention methodology looks at the problem from the point of view of the safety manager. This chapter focuses on the line manager's role and decision-making process.

THEORY

Risk management is a term generally credited to the insurance industry and it has different meanings to different people. As applied to aviation safety, it is based on some fairly simple ideas.

First, there is always some amount of risk in whatever we do. Flying is certainly no exception. Some risks we can "engineer" out of the system and some we can control or reduce. What we cannot do, though, is eliminate all of them.

If that makes sense, then the job of the aviation safety manager is primarily one of accurately identifying the risks and communicating that knowledge to the appropriate line manager. They also provide advice or recommendations on risk control actions. Ultimately, the decision on acceptability or what to do about the risk belongs to the line manager. The unacceptable risks must be avoided, eliminated, or somehow reduced to the point of acceptability. If the risks remain unacceptable, then that mission should not be flown. Because decisions on risk acceptability are (or should be) managerial decisions, we call this process "risk management."

The second idea involves the level at which risk management decisions are made. Consider these points:

1. There is risk out there.

2. If line managers don't make decisions on risk acceptability, they have merely bucked the decision down to someone who is confronted with the risk and must make the decision. We have put the decision in the hands of the individual least able to make an objective evaluation of it. The line managers lost their chance to make the decision correctly and must now accept the resulting decision which may have been made for the wrong reasons.

Looking at this another way, decisions on whether or not to accept a risk should be based strictly on the magnitude of the risk and the benefits of accepting it. Nothing else counts, including personal convenience, supreme self-confidence, peer pressure, or any of the hundreds of other reasons someone may decide to take a risk. Furthermore, it would be nice to make these decisions in an atmosphere where there is plenty of time, plenty of information, and no need to keep the desk straight and level while figuring out what to do next.

Remember, if we don't elevate risk management decisions to the proper level, we are merely delegating the authority to make them down to the cockpit — and we are going to have to accept the resulting decisions.

The minimum equipment list (MEL) is a good example of risk management in action. We have decided (and it was not easy) what equipment deficiencies our pilots may or may not fly with. That is one less problem the pilot has to worry about and we have reduced the chance that the pilot will accept a risk for the wrong reasons.

Question. Aren't we infringing on the inherent rights of the pilot-in-command (PIC) to make all decisions related to the flight?

I don't think so. In the first place, there is no such inherent right. The PIC has ultimate responsibility for the safety of the flight and acquires some additional rights in emergency situations, but the PIC does not have any inherent right to not comply with established company standards.

Even in emergency situations, the company has the right to specify which considerations will be given priority. First priority, obviously, would be safety of the passengers and aircraft. Availability of maintenance and scheduling convenience might be considerations, but not primary considerations. That's risk management.

APPLICATION

The risk management process follows a fairly logical pattern. As with any management tool, it is possible to get carried away with the technique itself and create more paper than progress. A lot of what we do in aviation is either simple or common and it is pointless to generate a lot of activity on something we already know how to do. In most flying operations, for example, the process of starting engines, taxi, takeoff, and departure is fundamental to almost anything else we do and probably doesn't require a lot of study. In general, we should apply risk management techniques to those parts of the mission which are neither simple nor common. If we are going to try some sling loading or long-line work with our helicopter, maybe that's the only part we need to worry about.

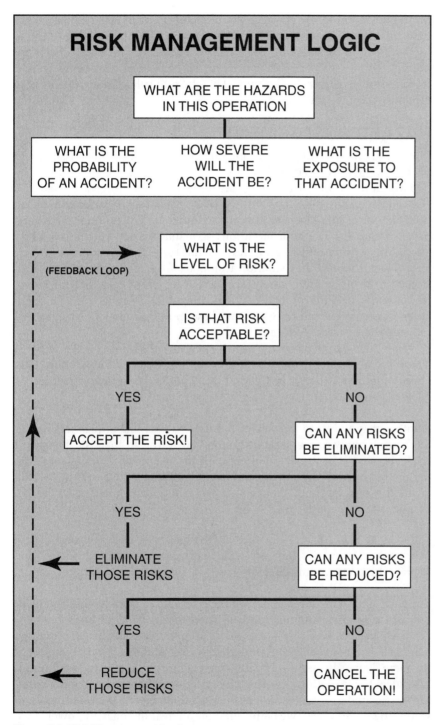

Figure 6-1. Risk Management Logic

Maybe we're in the law enforcement or emergency medical response business. Instead of making a normal engine start/taxi/takeoff, we want to "scramble" our aircraft into the air in less than five minutes. That's not normal, simple, or common and might be something that could benefit from risk management techniques. Let's take that last example and play around with it a little.

HAZARD ASSESSMENT

Consult Figure 6-1. Step one at the top is to make an accurate assessment of the hazards involved. This is a vital step and it is the step that is frequently done poorly or not at all. As a result, we are forced to make our risk management decisions with either inaccurate information or no information at all. This won't come as news to professional managers, because that's a common situation in management. You never know everything you would like to know at the time you must make a decision. Nevertheless, that shouldn't stop us from trying to get the best information. In aviation safety, we have a tendency to either minimize the obvious hazards or ignore them altogether. Maybe some of them should be ignored, but only after we have put them down on paper and realistically considered them.

There are a couple of ways to assess the hazards of an operation. One simple method is listed in Chapter 11. This is essentially a method of subjectively ranking risks in relationship to each other.

Another way is to use the risk or hazard analysis techniques in Chapter 18. In risk analysis we assign a numerical rating to the risk. In hazard analysis, we list each hazard along with the means of reducing or eliminating that hazard. If it can't be reduced or eliminated, we say so. We look at all the hazards (and their solutions, if any) and make a subjective assessment of the total risk.

A third way is to subjectively evaluate the hazards based on probability of occurrence; severity if they do occur; and total exposure to them. This logic is the basis for this chapter.

Suppose our organization really wants to be able to launch our airplane or helicopter on five minutes' notice. There are several obvious hazards. Since we need to save time somewhere, all possible cockpit switches must be preset (or "cocked") to a standard position. If they are not, the pilot is in some jeopardy assuming that the cockpit is correctly configured. Likewise, the takeoff trim setting must be correctly computed and preset. Maybe our radar or navigation system needs longer than five minutes to warm up or erect. If so, we better plan on preheat or constant power if we really intend to launch in five minutes. The point is, a little constructive thinking about what can go wrong will usually identify the majority of the hazards involved. What we want to do is anticipate them; not discover them.

RISK ASSESSMENT

Step two is to take your total assessment of the risk involved (be honest, now) and ask the line managers if they are prepared to accept that risk. You can see that if you have fooled yourself, and the line managers, on the assessment of the hazards involved, you are likely to fool them here, too. They will be taking a bigger risk than they want to take — and they won't know it. This is the "uninformed risk" mentioned in an earlier chapter.

If they conclude that the risk is acceptable, then they should go ahead with the operation and not waste any more time agonizing over the hazards. Granted, an accident could still occur, but if your logic in assessing the risk is sound, you shouldn't worry about that possibility. If you want to worry about something, worry about the accuracy of the information you were given on the nature of the hazards. That's what the line managers based their decision on and their decision can be no better than the information they were given.

Suppose, though, that they decide that the risk is not acceptable. Now what?

HAZARD ELIMINATION

Step three is to look at each of the hazards find those that can be eliminated. By keeping ground power on the aircraft, for example, the problem of erection of the navigation system may go away. Does that change your total assessment of the risk? Maybe, maybe not.

Suppose that none of the hazards can be eliminated and the total risk remains unacceptable. Now what?

HAZARD REDUCTION

Step four is to look for hazards that can be reduced. What you would like to do is to reduce the exposure to a particular hazard; reduce the probability that it will occur; or reduce its severity if it does occur. By doing this, you are trying to drag the total risk assessment down to something acceptable. Maybe you develop, for example, a special "cocking" checklist for configuring the cockpit for scramble operations. This won't absolutely guarantee that all the switches will be correctly positioned, but it will certainly reduce the possibility that they aren't. Furthermore, by specifying a standard fuel load for all scramble operations, maybe you can reduce the possibility that the plane will be mis-trimmed at takeoff. By now, maybe the line managers are willing to accept the remaining risks and fly the mission.

Suppose, though, that you've gone through this exercise of hazard elimination and hazard reduction and the total risk is still unacceptable. Now what?

Easy. Cancel the mission! Don't fly it! Try and follow along here. Based on an accurate (we hope) assessment of the hazards, the line managers have judged the risks to be high and unacceptable. They have seriously considered eliminating or reducing the hazards and the total risk still remains unacceptable. There is really not much more they can do except cancel the mission. They have made a series of logical managerial decisions based on sound information.

RISK ACCEPTANCE

If, in spite of all logic, they insist on flying a mission involving unacceptable risks, they are kidding themselves. They are, in fact, saying one of two things.

1. The risk involved in this mission is really acceptable, but I don't like having to accept it, or

2. I choose not to take any action to eliminate or reduce the hazards involved in this mission.

RISK MANAGEMENT APPLIED TO ACCIDENT ANALYSIS

Let's suppose an accident occurs. Let's turn this risk management idea around and apply it to an analysis of the accident. Figure 6-2 shows one way to do this. This is very similar to the top branches of a MORT (Management Oversight Risk Tree) chart. Here, we use the term LTA (Less Than Adequate) which is a catch-all phrase to describe something that wasn't very good. An analysis might go like this.

If the accident involved an acceptable risk, then we should accept the accident. That was always a possibility. On the other hand, if it involved an unacceptable risk, then one of two factors must have occurred.

The first factor involves our risk prevention scheme. It didn't work because we either didn't select adequate prevention methods or we didn't implement them.

The second factor involves what the MORT people would call management factors. Our prevention policy was flawed; our implementation of that policy was flawed; or our assessment of risk wasn't very good. Perhaps we made no assessment of risk at all, or if we made one, it wasn't accurate.

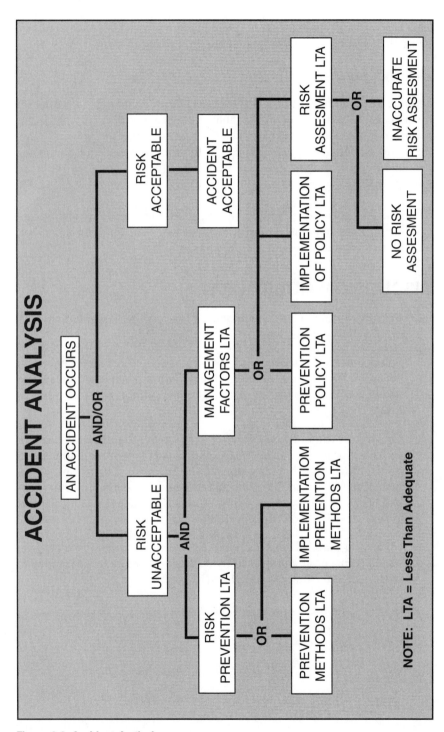

Figure 6-2. Accident Analysis

This type of analysis leads us to decide where our risk management system failed; assuming we were using one in the first place.

SUMMARY

Perhaps the chief benefit of this risk management concept is that it forces the manager to put money on the table and make an informed, intelligent decision. It also lets the manager see the results of that action — or inaction. The acceptance of risk belongs to the line manager along with the results of whatever decisions have been made (or not made) on reducing the hazards.

All in all, it is a useful technique, but, as stated earlier, the whole process is no better than step one. The risk management decisions can be no better than the original assessment of the hazards.

DISCUSSION QUESTIONS

1. Identify the areas in which your company has standards which exceed federal requirements.

2. Select some hazard associated with flying (e.g. Controlled Flight Into Terrain (CFIT), structural icing, engine failure.) What actions can be taken to eliminate the hazards and control the risks to acceptable levels.

3. You are the safety manager for a large primary flight training school that has had a series of accidents and incidents involving touch and go landings in aircraft with retractable gear. The Chief Flight Instructor has asked for a risk analysis and assessment of this problem. How would you go about conducting such an analysis and assessment? What are the considerations?

4. Under the topic of Risk Acceptance, the author listed two reasons why a manager might elect to fly a mission in spite of unacceptable risks. Can you think of any others?

INTRODUCTION TO SECTION 2

THE HUMAN ELEMENT

If you trace the history of an aircraft accident back far enough, you will always find the human element involved somewhere – maybe way back in the design of the aircraft or the initial training of the pilot. Although this is not a book on aviation psychology or human factors, we can't ignore the fact that a large percentage of our problems are not related to the aircraft; but to how we operate it and maintain it. The next three chapters explore some basic ideas about risk, punishment and motivation. Chapter 10 summarizes some of the human factors problems confronting us.

THEORY OF RISK

As we have already stated, aviation safety is very much a people problem. Accidents are related more to the way the equipment is used than to the equipment itself. Few accident sequences begin with a component failure. If you want to get philosophical, all aircraft accident causes (or component failures) are people-related. The airplane was either inadequately designed, improperly manufactured, incorrectly maintained, or misused by the pilot. Things don't just sit there and break by themselves. There is some human input somewhere.

Granted, we can sometimes solve a "people problem" with an equipment solution. We can "idiot proof" the machinery. We can rig the landing gear, for example, so that it absolutely cannot be retracted on the ground and we can quit worrying about that type of accident. There is a limit, though, to how far we can go in that direction. Short of welding it in the down position, we have yet to figure out how to rig the landing gear so that the plane absolutely cannot be landed with the gear retracted.

Eventually, we have to place considerable reliance on human beings who come to us with about the same capabilities and limitations they had when the airplane was invented. They haven't changed much. They can still only reach so far, pull so hard, and keep track of only so many things at once.

This is not a book on psychology or behavioral theory, but we can't ignore the human factors side of the problem just because we don't happen to be psychologists. We must deal with it daily and it would be helpful to develop a few ideas on what works and what doesn't.

WHY DO PEOPLE TAKE RISKS?

For openers, let's discuss some ideas about risky behavior. This is really the nub of our problem. We have pilots and maintenance technicians out there taking risks and shortcuts and doing all sorts of undesirable things, any one of which could conceivably lead to an accident. Why?

Let's suppose that we're running a commercial helicopter operation. One of our pilots — call him Charlie — takes off with his helicopter loaded well above the maximum allowable gross weight; flies in weather that is occasionally below our company minimums; delivers his load where it belongs and returns without incident. Has that ever happened in the real world? Certainly!

Charlie took a number of risks. We don't know why, but if we were to list all the possible reasons, we might come up with some of these:

1. Undisciplined. Charlie thinks that rules are mainly for other people.

2. Highly motivated. Charlie knows that this means money for the company and he really wants to deliver that load.

3. Ignorant or untrained. Charlie doesn't understand why we establish gross weight limits. No one ever taught him how to evaluate a mission and the weather.

4. Correct equipment not available. A larger helicopter which is IFR certified and could easily carry the load is out of service.

5. Time pressure. The load is needed now; not tomorrow.

6. Supervisory pressure. Charlie knows (or believes) that the chief of flight operations wants that load delivered — now.

7. Action is tolerated. Regardless of the company standards, that type of flying is routinely done and condoned.

8. Small risk, big benefit. We'll discuss this one later.

We could probably come up with another 15 or 20 possible reasons, but these are enough to make the point. If number 1 is correct, then we are going to have to get rid of Charlie. Our equipment is just too expensive to let anyone touch it who is not going to fly it the way we want it flown. Our chances of changing the behavior of someone who has no intention of following our rules is not good.

If number 2 is correct, we've got ourselves a good employee, but his enthusiasm is aimed in the wrong direction. We can salvage him.

If any of numbers 3 through 7 are the problem, then our management system is at fault; not Charlie. We can change any of those and remove the reason for the risky behavior.

CAN WE CHANGE THE BEHAVIOR OF THE RISK-TAKER?

Number 8 (small risk, big benefit) leads to some interesting ideas and may explain a lot about risky behavior. From Charlie's point of view, the risk was a small one. He has done the same thing many times before and he didn't see any problem with it. On the other hand, he considered the chances of being in trouble with his supervisor if he didn't deliver the load to be quite high - perhaps 100%. The benefit, in this case, was in not getting fired and in Charlie's mind it was a very big benefit compared to the risk. In any small risk, big benefit situation, we should always expect the individual to take the risk. All of us would probably do the same thing. We routinely take risks every day just in going to work or crossing the street. We all have a built-in logic circuit which automatically compares the risk with the benefits and tells us that it's okay to cross in the middle of the block; there is no traffic coming.

In operating aircraft, though, it's not okay. We want them operated correctly all of the time; not just when it is convenient. If we think that Charlie is using this small risk, big benefit logic, we may be able to change his behavior by simply removing the benefit. In this case, he must learn that he is not going to get fired for following the rules and meeting our standards regardless of whether the load gets delivered or not. We can go further, in fact, by letting him know that discipline is always going to be the result of violating the rules and standards - regardless of whether the load gets delivered or not.

If the load is consistently not getting delivered, then we need to critically examine our methods; but not our pilot who is doing exactly what we want him to do.

In actual practice, though, that's not what we do. Charlie comes back from delivering the load and we pat him on the back and tell him what a great job that was. We have just reinforced the incorrect behavior and we can reasonably expect Charlie to do exactly the same thing next time.

Joe is another one of our helicopter pilots. We send Joe out on the same mission. Joe takes one look at the load and the weather and turns it down. We don't exactly criticize or punish Joe for this, because we know he is technically correct, but we don't give him a pat on the back, either. Joe sees Charlie getting all the back pats and he rapidly decides to start behaving like Charlie. Now we've got two pilots trained to do it wrong and we can't understand why.

This situation occurs more often than you might suspect. What's happening here is that our reward system is working backwards. We are rewarding the behavior that we are trying to discourage and doing nothing to encourage the behavior we really want.

RESULTS VERSUS METHOD

It is my personal view that in aviation we have a tendency to reward results rather than method. This leads to the situation where the risky behavior is tolerated, even encouraged as long as it gets the job done. If an accident occurs, though, watch out. Now, we're going to get a rope and hang somebody for violating a standard that was on the books, but everybody was ignoring.

Skinner, the gentleman who worked with mice and developed operant conditioning theory, taught us that we can obtain the behavior we want by consistently rewarding the correct behavior and punishing (or withholding reward for) the incorrect behavior. Why do we think that won't work with people?

We probably think that way because we can tell people how we want something done and they can read it in the Ops Manual. Mice don't listen well and they can't read. The flaw in that reasoning is that people do not respond to what they hear (or read) as much as they respond to what they are rewarded or punished for. Skinner was right!

If we were all consistent managers, we would set our standards for operation and reward or punish conformance with those standards. If the results were not what we wanted, then we would change our standards; but we would not change our reward-punishment system. This way, we would build a strong work force of people who knew if they followed the rules, they would succeed and be rewarded.

Bottom line. Risk-taking is normal human behavior. When a risk unacceptable to us is taken, there is usually a reason for it. By finding out what it is, we may be able to change the behavior. Frequently we may discover that the reason for the behavior is not with the individual at all. It is in our management system — and we can fix that.

ATTITUDES

Another way of examining this problem of risk is to examine the attitudes of people who take risks. It is generally felt that attitudes can be changed while personality traits are relatively immutable. Considerable work has been done in this area by The Ohio State University Aviation Psychology Department. Both the Federal Aviation Administration and Transport Canada have developed Aeronautical Decision Making (ADM) training programs based on this research. See also Chapter 10.

As part of this research, five hazardous attitudes have been identified and defined which can be recognized and corrected by both individuals and supervisors. The following description of these attitudes is derived largely from FAA Advisory Circular 60-22, *Aeronautical Decision Making*.

1. **ANTI-AUTHORITY**: ("Don't tell me!") Some people do not like anyone telling them what to do. We probably all have periods of time when we feel that way. The person who consistently displays this attitude is the one who resists rules and regulations as a matter of personal policy. (Antidote: Follow the rules. They are usually right.)

2. **IMPULSIVITY**: ("Do something — quickly!") This describes people who react without thinking to almost anything. They never analyze a situation or consider alternatives. They never have time. Actually, there are very few actions on an airplane that have to be taken immediately. Failure to analyze a problem leads to things like shutting down the wrong engine. (Antidote: Not so fast. Think first).

On the other hand, there are some situations in which "impulsive" actions are required. An example is a Ground Proximity Warning System (GPWS) "PULL UP!" warning. The pilot must instinctively react to that without analyzing it or considering alternatives. Because that is an abnormal reaction for most pilots, it has led to something called the "delayed response syndrome." The GPWS actually provided adequate warning, but the plane hit the mountain anyway because the pilot was analyzing it rather than reacting to it. This creates a problem. We want the pilot to stop and analyze his problems most of the time, but here, we want him to act impulsively.

The problem may be that early GPWS equipment (which relied on the radar altimeter) did not and could not give the pilot enough warning to analyze the situation. Enhanced GPWS equipment will be based on an entirely different method (satellite GPS) and should give the pilot better situational awareness of position and obstructions and a series of graduated warnings allowing analysis. That's the engineering solution (Chapter 5) in action.

3. **INVULNERABILITY**: ("It won't happen to me.") To some degree, we all feel invulnerable. If we didn't, we would never drive a car — or fly an airplane. We cannot do what we do if we are afraid of it. There is a fine line, though, between overconfidence and prudence. Pilots who lack any sense of prudence are more likely to take unacceptable risks. (Antidote: It could happen to me.)

4. **MACHOISM**: ("I can do it.") Some pilots view each flight as a new requirement to prove their skills. They treat each landing as a competitive event and they are inclined to take additional risks to prove themselves. These are the ones who will almost never make

a go-around or a missed approach. They see that as a personal failure. (Antidote: Taking chances is foolish.)

5. **RESIGNATION**: ("What's the use?") This describes the pilot who just quits when he comes up against a difficult situation. This is sometimes a cultural problem. Some people have a strong belief in luck, fate, the will of God, and so on. Unfortunately, they are flying an airplane that does not depend on luck, fate, or the will of God. It was designed to survive the single failure or error. Our method of training pilots assumes that there are always alternatives — if the pilot will use them. (Antidote: I'm not helpless. I can make a difference.)

CAN WE IDENTIFY RISK-TAKERS THROUGH THEIR BEHAVIOR STYLES?

Maybe. We're pretty good at identifying unsatisfactory behavior patterns AFTER an accident occurs, but we are not very good at identifying that same behavior pattern before an accident.

The problem is that few people exhibit really extreme behavior that is totally unacceptable. Most of us have behavior or personality quirks which are not unique or unusual; but could be unsatisfactory in certain situations. Identifying unsatisfactory behavior (or at least behavior that we don't like) is easy enough, but equating that with a potential accident is difficult.

In 1971, an international study on accident proneness (Shaw and Sichel quoted in FAA Pamphlet 8740-38, see Bibliography) examined a large number of accidents and attempted to characterize the behavior that was consistently present in accidents and compare that with the behavior of people who had never been involved in an accident.

ABNORMAL AND UNACCEPTABLE BEHAVIOR

This behavior is extreme and seldom found in aircraft accidents. (The Shaw and Sichel study examined all types of accidents.) People in this group have one or more of the following behavior characteristics:

1. Mentally defective or psychotic

2. Unintelligent, unobservant, unadaptable

3. Disorganized, disoriented, or badly disturbed

4. Maladjusted

5. Distorted perception of life or distorted sense of values

6. Emotionally unstable

7. Exhibits uncontrolled aggression

8. Anti-social attitudes; criminal tendencies

9. Suicidal tendencies

BEHAVIOR USUALLY CONSIDERED NORMAL

Most of us probably have one or more of these behavior traits. These are the ones that consistently show up as factors in aircraft accidents. A person exhibiting a significant number of these may be at risk. In reading these, perhaps you'll recognize someone you know.

1. Selfish or self-centered

2. Highly competitive

3. Overconfident

4. Irritable and cantankerous

5. Holds grudges, harbors resentment

6. Blame-avoidant, always has an excuse

7. Intolerant, impatient

8. Antagonized by, or resists, authority

9. Frustrated and discontented

10. Feels inadequate, must continually prove themselves

11. Anxious, tense, panicky

12. Overly sensitive to criticism

13. Helpless, or constantly in need of guidance

14. Chronically indecisive

15. Cannot concentrate

16. Easily influenced or intimidated

17. Careless or frivolous

18. Does not recognize own limitations

19. Predisposed to alcohol or drugs

20. Lacks common sense

21. Immature, foolhardy, impetuous

22. Irresponsible, hypersensitive

23. Unrealistic goals

24. Lacks self-discipline

BEHAVIOR PATTERNS OF GOOD ACCIDENT RISKS

Just as no one is totally free of all the characteristics listed above, it cannot be said that the people with the behavior characteristics listed below will never have an accident. Nevertheless, people who do not make accident-causing mistakes in an airplane tend to have these behavior characteristics.

1. Well-balanced, well-controlled

2. Mature

3. Healthy and realistic outlook and goals

4. Satisfactory interpersonal relations

5. Kindly and tolerant attitudes toward others

6. Well-developed social and civic conscience

7. Ingrained sense of responsibility

8. Moderation, and adequate control over impulses and emotions

9. Positive attitudes

10. Accurately able to assess situations and act decisively

11. Contented, cheerful, adaptable, and accepting

12. Reasonably intelligent

13. Aware of their own weaknesses and limitations

While the final chapter on risk theory has not yet been written, this idea of training pilots to recognize and cope with hazardous attitudes and unsatisfactory behavior styles has a lot of merit.

SUMMARY

We are all risk-takers. Risk-taking is a normal human activity. The differences among us are in how we approach the risks and why we take them.

DISCUSSION QUESTIONS

1. You have a pilot who has taken an unacceptable risk because he thought it would help the company and that is what the company wanted him to do. What arguments are you going to use to try and change this attitude?

2. Pick a pilot of your acquaintance and cite the abnormal, normal, and desirable behavior patterns that pilot exhibits. On the whole, is this pilot a good accident risk?

PUNISHMENT: DOES IT PREVENT ACCIDENTS?

Most people would agree that rewarding correct behavior is more effective than punishing incorrect behavior. We will talk about developing aviation safety awards programs in Chapter 16. A discussion of the value of punishment is more appropriate here in our examination of the human element in aviation safety.

Let's suppose your organization has just had an aircraft accident. It didn't kill anyone, but it did a lot of damage. It destroyed one of your aircraft.

The investigation is in progress, but it doesn't take a genius or a big report to tell you what happened. The pilot screwed up — badly!

Anyway you look at it, the pilot's actions were absolutely unacceptable. You are sitting at your desk thinking of all the bad things you would like to do to the pilot.

Questions. Will this do any good? Will it change the pilot's behavior? Will it change the behavior of your other pilots? Will it prevent this type of accident in the future?

Good questions! You deserve answers to them before you reach for your skinning knife. Let's discuss a few ideas.

DISCIPLINE

This word has different meanings depending on how it is used. When we speak of disciplining someone, we are using it in a negative sense in that we are applying a form of punishment in the hope that someone's behavior will be corrected because of it. On the other hand, when we speak of a group as "disciplined" or of pilots as "well disciplined" we mean it in a positive sense. We mean that particular group may be expected to consistently conform to whatever rules guide their behavior. They do it not because they fear punishment, but because they have been trained that way and they are individually convinced of the wisdom of conformance as a means of achieving objectives.

In my view, pilots are "disciplined" and I prefer to use the term in its most positive sense. Adverse actions are punishment, not discipline.

PUNISHMENT

This can be loosely defined as any perceived adverse action. The key word here is "perceived." Punishment is very much in the eyes of the punishee. Regardless of what you may call it, if it resulted directly from the accident and it is adverse to the interests of the individual — it is punishment. Thus the fairly routine procedure of grounding a pilot following an accident can be perceived as a form of punishment, whether you mean it that way or not. (If you don't mean this as punishment, you can remove most of the stigma by, first, making it automatic for every pilot involved in an accident regardless of circumstances and, second, explaining to everyone what is going to happen before an accident occurs. Prompt restoration of flight privileges will also help.)

Let's talk about punishment. Our concepts of punishment probably come to us from primitive times where we used it for simple revenge. An eye for an eye - even the score - that sort of thing. Some countries of the world have not moved too far from that. More recent concepts of punishment see it as a means to protect society (incarceration) or a deterrent to others (public, or at least publicized punishment). Finally, of course, we see punishment as a means of ensuring that the individual will be deterred from similar behavior in the future. Thus the three principle reasons for punishment are revenge, correction of the individual, and deterrence of others. To those we might add a fourth; personal satisfaction. In the absence of any other good reason, punishing someone seems to make us feel better. At least we've done something!

Let's get back to our aircraft accident and the pilot who erred. Before we apply punishment, let's examine our reasons for punishment.

REVENGE

DO WE WANT REVENGE? Maybe, but how much are we going to get out of the pilot's body — or bank account? It is a little unrealistic to expect the pilot to pay us back for the airplane. Before we let the pilot fly it, we should have covered ourselves with insurance. In addition, we should have subjected the pilot to some sort of training and certification process to assure ourselves of acceptable flying ability. Knowing what subsequently happened, we might wish that we had either trained the pilot better or withheld certification, but it's a little late now. Our revenge, if any, is going to come from the insurance company. Punishing the pilot isn't going to help.

PROTECTION OF SOCIETY

DO WE NEED TO PROTECT SOCIETY FROM THIS PILOT? Probably not. As long as we are talking about errors of judgment or technique and not willful violations of flying regulations, society is not in much danger. We may, in the extreme case, conclude that this person should never have been certified as a pilot in the first place. If so, who is at fault? We who trained and certified the pilot or the pilot who merely discovered the hard way that the training was inadequate? Maybe society needs protection from a system that will not prevent an individual from eventually achieving PIC status based entirely on longevity.

CHANGING INDIVIDUAL BEHAVIOR

DO WE NEED TO CHANGE THE BEHAVIOR OF THIS PILOT? If we are still talking about errors of judgment or technique, it is safe to say that the pilot had absolutely no intention of having that accident in the first place. Now that it has occurred, the pilot has even less intention of having it again. To cite a simple example, the pilot who has landed with the gear retracted is unlikely to ever do so again. Applying punishment won't improve on that. Punishing a pilot who was guilty of some lesser infraction (which the pilot might do again) isn't entirely effective either. Sometimes punishment merely teaches the pilot to not get caught in that infraction again. An entire industry (vehicle radar warning detectors) relies on this principle. That is obviously not satisfactory in aviation safety.

AN EXAMPLE TO OTHERS

DO WE NEED TO MAKE AN EXAMPLE OF THIS PILOT TO OTHERS? This is an interesting question and it can be argued a number of different ways. My view is that it depends entirely on whether the other pilots were planning on doing the same thing our prospective punishee did.

If the accident was genuinely the result of mistakes and misjudgments, punishment probably has zero effect on others. They weren't planning on making those mistakes in the first place and seeing another pilot punished won't change their minds. On a negative note, the punishment could influence them to avoid the circumstances where there might be an opportunity to make the same mistake. Maybe that's what we want. Be careful, though. That's how we develop students who have never been taught the hard things; instructors who won't get off the controls; and pilots who can't operate their airplane in the corners of the flight envelope.

On the other hand, let's suppose that our other pilots were planning on doing the same thing that got this pilot in trouble. They were also planning to ignore certain procedures, restrictions, whatever. Here, punishment can be very effective providing it is applied to the act; not the results. By that I mean that you always punish the pilot who disregards your rules regardless of whether it results in an accident or not. You are punishing the pilot's actions; not the results of those actions. That is an effective way to manage all of your pilots. If you wait for an accident to occur and then apply punishment, you are behaving inconsistently and you lose any benefit that punishment might have on the rest of your pilots. They realize that you are willing to tolerate their misbehavior as long as they don't have an accident. This, you'll notice, complements some similar ideas in Chapter 7.

Another inherent weakness in this idea of punishment as a means of deterring others is the short term effects of that action. There is a certain amount of turnover in any organization and the effects of punishment are completely wasted on people hired after the situation occurred. Granted, we could use the circumstances of the incident as a teaching tool for new hires or we could incorporate those ideas into our initial training. Here, though, we are taking some positive action other than just punishing the individual. We are, in fact, admitting to ourselves that there is more to be done than just punishing someone.

PUNISHING JUDGMENT OR TECHNIQUE

On the whole, punishing poor judgment or technique doesn't seem to satisfy any of the classic reasons for punishment (unless, of course, you include "making me feel better" as a reason). On the negative side, there are a lot of arguments against it.

1. It can have some negative reactions among the other pilots if it is perceived as undeserved or if it creates unreasonable fear.

2. It does not change the circumstances of the accident. It is likely that the same circumstances occurring again will produce the same result.

3. Fear of punishment inhibits internal communications. If you do not believe this, try comparing the number of hard or heavy landings made to those actually reported. Your ability to manage a successful flying operation depends to some extent on your knowledge of what problems exist and need your attention. If your people are unwilling to bring problems to your attention, you are managing in a vacuum. You think you know what's going on, but you really don't. If you want to create the atmosphere where pilots will not bring problems to your attention, try inconsistent and undeserved punishment.

To summarize, there is nothing wrong with punishment fairly and consistently applied. You can use it to change behavior providing you consistently punish the behavior and not the results. Used this way, you can even use it to change the behavior of others. You cannot, however, punish a judgmental error and expect that error will never occur again. Not only have you not prevented the future error; you have also missed the opportunity to take some other action (training; a change in procedures?) which might have prevented the future error. Moreover, punishment is frequently a short term solution to a long term problem. Sometimes we are better off if we waive our opportunity to punish (short term satisfaction) in favor of future knowledge of this situation (long term prevention).

As an example of this, consider the following true story.

Back in the 1960s, the United States Air Force went into the oil analysis business as a means of determining turbine engine health and predicting failure due to excessive wear of bearings and accessory drive gears. It involved spectrographically analyzing an engine oil sample after each flight (or several flights) and keeping a history of the amount of various metal elements found in the sample. If the volume (in parts per million) increased, the engine was wearing abnormally and should be changed. The program saved both aircraft and lives.

The original sampling bottles were small bottles used by pharmacies to dispense pills. Only a small sample of oil was needed and these pill bottles were sterile and didn't contaminate the sample.

This created a problem with the J-57 engine which, in various models, was used in five different Air Force aircraft. The bottle, if dropped during the sampling process, would sometimes fall into the oil tank filler neck. Once in the tank, the bottle would rattle around and eventually wedge itself into the standpipe in the bottom of the tank where it was a perfect fit. This might happen on the next flight or the tenth flight; but it would eventually happen. With the oil flow blocked, the engine would only run for a few minutes before failing.

This cost the Air Force a lot of engines and several accidents. In analyzing it, the Air Force decided to look at the units that were <u>not</u> having that problem. That led to some interesting conclusions. The units that were having the problem would routinely punish a technician for dropping a bottle in the tank — if they knew who he was. The other units would reward (or at least thank) a technician for telling them that a bottle had been dropped in the tank. The difference was in the perception of punishment as a means of preventing unintentional errors and in the realization that it was better to have knowledge of the problem than discover it through an engine failure.

The solution to all this was absurdly simple. Use sampling bottles that were too big to fit into the tank!

To go back to the original question, punishment may do a lot of things, but preventing accidents is rarely one of them.

THE BLAME CYCLE

Looking at this another way, some psychologists define this urge to punish as part of the "blame cycle." When an error occurs, we have a tendency to assume that it results from some personal characteristic such as laziness, incompetence, carelessness, inattention, and so on. This makes the error somewhat deliberate, or at least the fault of the person making the error. The solution, therefore, is some form of punishment; perhaps exhortations (Be Safe, Prevent Accidents!), warnings, or sanctions. When this doesn't prevent the error, we naturally assume that there wasn't enough punishment. A few more strokes of the wire brush ought to do the trick.

This ignores some basic facts. Errors are results; not causes. Errors are more likely to be the result of situations that provoke errors or tasks that encourage error than they are of the lazy and careless. This is particularly true in aviation where we can say that the pilot had absolutely no intention of making that mistake and sincerely wishes that it had not been made!

There are some ways out of this cycle. One is to accept the idea that it is a lot easier to change the situation or the system than the individual. If the cause of the error is actually situational or systemic, punishing the individual just isn't going to work.

As an example, maintenance technicians were being regularly threatened with extreme punishment if they didn't refer to the technical manuals as they performed maintenance. One quick look at the situation explained why. The technicians had no inherent objections to using the manuals, but they were hard-bound in four-inch thick books, wouldn't stay open to the page they wanted, and there was no place to put the manual to refer to it as you worked on the plane. Now why do we think that punishing the technician is going to make the manual easier to use?

Another solution is to identify the nature of the common errors and focus on eliminating the most common. One technique for this is called Pareto Analysis. Basically, this involves logging all errors made in a particular operation and ranking them by frequency and percentage of all errors. This involves waiting for a lot of errors to occur, but it does allow focusing on those that occur most frequently; not on those that seldom happen.

ERROR TOLERANCE

We ought to accept the idea that humans have a lot of advantages over machines, but perfection isn't one of them. Humans make errors. If you agree with that, then it should be obvious that our operations should be designed so that a single human error does not result in a catastrophe.

As a case in point, some years ago there was a runway incursion accident at a major airport in the United States. This occurred during night operations where a departing aircraft was cleared onto the runway, "Position and Hold," for an intersection takeoff. The controller forgot the plane was on the runway and couldn't readily see the plane due to darkness. The controller cleared another plane to land on the same runway with disastrous results. That was a single human error and the system could not tolerate it. That particular error (forgetting that a plane is occupying the runway) has occurred a number of times before and will no doubt occur again. It happened, in fact, at that same airport about six months prior to that accident.

It happened on a different runway, though, and that situation could tolerate the single error. The runway had a displaced threshold and the landing aircraft flew directly over the aircraft holding for clearance at the end of the runway. That scared a lot of people, but there was no damage or injury.

In the first situation, the controller making the error was punished. In the second situation, the one resulting in an accident, the principal thrust of the investigation was toward making sure that a controller would never make that mistake again.

That's silly. Of course that mistake will be made again. The thrust should have been toward adjusting the system so that a mistake can be tolerated.

How? Well, without even discussing the lack of surface movement detection equipment in the control tower, we could ban intersection takeoffs. We could eliminate "position and hold" clearances. We could displace the thresholds on all our runways. Finally, if we have enough runways, we could limit takeoffs to one runway and landings to another. That's an easy type of accident to eliminate, but punishing the person who made the mistake isn't one of the ways to do it.

RESOLUTION OF ERROR

Let's approach this from a slightly different direction. Our pilot has made a serious error and we are contemplating punishment. Before we act, let's walk through a logic exercise to try and determine why the error was made. This works best when applied to a specific situation, but the basic idea is shown in Figure 8-1.

Starting at the top of the chart, we ask ourselves if the pilot was aware that the action was wrong. If the answer is "yes," we may be dealing with a genuine disciplinary problem, but we may also be dealing with any number of other reasons why a pilot may have deliberately chosen to violate a rule or a standard. As pilots, we've all been there and done that. Perhaps the pilot had a "drop dead" time for takeoff and was taking a few shortcuts to make it. Perhaps we pressured the pilot into taking the plane "as is."

If the pilot did not know better, then we either exposed the pilot to something beyond the pilot's knowledge and ability or we neglected to ensure the pilot's proficiency and currency in certain procedures. Maybe we upgraded the pilot to PIC too soon. There are no shortcuts to experience and a pilot can meet the technical qualifications long before enough experience has been accumulated to cope with everything that might come up.

The point of this exercise is to show where punishment is effective and where it is not. You can hardly punish a pilot for a lack of training and expect to prevent anything.

You may notice some commonality between this chapter and the preceding one on risk. That's true. Error and risky behavior have a lot in common. The correction of either starts with an understanding of why it occurred in the first place.

DISCUSSION QUESTIONS

1. In the story of the oil sampling bottle, changing the size of the bottle was an example of what type of preventive action? If larger bottles were not immediately available, what other actions could have been taken?

2. Think of an aviation situation, perhaps involving FAR enforcement, where the result of the enforcement action was not to change the behavior, but to merely encourage pilots to not get caught in that behavior.

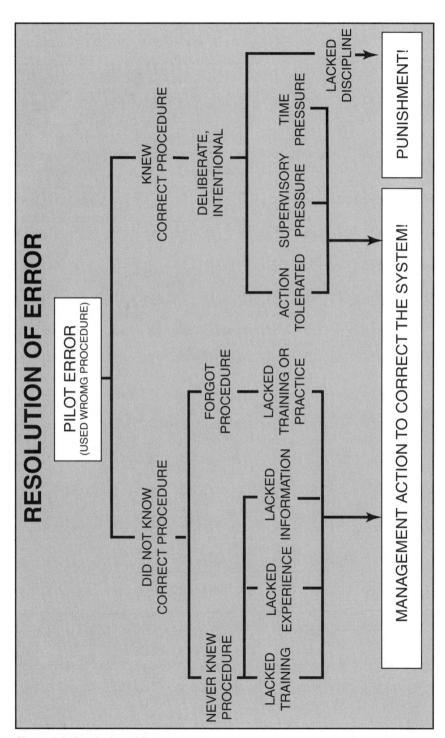

Figure 8-1. Resolution of Error

MOTIVATING SAFE BEHAVIOR

Realistically, there are some things in the human factors arena that we can't do much about. Other than acknowledging them, we can't do much about a pilot's basic physiological capabilities and limitations; nor can we change the environment in which the pilot works. That's the plane we bought and the cockpit came with it. We're stuck with it.

There are some things we can change. We can, for example, change the operational, support, and supervision factors that influence a pilot's actions, and we can change the way a pilot behaves. We can turn a non-checklist user into a checklist user if we approach it in the right manner. (We can also change a checklist user into a non-checklist user just as easily; it will work either way.)

We can do this by understanding something about what makes people want to do things. We take advantage of this by making sure that what they want to do matches what we want done. This is called motivation and the man with the simplest (not necessarily the best) explanation of this was a psychologist named Maslow.

Maslow defined motivation as the drive to fill an open need. Maslow developed a hierarchy of needs and it was his thinking that people are driven to satisfy those needs from the bottom up. Once a need was satisfied; it no longer motivated. In theory, the way to change behavior is to find out what needs are unfilled and provide the individual with an opportunity to fill those needs — your way.

PHYSIOLOGICAL NEEDS

On the bottom of Maslow's hierarchy are physiological needs; air to breathe, food to eat, and water to drink. There is nothing useful to us here, because the people we work with already have those needs satisfied. They no longer motivate. An example is going to the grocery store after a big meal. Since you are not hungry, you are not motivated to buy a lot of food.

SAFETY NEEDS

On the next level, Maslow listed safety needs which he defined as the need to feel secure or free from danger or threat. If something threatens us, we tend to drop whatever else we are doing and remove that threat.

This is the level at which a large number of our safety programs are aimed — and they are not very effective. We spend a lot of our time trying to get people to do things a certain way — or not do them — by threatening them with an accident. It just doesn't work. An example are the campaigns to get people to wear seat belts in automobiles by promising them fewer injuries if they have an accident. The problem is that people who drive automobiles are not afraid of them and have no intention of having an accident. There is no unfilled need in the form of threat or danger. The absolutely predictable reaction to this type of campaign is, "I am not going to have an accident; therefore there is no reason to wear a seat belt." We have been trying to motivate people at a level where their needs are already filled.

We can elevate the same reasoning to the aviation business. Pilots are not afraid of airplanes. Attempting to change their behavior by threatening them with an accident — a fear they do not have — isn't going to work.

SOCIAL NEEDS

The next level of needs in Maslow's hierarchy is the social level. We all have a need to belong to and be accepted by a group and we are willing to change our behavior to whatever is necessary for that social acceptance. There are always unfilled needs at this level (and above) and this can be a very powerful motivational force.

Pilots want to be recognized as pilots and be accepted by other pilots. If the image of a pilot required a mustache, you can bet that those that could would grow one and those that couldn't would think seriously about pasting one on. Likewise, if one of norms in a particular organization is that checklists are always used on every flight; everyone will use the checklists. If, on the other hand, a "good old boy" network exists and using a checklist is the sign of a wimp, you can bet that few people will use the checklists. This social acceptance thing can go either way on you. As a matter of fact, when you note an unsafe behavior pattern among a group of pilots, you might just check and see how high up it goes. It probably originates with the senior pilots in the organization, because they are the ones who set the standards for behavior.

This leads to some good news. If you contemplate changing the behavior of a group, you only need to change the behavior of a few people — the formal and informal leaders of the group. If they change, the others will usually change, too.

One interesting way to study this phenomena is something called group dynamics. In any given group, there is a Designated Leader, one or more Informal Leaders and the "Ins" and the "Outs."

The designated leader is, of course, the person in charge of that group. A designated leader may also be an informal leader; but not always. The informal leaders are those members of the group who are respected by the others and, by their actions, establish the norms for the behavior of that group. In a flying operation, these are typically the Chief Pilots, Check Airmen, Instructors or maybe just the old gray-haired Captain who has a million hours and has been around forever.

In some groups, the informal leader only leads in specific areas. In meetings of the company executives, the Director of Safety should be the informal leader when the discussion turns to something related to safety.

The "Ins" are the members of the group who are accepted by the rest of the group. The "Outs" are members of the group who are not accepted. A person new to the group usually starts as an "Out," but becomes an "In" fairly quickly. The permanent "Outs" are those whose behavior or ability consistently offends the rest of the group. They are consistently ignored. Every group has a few "Outs" and changing their behavior is very difficult. That's probably why they are an "Out."

As an aside, it is fairly easy for the Director of Safety to become a permanent "Out." Just consistently demonstrate that you're following some agenda other than helping the organization achieve its goals and you'll be talking to yourself. Nobody will listen to you.

Back to the point of all this, changing group behavior is largely a matter of changing the behavior of the designated and informal leaders. The "Ins" will readily change. Maybe some of the "Outs" will change, but don't bet on it.

As an example, one organization had a difficult problem with propeller safety. All of their maintenance personnel had been trained on turbine engines and the acquisition of some prop jobs created safety problems. The maintenance technicians had no particular fear of propellers and had the bad habit of walking through the propeller arc when it wasn't running; something a recip technician would never do.

The results were predictable. Two technicians dead over a two-year period. Everyone agreed that the problem was one of bad habits, but the prospect of changing the behavior of a large group of people looked impossible.

The Director of Safety assembled the designated and informal leaders and asked them to change their personal propeller habits, which were among the worst. They agreed. That took about a week and that was all that was necessary. After two weeks, you couldn't find anyone in that organization who wasn't walking around the propeller and avoiding its arc.

EGO NEEDS

Maslow's fourth level in his hierarchy is the ego level. We all need to get satisfaction out of what we do. That is probably the biggest single reason why pilots are pilots. They get an enormous amount of satisfaction from flying the airplane, and they will tend to fly it in the manner that satisfies them most.

The way to take advantage of this is to make sure that they do get satisfaction from flying it correctly and they do not get satisfaction from flying it incorrectly and violating the organization's safety standards. This is essentially the same message expressed in Chapter 7.

How do you reward them for flying the planes correctly when they would secretly rather be doing aerobatics or flying under the bridge? "Off on time, flown as scheduled, no problems," ought to be worth an occasional "attaboy" (or an "attagirl" where appropriate). There is a saying that flying is boring only if you do it right. There is considerable truth to that and boredom deserves an occasional reward if you want it to continue. If you do that often enough, that will become the norm and it will be satisfying.

In addition, the pilot who takes some action in the interest of safety (missed approach, weather diversion) deserves an "attaboy." At the time the pilot did that, there must have been some concern about how that was going to be received. The news that it was considered a good decision is a form of reward. Lack of any such reward breeds suspicion that maybe it wasn't such a good decision after all. Criticism, as you might guess, kills the whole program. No more missed approaches.

SELF-FULFILLMENT NEEDS

The top of Maslow's hierarchy is the self-fulfillment level. We all have a need to somehow make a contribution or to leave our mark on something and be able to say, "That's mine. I did that." The book you are reading was written in part to satisfy the author's self-fulfillment needs.

Many people wander through life without ever satisfying that need. They never have an opportunity to make a contribution. No one ever asks them for their help.

Aviation safety, as it turns out, can offer people an opportunity to fill that square. It goes back to the idea of participation mentioned several times in this book. If you ask people to help or participate by serving on a committee, contributing their ideas, speaking at a safety meeting, assisting with an investigation — whatever — you are offering them an opportunity to make a contribution and you are gaining participation in your program.

SUMMARY

You can change behavior if you concentrate on what needs are unfilled and provide people with an opportunity to fill them. Don't waste your time working on needs that are already filled. Caution: it is just as easy to change behavior in the wrong direction.

DISCUSSION QUESTIONS

1. Some airlines provide pilots with extremely accurate flight plans and predictions of fuel consumption and offer the pilots bonuses for using less fuel. What level of motivation is this? From an aviation safety point of view, what are some of the predictable results of this program?

2. Getting airline passengers to pay attention to the safety briefing has become almost impossible. What motivates passengers to not pay attention? What could be done to change that?

3. Identify some of the "informal leaders" in your flying organization and some risky behavior they engage in. How could you motivate these "leaders" to set a better example?

HUMAN FACTORS IN AVIATION SAFETY

This is a book-length subject all by itself. The book by Frank H. Hawkins, *Human Factors in Flight* is a good general treatment of the subject. The book by Robert A. Alkov, *Aviation Safety — Human Factors* is also excellent. See Bibliography.

WHAT DO WE MEAN BY "HUMAN FACTORS?"

At the present time, the term "Human Factors" lacks precise definition, although the Human Factors and Ergonomics Society would probably disagree with that. Perhaps the problem is that it is not precisely used. It means whatever people want it to mean at the time they use it. We read that the biggest problem in aviation is the human factors problem. I would not argue with that, but I would point out that has always been true. Aircraft accidents have always been dominated by the human element and we are just beginning to concentrate our efforts where they belong.

We're going to keep it simple and define human factors as the study of the interaction between humans and their environment. By environment, we mean the tools, equipment, instruments, systems and vehicles that they use in their job in addition to the physical environment of the job itself. A component of human factors is ergonomics. This is loosely defined as the presentation of information to a person through the senses of sight, hearing, or touch. It is here, for example, that we decide that moving a switch up should turn something on and twisting a knob clockwise should increase something. A lever with a wheel on the end of it should have something to do with the landing gear, and so on.

Human factors is probably the most dynamic aspect of aviation safety in that it is constantly changing based on new ideas, new research, and new insights into the human problem.

HUMAN FACTORS DIFFICULTIES

This human factors business is fraught with difficulties and getting anything changed on the basis of human factors involvement is usually an uphill battle.

For one thing, we are reluctant to openly discuss human factor-type problems. None of us wish to admit to a weakness and a chief pilot cannot afford to admit that any of the assigned pilots have problems. To do so would invite criticism on why they are allowed to fly. As a result, it is rare to find anything in the records that would give us a clue as to why a pilot acted in a particular manner. If the pilot is no longer alive to explain it, anything we come up with as investigators is largely speculation. Informed speculation, perhaps, but still speculation.

For another thing, we don't keep track of our pilots' previous experience as well as we think we do. Frequently, our actions can be explained by our previous experiences, if someone knew what they were. Predicting negative habit transference, for example, starts with knowing the original habits. Several years ago, one of the questions on the application for U. S. Army pilot training was, "Do you have any experience with bobsleds?" That looked like a trick question, but it was based on some rudimentary human factors logic. In those days, training planes had tail wheels and learning to steer them with your feet was a fairly tricky business. The Army learned that people who knew how to steer a bobsled were in a lot of trouble because the bobsled is steered exactly backwards from an airplane. If you want the bobsled to go to the right, you push in with your left foot. In a tail wheeled airplane, this generates an unwanted maneuver called a ground loop.

A third problem confronting human factors specialists is that they are in competition with the engineers and the bean counters. They can put numbers on their conclusions and ideas, but the human factors specialist cannot. The human factors specialist may strongly suspect that pilot fatigue is a problem and may have some evidence of unsatisfactory crew rest to support it — but there is no proof. Fatigue doesn't leave any evidence.

At the present time (1997) there is a movement afoot in the United States to require a pilot's training and flying performance records to be kept in a permanent form and be available to anyone who subsequently hires that pilot. With some experience as an aircraft accident investigator, I'm not optimistic that this will work. First, the present records on training and check rides rarely tell you anything about a pilot's actual performance. Even the FAA records are merely pass-fail type records. Second, the knowledge that anything put on paper will become chiseled in stone as part of a pilot's career will make the records even blander than they are now. At one time in the United States Air Force, flying proficiency was added to the annual performance report as a scored item. This seemed like a good idea, but the result was that all flying proficiency scores rose to the "magnificent" category. It effectively destroyed a measuring system which was none too good in the first place. It is really difficult to accurately establish a pilot's past performance except by interviewing people who instructed, checked or flew with that pilot.

HUMAN FACTORS IN AVIATION MAINTENANCE

In 1988, An Aloha Airlines B737 lost a large part of its roof while on approach to Kahalui airport in Maui, Hawaii. That accident hit the industry like an icicle driven into the pit of its stomach.

> "That can't happen!"
> "But it did!"
> "But it can't happen!"
> "You're not paying attention. It happened!"

After the dust settled, it became apparent that our ability to inspect airplanes for cracks wasn't anywhere near as good as we thought it was. This generated a lot of activity on the question of human factors and maintenance errors.

First, all of our non-destructive inspection (NDI) methods ultimately involved a human being looking at the results and interpreting them correctly. These methods include radiographic, eddy current, ultrasonic, magnetic particle, dye penetrant and the number one method; visual inspection. There are some automated inspection schemes on the horizon, but they are not in general use yet.

Second, many if not most of the inspection procedures are dull, boring and tedious. They require meticulous attention to the scope, meter, x-ray, or whatever. We can say with certainty that the best maintenance technician out there cannot detect 100% of the detectable cracks 100% of the time. One solution to this is to set the inspection interval so that detectable cracks are inspected at least twice before they grow to critical length. If you dabble in probability statistics, you realize that while this improves the likelihood of detection, it doesn't guarantee it.

The DC-10 crash at Sioux City, Iowa in July of 1989 resulted primarily from the violent failure of the number two engine compressor disk and subsequent loss of all hydraulics. (NTSB/AAR-90/06, PB90-910406). In their statement of probable cause, the National Transportation Safety

Board said, "...the probable cause of this accident was the inadequate consideration given to human factors limitations in the inspection and quality control procedures used by United Airlines' engine overhaul facility which resulted in the failure to detect a fatigue crack originating from a previously undetected metallurgical defect located in a critical area of the stage 1 fan disk. . . ."

That sentence, translated into English, means that our inspection techniques are not adequate and errors are very much a human factors problem. The corresponding NTSB recommendations made more sense and addressed the need for better research and development in the NDI field.

Back to the idea of human factors in maintenance, almost everything we know about human factors as applied to the pilots or the air traffic controllers also applies to the maintenance technicians. They are humans. They make mistakes, and they make them for the same reasons pilots and controllers make them. The problem confronting maintenance management is to either limit those errors or contain them so that they are caught before harm is done.

With a metal part, we know that if we put too much stress on it, it fails — suddenly. Parts built to the same standard tend to fail under the same amount of stress. Humans don't behave that way. If we put too much stress on a human, the error rate goes up. On the other hand, if we don't put enough stress on them, boredom sets in and the error rate still goes up. To make matters worse, different people may respond differently to stress. Any of us can have a "bad hair day" and make errors at stress levels well below normal. When and why this happens is not as easy to determine as it is with a metal part, but we know that if we can identify stresses and keep them under control we can reduce (but not eliminate) the error rate.

With respect to containing the errors, this is the essence of Total Quality Management (TQM) or ISO-9000 standards.

When dealing with individual maintenance errors, a good place to start is to assume that no one really intends to make an error. Before we can decide what to do about it, we need to determine (honestly) why it was made in the first place. Chapter 8 dealt with this idea and Chapter 18 offers some analytical methods that may be useful.

Another useful step would be to obtain a copy of the FAA's *Human Factors Guide for Aviation Maintenance*. See Bibliography.

IMPROVING OUR UNDERSTANDING OF HUMAN FACTORS

First, the more we know about our pilots, the better we should be able to judge or predict their performance based on their past experience. Whatever our recordkeeping system is, it is probably not good enough. We definitely need to track experience in various types of aircraft as that heavily influences habit patterns.

Second, if we expect to make progress, we must absolutely divorce our human factors inquiries from any sort of punishment or adverse action. If we do not guarantee anonymity, we simply will not learn of human factors problems. The FAA and NASA have confirmed that with their Aviation Safety Reporting System.

Third, we have to take advantage of the information already available to us. If we have flight data recorders and cockpit voice recorders, we must be able to use that data for performance improvement. To not do so is ridiculous. Some international airlines are doing this now and are very satisfied with the results.

Fourth, we must consistently and routinely collect human factors data on all accidents and incidents. It is unlikely that we can ever tie a specific human factors event to a specific accident other than to say that the factor was present and possibly a cause. If, though, we collect these data over a period of time, we may eventually be able to say, "In this type of accident, this factor is consistently present to a degree greater than chance frequency. It is undoubtedly a cause of some of these accidents and we should correct it."

Fifth, we should continue to explore ways to improve our behavioral training. This is also a dynamic field and some types of training are showing a lot of promise.

TRAINING INVOLVING HUMAN FACTORS

In thge past we have provided training that envolves human factors. We just didn't use the label. Now that human factors is recognized for it's true value, we have a better understanding of how to go about designing our program.

LINE-ORIENTED FLIGHT TRAINING (LOFT)

This type of training has been around for a while and it is generally accepted as a better approach to training in that it emphasizes crew coordination in a realistic environment.

CREW RESOURCE MANAGEMENT (CRM)

This is something of a buzzword in the industry. It has different meanings to different people. Basically, it refers to the management and utilization of all the people, information, and equipment available to the crew. It really could be applied to any activity involving a team, a lot of equipment, and a dynamic situation. A hospital emergency room would qualify. It is my view that pilots probably need this (or something like it) because there is nothing inherent in the training of a pilot that teaches much about management of people and interaction with them.

Professional pilot training puts a heavy emphasis on operating the airplane and its systems and stresses self-reliance. A pilot's initial experience is likely to be in a small airplane where there is no copilot. In some cases, the only other person on the plane may be a passenger which really reinforces the pilot's need for self-reliance. Eventually, the pilot moves into a multi-crewed airplane, probably as a copilot. What copilots learn about being a captain probably comes from the captains they fly with — who, as it turns out, don't know much about being a captain either. Thus when the copilots become captains, their management style is based on experience and not on any particular knowledge on how it ought to be done.

In the meantime, the pilot's old college roommate entered the world of business; not flying. While the pilot was learning to steer the plane, the roommate was learning how to get along with and manage people. The roomie can't fly a plane for beans, but is way ahead in the dealing with people business.

Finally, we realize that our pilots are missing an essential skill; the ability to manage all of their resources, including other crewmembers, in a dynamic and sometimes stressful environment. CRM training is basically an effort to develop that skill very quickly. Is it effective? Not in every case, but it is getting better. Two conclusions are pretty well accepted. First, it is not a one-time training activity. It must be regularly reinforced. Second, the flying culture within an organization must be adjusted to accept CRM principles. Just training the crews without changing the culture is not good enough.

JUDGMENT AND DECISION MAKING TRAINING

Can judgment and decision making be improved through training? Yes. After 12 years of research into and testing of Aeronautical Decision Making (ADM), researchers concluded that pilots who had received ADM training made significantly fewer inflight errors than those who had not received the training. This is described in FAA Advisory Circular 60-22 and a series of six ADM training manuals. See Bibliography. It seems likely that this type of training will become a part of recurring training in all aviation operations. This topic was also discussed in Chapter 7.

ADM teaches a logical approach to decision making. One of these is the DECIDE model.

1. Detect. The decision maker detects the fact that a change has occurred.

2. Estimate. The decision maker estimates the need to counter or react to the change.

3. Choose. The decision maker chooses a desirable outcome.

4. Identify. The decision maker identifies actions which could successfully produce that outcome.

5. Do. The decision maker takes the necessary action.

6. Evaluate. The decision maker evaluates the results of the action.

ADM training also encourages self-assessment and advocates the use of the I'M SAFE checklist.

1. Illness. Am I sick?

2. Medication. Have I been taking medication?

3. Stress. Am I under any psychological pressure for any reason?

4. Alcohol. Have I been drinking?

5. Fatigue. Am I adequately rested?

6. Eating. Am I adequately nourished?

HUMAN PERFORMANCE CONCERNS

There are several ways to categorize human factors problems and areas of concern. The problems can be either physiological or psychological (or even physio-psychological.) In addition, the problems can be influenced by individual personality or the social environment. These would be termed psychosocial factors. The following list is by no means complete. It was compiled from many sources; primarily the U.S. Air Force. It is useful as a reminder of the various possibilities when considering human factors problems.

HUMAN PERFORMANCE FACTORS

1. PHYSIOLOGICAL FACTORS

   A. Biodynamic
     - Hypoxia
     - Hyperventilation
     - Ear/sinus block
     - Pneumothorax
     - Decompression sickness
     - G-induced loss of consciousness

B. Sensory
  • Visual Illusion
  • Vestibular Illusion
  • Noise
  • Vibration
  • Misperception of speed/distance/position
  • Spatial disorientation

C. Pathophysiological
  • Drugs
  • Alcohol
  • Nicotine/caffeine
  • Nutrition
  • Dehydration
  • Physical fitness
  • Sudden incapacitation
  • Toxic exposure (poison, carbon monoxide)
  • Motion sickness
  • Thermal stress

2. PSYCHOLOGICAL FACTORS

A. Proficiency
  • Total experience
  • Recent experience
  • Negative habit transfer
  • Learning ability
  • Memory ability
  • Technical knowledge

B. Situational awareness
  • Inattention
  • Channelized attention
  • Distraction
  • Boredom
  • Fascination
  • Temporal Distortion
  • Confusion
  • Habit interference
  • Misread/misinterpreted instruments

C. Fatigue
  • Physical fatigue
  • Motivational exhaustion
  • Sleep deprivation
  • Circadian rhythm desynchrony

    D. Perceptual-motor capabilities
- Task oversaturation
- Confusion of controls
- Inadequate coordination
- Flying skill deficiency
- Overcontrol

    E. Judgment and decision making
- Failed to use accepted procedures
- Selected wrong course of action
- Delayed taking necessary action
- Rushed in taking action
- Procedural error
- Inadvertent operation of control
- Get-home/get-there-itis
- Ignored caution/warning

3.   PERSONALITY FACTORS

    A. Emotional State
- Apprehension
- Panic
- Anger
- Depression
- Irritable
- Carefree
- Elation

    B. Behavior
- Preoccupation
- Excessive motivation to succeed
- Lack of discipline
- Lack of confidence
- Overconfidence
- Gamesmanship
- Overaggressive
- Complacent

    C. Personality style
- Narcissistic
- Explosive
- Impulsive
- Invulnerable
- Macho
- Passive aggressive
- Submissive
- Conservative

- Loner
- Authoritarian

4. PSYCHOSOCIAL FACTORS

A. Peer influences
- Other pilots
- Other crewmembers on same crew

B. Personal and community influences
- Career progression
- Interpersonal relationships
- Marital problems
- Family problems
- Legal problems
- Financial problems
- Community problems

C. Communication factors
- Misinterpreted communications
- Disrupted communications
- Crew coordination
- Communications discipline

D. Operational factors
- Mission demands
- Supervisory pressure
- Adequacy of supervision
- Competency of other crewmembers

5. PHYSICAL FACTORS

A. Visibility
- Outside from the design-eye reference point
- Inside from the design-eye reference point

B. Reach
- Location of switches and controls
- Tactile identification of switches and controls
- Visual identification of switches and controls

C. Strength
- Small muscle vs large muscle
- Size, stature

D. Dexterity
- Fine (as opposed to coarse) movements
- Normal finger/hand/arm motions

And the list goes on. Human factors is a growth industry. There is much to be done.

DISCUSSION QUESTIONS

1. A pilot is transitioning into a new aircraft. In the new aircraft, the electric trim button is in the same location as the transmit/interphone button in the old aircraft. What human factors problem can you reasonably expect to occur? Using the list of possible human factors problems, what would you call this problem?

2. In a corporate aircraft, the two pilots normally alternate legs with one flying the plane and the other handling the radios and the paperwork. In doing this, though, they also swap seats. The pilot flying the plane always flies from the left seat. Do you see any potential human factors problems here?

3. Identify five aircraft accidents, each involving at least one of the five human performance factors listed in this chapter. How could a safety program identify these problems before they become accidents?

INTRODUCTION TO SECTION 3

AVIATION SAFETY PROGRAM ELEMENTS

By now, you have probably decided where you are going to fit an aviation safety program into your organization and what you expect it to do. Your next step is to choose the elements that will make up your program. Chapters 11 through 18 each address an element commonly found in aviation safety programs. None of these are mandatory. If, for example, you don't want an aviation safety awards program, skip that chapter.

Chapter 19 provides some ideas on how to manage the office and the paperwork. This is mainly for pilots who are uncomfortable in anything that doesn't resemble a cockpit. I have a lot of sympathy for that feeling as I spent a year or two mis-managing the office and the paperwork. I've been there.

Finally, Chapter 20 provides a sample aviation safety program based on everything covered so far.

INTERNAL REPORTING SYSTEMS

We need a method of collecting information about what's going on (with respect to aviation safety) within our organization and our industry.

In a very small organization (or even a small branch within a large organization) this is not a problem. Everybody knows what's going on and most of them probably saw it. As an organization grows or becomes dispersed, it needs to develop some systematic method of collecting data or it simply can't function. Aviation safety is no different. The program is very dependent on current information. The idea that the Director of Safety can sit in the office at the corporate headquarters and issue safety advice without knowledge of the problems is ludicrous.

Before we get into this, let's establish a couple of ground rules. First, we're not worried about the reporting of aircraft accidents that produce serious damage or injury. They are going to be reported if only because the law requires it. As stated earlier, though, we can't run an aviation safety program based solely on accidents. We don't have that many. We need to know about the incidents and the hazards. Second, we are going to avoid duplicating any existing reporting system. It is frustrating in any business to have to prepare two or more reports on a single event and we are not going to build our own private safety reporting system in ignorance of reports that already exist.

Suppose, for example, our pilots are required to file a "Captain's Report" or a "Trip Report" at the completion of each flight. Perhaps that report already contains information we need, or perhaps it could with the addition of another block marked, "Aviation Safety Items." Another example. Surely our maintenance people are collecting data on equipment failures and system deficiencies. Let's use their data as much as possible.

Still, we are probably going to have to set up a reporting system for events that won't be reported by any other method. Here are some ideas on how to do that.

INCIDENT REPORTS

Until something changes, you should take advantage of the fact that the term "Aircraft Incident" is very broadly defined. (See Chapter 3 for definitions.) Within your organization, you are free to define that term any way you like. Ideally, an incident should be a precursor or a predictor of an accident. If we can prevent the incident from occurring, we can logically prevent the associated accident from occurring. Carrying that logic in the other direction, if our defined incident is not a precursor of an accident, then preventing it isn't going to do much good. As an example, inflight precautionary engine shutdowns are commonly reported as incidents. Actually, that situation does not generate a lot of accidents. That is not to say that the inflight shutdown is not important, but let's let the maintenance people handle it. That goes back to the idea of not duplicating an existing data collection system. The data's there if we need it.

Take a look at the NTSB "Incidents" listed below. You would agree, I think, that those are all serious events. You should also agree, though, that not all of those events are producing large numbers of aircraft accidents. The correlation isn't there. Reducing those incidents, serious as they may be, will not significantly reduce aircraft accidents. Look also at the USAF list of Class C Mishaps (Incidents). This is a better list as many of them are correlated with some of the accidents experienced by the USAF.

NTSB INCIDENTS

1. Flight control system malfunction or failure.

2. Inability of any required flight crewmember to perform normal flight duties as a result of injury or illness.

3. Failure of structural components of a turbine engine excluding compressor and turbine blades and vanes.

4. Inflight fire.

5. Aircraft collide in flight.

6. Damage to property, other than the aircraft, estimated to exceed $25,000.

7. For large multiengine aircraft (more than 12,500 pounds maximum takeoff weight):

   A. Inflight failure of electrical systems which require the sustained use of an emergency bus powered by a backup source such as a battery, auxiliary power unit, or air driven generator to retain flight control or essential instruments.

B. Inflight failure of hydraulic systems that results in sustained reliance on the sole remaining hydraulic or mechanical system for movement of flight control surfaces.

C. Sustained loss of the power or thrust produced by two or more engines.

D. An evacuation of an aircraft in which an emergency egress system is utilized.

UNITED STATES AIR FORCE INCIDENTS (CLASS C MISHAPS)

1. Inflight fire.

2. Massive fuel leakage in an engine bay.

3. Any wire strike by fixed or rotary wing aircraft.

4. Engine case penetration, rupture, or burn-through from internal engine component failure.

5. Loss of thrust sufficient to prevent maintaining level flight at a safe altitude, or which requires the pilot to jettison stores.

6. Emergency or precautionary landing of a single engine aircraft, including helicopters, with imminent engine (or rotor drive system) failure confirmed after landing.

7. Unselected propeller or thrust reversal.

8. Engine flameout, failure, or emergency shutdown to minimize damage to malfunctioning engine.

9. All cases of departure from intended takeoff or landing surface (runway, helipad, landing zone, etc.) onto adjacent surfaces.

10. Flight control events resulting in an unexpected, hazardous change of flight attitude, altitude, or heading.

11. Spillage or leakage of radioactive, toxic, corrosive, or flammable material from aircraft stores or cargo.

12. Inflight loss of all pitot-static instrument indications.

13. Inflight loss of all normal gyro-stabilized attitude indications.

14. Physiological mishaps including any episode that produces abnormal physical, mental, or behavioral symptoms that are noticed by other individual crewmembers. Specific physiological mishaps include:

A. Decompression sickness.

B. Illness causing incapacitation inflight.

C. Hypoxia (suspected, probable, or definite.)

D. G-induced loss of consciousness

E. Trapped gas disorders.

F. Spatial disorientation of any type (including visual illusion) resulting in unusual attitude.

G. Symptoms or health effects caused by toxic, noxious, or irritating materials such as smoke, fumes, or liquids.

H. Traumatic strains or injuries that are the result of required mission demands or activities.

I. Any other condition or event the medical professional determines as significant to the health of the aircrew and provides useful safety information.

The best example of a good correlation between an incident and an accident is the relationship between a near mid-air collision and an actual collision. The difference between the two is largely a matter of luck and the near collision could easily have been a real one. One obvious way to prevent collisions is to collect data on the near collisions and work on preventing them.

It is not possible to construct a list of incidents that would be appropriate for every organization. It depends very much on the equipment and the type of flying. Fixed wing operations will always have a different list of incidents than rotary wing operations. Here is a list that is appropriate for fixed wing air transport operations. These "incidents" are all precursors of transport-type accidents.

1. Near mid-air collision.

2. Any instance of inadequate terrain separation.

3. Any unstabilized approach which is continued.

4. Any departure or excursion from the runway.

5. Aborted takeoff above 100 knots.

6. Weather-related injury or damage.

7. Any runway incursion.

8. Any landing on wrong airport or wrong runway.

9. Altitude deviation (Unintentional.)

10. Navigation deviation (Unintentional.)

Several international airlines have well established internal reporting systems. The following list was compiled from several sources.

1. Any defect which adversely affects the handling characteristics of the aircraft.

2. Failure of pressurization system.

3. Failure of navigation or communications systems.

4. Inadvertent incorrect operation of flight controls.

5. Severe turbulence.

6. Loss of any external part from the aircraft.

7. Rejected takeoff.

8. Runway excursion.

9. Missed approach below decision height.

10. Landing on wrong runway or at wrong airport.

11. Inadvertent engine shut down.

12. Ground Proximity Warning.

13. Stall warning.

14. Door warning (inflight.)

15. Significant fuel leak.

16. Crewmember incapacitation.

17. Fire, explosion, smoke or toxic fumes.

18. Critically low fuel quantity.

19. Significant fueling error.

20. Significant cargo loading error.

21. Insecure load, leakage or fumes from cargo.

22. Injury to any person while in or on the plane.

23. Damage to non-company property.

24. Inadequate or failed ground facilities (navaids, communications, lights, etc.) creating a hazardous situation.

25. Lightning strike or bird strike.

26. Damage to aircraft by ground equipment.

You should be able to construct a similar list which is relevant to your type of flying. Beyond that, you may wish to define some reportable incidents which are related to your type of airplane or helicopter. Here's one way to do that.

Assemble some of the senior check airmen or instructors who fly the aircraft and ask them to come up with a list of events that might be considered serious. The lists shown above might be a good starting point. With a few minutes of brain storming, this will usually produce a list of 30 or 40 possibilities.

Next ask the group to rate each event in terms of its seriousness on a scale of one to ten. Ten would be very serious and one would be nuisance level. A group of professional pilots will usually agree within a number or two of where a particular event ought to be ranked. After this is done, you'll notice that there are usually a couple of obvious break points. The serious events are clustered around 8, 9 and 10. There is another cluster in the 5-6 range and the non-serious events are down at the 1-2 level.

This pretty well establishes your reporting system for that type of aircraft and mission. The serious ones ought to be reported, investigated, and resolved. The middle ones are reported, but primarily for data collection purposes. If they are increasing, they can be investigated selectively. The nonserious ones shouldn't be reported at all. Even though you might like to know about them, the truth is that your reporting system is limited by what the people filing the reports will tolerate. They are not paid to do nothing but send reports to you. Besides, if you are focused on the serious ones, you won't have time for the nonserious ones.

There are a couple of advantages to using a group to develop this scheme. Aside from the extra ideas contributed by the group, you have gained participation in the aviation safety program. This is an important idea and it will be repeated throughout this book.

Additionally, your incident reporting system is now one that the people in the organization helped develop; not one that was imposed on them. You have obtained their agreement that this is a reasonable system and you should have little trouble making it work.

A small word of advice. Reporting systems always grow. They never get smaller. More and more events are added and more data is required for each event. The reporting system takes on a life of its own and it begins to consume the rest of the safety program. Don't let this happen. At least annually, sit down and review the system and ask if you still need all that information on that event. Review the events that have been added recently and ask if you still need those reported. Look for events that no longer need to be reported and eliminate them.

HAZARD REPORTS

Another type of reporting system you will need is a hazard reporting system. The basic idea behind a hazard reporting system is to provide a method for the pilots and maintenance technicians to bring hazards to your attention without any fear of retribution for having reported the situation. Management benefits if only a few of the hazards submitted are serious and worth resolving. They also benefit if the employees feel that they are participants in the safety program and that management is interested in their ideas.

Aviation lends itself pretty well to a hazard reporting system. Almost everyone involved in aviation has a strong personal interest in safety and it doesn't take much to get them involved. Also, hazards frequently occur in aviation which are known only to the pilot, the crew member, or the maintenance technician that experienced them. If we can't get them to tell us about it, we may lose an opportunity to prevent something really serious. Worse, we may find out about it the hard way — by having an accident.

Here are some basic guidelines on how to make a hazard reporting program work.

1. Don't waste a lot of time trying to define what constitutes a hazard. While incidents need to be narrowly defined, hazards do not. If the employee thinks it's hazardous, you want to hear about it.

2. On the other hand, you must reserve the right to reject a hazard report which represents personal heartburn or describes a problem which is beyond anyone's capability to solve. If you don't do this, you lose control of the program to the employees. Granted, you have to accept a certain amount of "garbage" with a system like this, but you don't have to process the report and pretend that it isn't garbage. If you reject a hazard report, you should do it with a personal note and an explanation. Sometimes, the problem really belongs to someone else (finance, personnel) and you can help by routing it to the correct office. You don't want to destroy that employee's participation in the safety program and if you can help with the non-safety problem, it is usually worthwhile.

3. Keep the program simple. Keep the forms simple and make them readily available at the location where they are most likely to be used. People are basically lazy and they won't use a program that requires a lot of effort on their part. Take advantage of modern technology. Connect an answering machine to a hazard reporting line. Publish your fax number. Accept hazard reports on e-mail. Don't reject a hazard report merely because it is on the wrong form

or in the wrong format. It doesn't really matter how you get the information.

4. Advertise the program. Since this is an optional program (no one has to use it) results will vary directly with the amount of advertisement. Publish the results of the program in the form of an occasional bulletin. A successful program that is accomplishing something is its own best advertisement. The U.S. Navy's "Anymouse" program is a good example of a program that feeds on itself and gets bigger each year.

5. Accept anonymous reports. Remove any inhibiting factors.

6. Acknowledge all reports. Always provide feedback. People will not use a system if they are convinced that no one cares and nothing is happening to their reports. Acknowledge the anonymous ones in a bulletin.

7. Develop some method of prioritizing the hazards. All hazards are not equally hazardous and they do not deserve an equal share of your time and your company's money. One of many methods for doing this is shown in Figure 11-1. This is one version of a Risk Assessment Matrix, or Hazard Priority Assessment. In this system, the probability that an event will occur is assigned numbers from zero to two. If the event does occur, the expected severity is assigned numbers from one to three. The numerical rating of the hazard (or risk) is the sum of the probability and severity numbers. Thus the hazard assessment will be a number between one and five, with five being the least serious. This assessment is entirely subjective and is merely a method of prioritizing your problems and allowing you to concentrate your preventive efforts where they will do the most good. As mentioned, there are other versions of this chart. The U.S. Department of Defense uses one that offers four levels of probability and severity and the numbers one through six with the lower numbers being the most serious. The basic idea, though, is the same.

RESOLVING HAZARD REPORTS

Part of your aviation safety program should be a method of resolving hazard reports that are received. Keeping in mind that you personally can rarely correct a hazard, it should be an established part of your program to route the hazard report to a line manager for review and correction. Generally, this is how it should work.

1. Acknowledge receipt. Confirm that it does exist and determine its seriousness.

2. Re-write the hazard report if more explanation is necessary and add any additional information available to you.

HAZARD PRIORITY ASSESSMENT

PROBABILITY

		PROBABLY WILL OCCUR 0	MAY OCCUR 1	UNLIKELY TO OCCUR 2
S E V E R I T Y	SEVERE 1	1	2	3
	MINOR 2	2	3	4
	NEGLIGIBLE 3	3	4	5

Figure 11-1. Hazard Priority Assessment

3. Forward the hazard report to the appropriate line manager with a reasonable suspense time and instructions to respond with corrections. comments, or both. A reasonable response time would be ten days or less. That does not mean that the hazard must be corrected in ten days; it means that the line manager should be able to evaluate the hazard and tell you what is going to be done. It is very helpful to have this procedure and responsibility in writing as part of the company aviation safety program. See Chapter 20.

4. When the response is received, notify the submitter (if known) of the action taken or planned. The completed hazard paperwork might then be added to the agenda of the aviation safety committee for review, or added to the safety inspection file for follow-up on the next inspection.

5. Publish the results. Print a one-line description of the hazard, the action taken or planned, and whether the hazard is open or closed. This is easily done on a computer with data processing software. Not only is this the best advertisement your program can have, the certain knowledge that the results will be published is sometimes an incentive to actually correct the problem.

HAZARD PROGRAM EVALUATION

The easy way to keep track of what you are doing is to assign a number to each hazard report received and enter it on a hazard report log, preferably in a computer. This log is merely a form with vertical columns listing hazard number, date, subject, seriousness, action agency, response, reply to originator, and report status. This can be done with almost any common data processing software. See Chapter 19.

Continually evaluate the program. The key questions are:

1.   Is anyone using the program?

2.   Is it doing any good? Has anything changed because of it?

A good hazard reporting program can be a very useful element in an aviation safety program. Several airlines have established excellent programs and they are very pleased with them. If you want the program to work, you must create the atmosphere where the pilots and maintenance technicians trust it and are willing to tell you what's going on.

NATIONAL AVIATION HAZARD REPORTING SYSTEMS

A word about some of the hazard reporting programs set up by some countries. Some of these were mentioned in chapter 3. The United States program is called the Aviation Safety Reporting System (ASRS) and it is managed by NASA as a disinterested 3rd party on behalf of the FAA. Flight crews should be aware of it and should use it. It not only has some benefits to the individual, but it contributes to the national data base of aviation safety related items. As an aviation safety manager, you should be a subscriber to the (free) ASRS bulletin, "Callback." It summarizes reports of current interest and it is usually worth distributing to your pilots. For more information, see FAR Part 91.25 and FAA Advisory Circular 00-46.

Beyond that, though, the ASRS doesn't directly help your program and won't replace your internal reporting system. The events reported through the ASRS system are not extensively investigated and there is no feedback to you on events involving your aircraft. You will still need an internal reporting system to provide you with a constant and reliable flow of information.

DISCUSSION QUESTIONS

1. You receive a hazard report that is full of grammatical errors and miss-spellings. It looks like it was written with a blunt crayon. Nevertheless, it is a valid report. The individual signed his name. How are you going to handle this?

2. You sent a hazard report to a line manager for evaluation and possible action. He sent it back with a strongly worded memo indicating that you were wasting his time and don't send him any more of these. How are you going to handle this?

3. You receive a hazard report from a pilot who says he has not been reimbursed for travel expenses in over three months. This is causing mental anguish and is becoming a hazard. How are you going to handle this?

INFORMATION DISTRIBUTION SYSTEMS

If our program is working well, we are going to collect a lot of information. Some of it will come from the bottom as a result of our internal reporting systems. What happened in Branch X may be important to Branch Y and the responsibility for getting that information to them is ours. If we are a large organization, some of the information will come from the top and must be distributed to where it is needed. Some of the information will come from the side, so to speak, from trade associations, professional societies, trade magazines, other operators, and so on. How do we handle this?

DISTRIBUTION PRACTICES

First, form the habit of sorting everything into four piles; critical, nice-to-know, future reference, and useless. Put the "useless" pile in the wastebasket (or perhaps the recycling bin) and the "future reference" pile into your reference filing system (Chapter 19.) The "critical" and "nice-to-know" piles get distributed to the people who need them.

Consider your office as a giant information filter. You've got the information. Your job is to get it to the people who need it and can act on it, and deliver it in a form that is useful to them. It is not helpful to just send copies of everything to everybody. This merely transfers the problem of sorting it out to the recipient. You can do better than that. Also, if there is an important article in a trade magazine (for example) don't just send out the whole magazine with a routing slip on it. Summarize the article. Tear it out and send just the article. Don't make people hunt for things that you've already found.

Second, develop some reliable, but separate distribution methods for the critical items and the nice-to-know items. Do not mix these together, because there is always going to be more nice-to-know trivia than critical information. The trivia will mask the important items. Worse, the aviation safety department will develop the reputation as a purveyor of junk mail which can be ignored. One secret to getting people to pay attention to you is to make sure that your critical information distribution is never contaminated with trivia. Eventually, people learn that if something is distributed in that fashion, it is probably important.

CRITICAL INFORMATION

Here are some common methods that can be used for critical information.

1. **FLIGHT CREW READING FILES.** These go by a number of different names and they are very common in flying organizations. The idea is that each crewmember must read and initial items in the reading file before each flight. The problem is that most reading files have already been contaminated with trivia and the crewmember suspects that they only need initialing. They aren't important enough to read.

The reading file system can work well providing each item in it is important enough to be read before the next flight and no item stays in the file longer than absolutely necessary.

2. **FLIGHT CREW BRIEFINGS.** If your flight crews attend a briefing before flight, it is easy to set up a system where the briefer covers critical items.

3. **DISPATCH SYSTEMS.** If you use a dispatcher, this a good way to get critical information to the crews when they pass through to pick up their flight plans.

4. **DIRECT MAIL.** This is used by airlines who seldom see more than a small percentage of their crews at any one time. The professional crewmember is expected to pay attention to information that is mailed directly to him.

5. **E-MAIL.** This is becoming very common in many companies. The advantages are rapid and simultaneous distribution to a number of people, plus the fact that they can receive the e-mail wherever they have computer access. The disadvantage is the possibility of the system being overloaded with trivia and ignored.

6. **FAX TRANSMISSION.** The fax machine is now common in most offices and many homes. Suggestion! Design a cover sheet that lets people know that what follows involves aviation safety and is important.

NICE-TO-KNOW INFORMATION

Here are some common methods used to distribute "nice-to-know" information.

1. **BULLETIN BOARDS.** A well-maintained bulletin board can enhance your aviation safety program, while a poor one can detract from it. In either case, you can't afford to use it for critical information as you cannot compel people to read bulletin boards.

2. **BULLETINS AND NEWSLETTERS**. These can be very effective, but, like bulletin boards, you can't guarantee that they will be read. Also, the time required to write, print and distribute precludes their use for critical information.

3. **INTERNAL COMPANY DISTRIBUTION**. In many organizations, this is the way crewmembers expect to get trivia. This probably explains why some crewmembers only empty their distribution boxes every other month. They know that if it is really important, someone will tell them about it.

4. **FLIGHT SAFETY MEETINGS**. Anyone who has been in the aviation business for very long has attended flight safety meetings. They are quite common in the military; less common in civil flying organizations. Flight safety meetings are nothing more than another method of distributing information. In some organizations they work very well; in others they do not. The big problem is attendance. If you can never assemble more than a third of your crewmembers at any one time, a flight safety meeting just isn't a realistic way to distribute information. A flight safety newsletter would work better.

MAKING INFORMATION DISTRIBUTION SYSTEMS WORK

Here are some general suggestions about information distribution. Each item that you distribute is going to carry a little bit of your reputation with it. People are going to subconsciously form an opinion of the aviation safety program based on what they see of it, hear of it, and get from it. You can easily become known as the junk mail king of the organization — if that's what you want.

If you are distributing paper, you have an obligation to make sure it goes to the right place. Maintenance technicians aren't terribly interested in air traffic control items. Fixed wing pilots dislike things with pictures of helicopters on them. If it is necessary to edit, rewrite or highlight something to make it relevant, it is probably worth your time to do so. If you are going to send out copies, make sure they are legible.

If you are going to get into the bulletin and newsletter business, you have to learn to think like an editor. People won't read something merely because it's important. It must also be interesting and attractive. This means headlines, good opening paragraphs, pictures, cartoons, highlights, and so on. No one has to read your newsletter and you have a very short time to capture their attention and make them want to read it. Suggestion.

Until you get good at it (or can afford a full-time editor) set up the newsletter masthead and logo, but don't commit to a specific publication schedule. Publish when you have something worth reading. (Instead of calling it a "periodical," you could call it a "spasmodical!") That will keep the quality up and your workload down.

Another suggestion. Give your newsletter or magazine a distinctive appearance and make it easily recognizable at a distance. One of the world's largest airlines has an excellent and very recognizable safety magazine. For the cover, they have selected a beautiful painting of one of their aircraft. OK so far. The magazine is distinctive and easily recognizable. Unfortunately, they use the same painting for every cover. All editions look alike and have for several years. It is not possible to glance at a copy of the magazine and tell whether it is a new edition or not. Another flight safety magazine established a very popular comic strip character which was always found on the back cover. The back cover of the magazine was widely read, but the interior was not. It took a few years for them to realize that it was better to bury the comic strip inside the magazine.

If you are going to have an aviation safety bulletin board, make it attractive. Keep it purged of non-safety information and keep it interesting. Train your people to realize that there will be something new on it every day and it will be worth reading. In theory, a bulletin board should be located where people congregate; not where they pass. Items on the board should be at eye level, easy to read, highlighted, and identifiable at a distance. As an example, people can recognize a cartoon from a good distance and will go to the board if they think it is a new one. Likewise, if you put something on the board, draw a circle around one paragraph and point to it with a big cardboard arrow, people will come closer to see what that is about.

In the United States, an employer is required to maintain an Occupational Safety and Health bulletin board and is required to keep certain forms and items posted on it. Don't use this bulletin board for aviation safety items. It is unattractive by government decree and nobody reads it. Establish a separate aviation safety bulletin board.

If you plan to hold safety meetings, make them good meetings. A poorly conducted flight safety meeting is a turn-off. Your reputation and that of your program is riding on each meeting. Your audience is well-educated and is able to spot a time-waster at a considerable distance. As a rule of thumb, it takes roughly four times as long to prepare a meeting as it does to hold it. Thus you ought to be willing to put at least two hours into preparing a thirty minute flight safety meeting.

Develop a roster of good guest speakers. These might come from mainte-nance, flight medicine, weather, FAA, manufacturers, and so on. Here are some hints on managing guest speakers.

1. Tell the speaker about the audience, their backgrounds and interests.

2. Give the speaker a specific time limit. I always use an odd time like 14 minutes and 20 seconds. That creates the impression that time is critical. Never give the speakers a time range (15-20 minutes) or (worse) tell them they can talk as long as they like. They will.

3. Tell the speaker you want an outline so you can distribute it to the audience. Actually, you want to make sure that the speaker has an outline and is not planning to just "wing it." Also, you want to know if the selection of subjects is appropriate for your meeting and if the subject will fit in the allotted time.

4. If you do decide to have flight safety meetings, there is almost no limit to the subjects that could be presented or discussed. Listed below are just a few possibilities.

FLIGHT SAFETY MEETING TOPICS
ACCIDENTS

- Review of current accidents
- Government investigation procedures
- Crewmember rights
- Airport emergency plan
- Company response plan

AIR TRAFFIC

- Local air traffic problems
- Mid-air collision prevention
- Collision avoidance equipment
- Military training areas and routes

AVIATION MEDICINE

- Visual limitations
- Substance abuse
- Self medication
- Visual scan patterns

- Circadian rhythm
- Fatigue
- Pilot incapacitation
- High altitude problems
- Jet lag
- Hearing loss
- First aid and CPR

AVIATION PSYCHOLOGY

- Landing illusions
- Habit patterns
- Cockpit communications
- Judgment and decision making

BRAKING

- Deceleration physics
- Runway condition and friction measurement
- Tires, anti-skid and braking technique
- Hydroplaning

EMERGENCIES

- Communications
- Available assistance
- Evacuation

EQUIPMENT

- Personal equipment
- Survival equipment
- Rescue equipment

FIRE PREVENTION

- Use of fire extinguishers
- Cockpit/cabin material characteristics
- Fueling safety

HAZARDOUS CARGO

- Recognition
- Manifesting and Marking
- Compatibility

HIJACKING AND BOMB THREATS

- History
- Procedures

MAINTENANCE

- Aircraft logs
- Determining aircraft status
- Logging discrepancies
- Maintenance procedures
- Foreign object damage (FOD)
- Future aircraft modifications

NOISE

- Abatement
- Hearing protection

OPERATIONS

- Pressure to accept flights
- Diversions
- Bird strikes
- Lightning strikes
- Incident reporting
- Cold weather procedures

SAFETY

- Hazard reporting system
- Aviation Safety Reporting System (ASRS)
- Risk management concepts

SURVIVAL

- Search and rescue
- Water survival
- Land survival

WEATHER

- Wind shear
- Thunderstorms
- Turbulence
- Icing

SUMMARY

The manner in which you distribute information deserves some thought. It is by far the most visible aspect of your aviation safety program and the one that will contribute most to other peoples' opinion of it.

That said, there is an awesome amount of information circulating in the name of aviation safety. You need to take advantage of all modern indexing and distribution methods to stay ahead of it.

At this writing, the Internet is emerging as a very useful reference tool for the Director of Safety. As you may have already discovered, it can burn up an incredible amount of time if you don't have an organized method of searching and downloading. Some useful Internet references are listed in the bibliography.

DISCUSSION QUESTIONS

1. Corporate headquarters sends you an entire NTSB accident report (about 80 pages) and tells you to distribute this to all pilots as critical information. How are you going to do this?

2. There is a lot of safety poster material available for bulletin boards. How are you going to determine which is worth posting and which isn't?

AVIATION SAFETY COMMITTEES

A committee – any committee – is a means of achieving group consensus and action on a particular problem. The action may be in the form of a recommendation or, if the committee has enough authority, directions to individual members or other agencies. A committee is not a group of people who sit around and listen to the Safety Director brief them on current statistics. That's not a committee; that's a meeting.

In the United States, some state OSHA plans require a Safety and Health Committee with equal representation from both management and labor. That is not a useful forum for solving aviation safety problems. If you want an aviation safety committee as part of your program, establish it separately from the OSHA committee.

USEFULNESS

As we are all aware, committees can be a colossal waste of time. They are poorly led; no one knows what they are supposed to do; and they lack the authority to do it anyway. They meet monthly or quarterly just for the sake of meeting and nothing much happens.

On the other hand, a well-run committee can be a positive asset to an aviation safety program. The members can contribute a lot of different ideas on a problem and, once they agree on what is to be done, they can initiate the action much faster than they could if the same problem was circulated via company memo. They also achieve participation in the aviation safety program. People get involved. They contribute. They begin to feel that it is their program; not the aviation safety manager's program.

Some organizations use committees very well. It suits their management style and the senior line managers are used to accepting the recommendations of a committee. Other organizations do not use committees well and are not fond of them. Imposing a committee on this type of organization seldom works. Remember. You don't have to have an aviation safety committee. There are other ways to achieve action on problems.

If you intend to form an aviation safety committee, here are some ideas on how to do it.

LEVEL

There is a tendency to form committees at the senior management level, which, in some cases, may be a mistake. In theory, a committee should be formed at a level commensurate with the problems to be addressed. A committee in flight operations at the Chief Pilot - Check Airman level may be much more useful for operational problems than one at the vice president level. Likewise a maintenance aviation safety committee can do a lot for problems occurring in the ground handling and maintenance phases. There is nothing wrong with having a membership that cuts across the organization both horizontally and vertically. If there is too wide a disparity top to bottom, there is some risk that the senior person present will automatically become the de facto chairman.

SIZE

Ideal committee size is five to seven people. There is nothing wrong with a few more (or less), but at some point, the committee gets so big it is difficult to manage. Unanimity is unlikely. Consensus is the best you can hope for.

CHAIRMANSHIP (CHAIR)

Since the committee is supposed to be an action group, the Chairman (chairperson, chair) should be a line manager. Having the Director of Safety chair the committee tends to weaken it. The Director of Safety (or the aviation safety manager) should be the recorder and take care of the scheduling, agenda, minutes, and so on.

PURPOSE

It is best to decide what the committee is supposed to do before assembling it. Here are some possibilities.

1. Review all incident reports for adequacy of corrective actions.

2. Review all hazard reports for adequacy of corrective actions.

3. Review aviation safety inspection reports for applicability and adequacy of corrective actions.

4. Provide recommendations or direct actions on aviation safety problems brought before the committee.

5. Review effectiveness of aviation safety program elements and make recommendations for future program improvements.

We should point out that it is not the task of the committee to decide what is to be done on all incidents or hazard reports. This leads to delaying resolution until the committee meets, which is a bad idea. The committee should look at the results, and decide whether they are acceptable or not. This has an added advantage. Once line managers realize that their response to incidents, hazards, or safety inspection items will be reviewed by the aviation safety committee, the quality of the responses tends to improve.

Some subjects lend themselves to committee action; some do not. As a general rule, committees work best where information is needed from several different sources, and the support and concurrence of several different line managers is needed for resolution. On the other hand, committees do not do well on problems that are clearly the responsibility of a single line manager, or are very routine or trivial. If a problem can be resolved through the normal management process, it should not be held up for committee action.

FREQUENCY OF MEETINGS

This depends entirely on the level of activity and on what is expected of the committee. If it is only going to meet quarterly, it would not be wise to delay action on anything for three months until the next committee meeting. On the other hand, there is no point in meeting if there is nothing to be discussed. One workable system is to schedule the committee to meet monthly, but cancel the meeting if there is nothing on the agenda. (If this happens regularly, something is wrong. Consider canceling the committee.)

COMMITTEE MANAGEMENT

This is the job of the Director of Safety or the aviation safety manager. Here are some suggestions on how to do it.

1. **SCHEDULE**. Get the meetings scheduled as regular events on everyone's calendar. It's a lot easier to cancel a scheduled meeting than schedule an unscheduled meeting.

2. **DEVELOP AGENDA**. Solicit agenda items early. Train the committee members to realize that only the published agenda items will be discussed. Bring the Chair into the planning phase to obtain approval of agenda items. If there are no agenda items, cancel the meeting.

3. **DISTRIBUTE AGENDA**. Print twice as many copies of the agenda as you need. Send a copy to each committee member, along with any additional material on any of the items.

4. **REVIEW AGENDA WITH THE CHAIR**. A day or so before the meeting, go over the agenda with the Chair. Discuss the background of each item and what results you would like to achieve from the meeting.

5. **PREPARE "DRAFT" MINUTES**. Most of the minutes can be "boilerplated." You already know when the meeting will take place; who is supposed to be there; and what subjects will be discussed. The only thing you don't know is how each agenda item will be resolved and what action will be required. Just prepare the minutes and leave space for these actions to be entered at the meeting.

6. **START ON TIME**. Wait only for the Chair. (If you have to consistently wait for the Chair, you may have a serious problem!)

7. **STICK TO THE AGENDA**. Don't solicit other items during the meeting by saying something like, "Does anyone have anything else to bring up?" Train your members to realize that if they want something discussed, they must get it on the agenda and give the other members a chance to consider it. In general, managers don't like surprises and bringing up subjects they are not prepared to discuss might be considered a CLM (Career Limiting Maneuver).

8. **RESOLVE EACH AGENDA ITEM**. Ideally, each item should be closed with a description of the agreed action, the designated action agency and the date by which action should be complete. If it is necessary to carry an item forward to the next meeting, there ought to be some indication in the minutes of why it was carried forward and what should happen prior to the next meeting.

9. **QUIT ON TIME**. If you did not get through the agenda, either carry those items forward or schedule another meeting. Usually, though, if the members realize that the meeting will end on schedule, they will adjust their discussion to complete the entire agenda. If, by chance, you finish early, quit!

10. **PREPARE FINAL MINUTES**. Get the signature of the Chair and make the minutes serve as an action document.

11. **DISTRIBUTE THE MINUTES**. Get these out within a day or two of the meeting before the members forget what they promised to do. If you don't do this, the members may conclude that the aviation safety committee isn't very important after all. In the published minutes, include a reminder on the next meeting and a request for agenda items.

12. **FOLLOW UP ON THE ACTION ITEMS**. When a required action has been completed (or not completed) let the Chair know. Once the members realize that you will always follow up on commitments made at safety committee meetings they will tend to meet those commitments.

CHAIRING A COMMITTEE

The chair is the key person in any committee. If the chair does not know how to chair a committee, it is unlikely that much will be accomplished. Almost any basic management text has a chapter on how to chair a committee. Here are a few guidelines.

1. **THEORY**. The purpose of any committee is to bring group judgment and deliberation to bear on a problem. In general, people tend to produce more ideas or "collective wisdom" when operating as a group than they would individually. This can work very well provided the group has good leadership and their attention is focused on the problem at hand. In the absence of good leadership, the dominant personality in the group will tend to take over the leadership role. That dominant personality may or may not have the ability to direct the group toward problem resolution.

2. **THE CHAIR'S TASK**. The job of the committee chair is to keep the group moving steadily toward the objective; to get the best possible contributions from the group; and to make sure the record (or minutes) accurately reflects the group's opinions and conclusions.

3. **STARTING THE MEETING**. Make sure everyone understands the agenda and has a copy of it. If they forgot to bring their copy, give them an extra one. Make sure they also understand the time constraints, i.e. when the meeting will end. If they know the agenda and the time limit, they will tend to help complete the agenda on time.

4. **CONTROL THE COMMITTEE**. Start an agenda item with pure ideas and discussion. Avoid letting anyone take an early position from which they cannot retreat. People who do this feel obligated to argue for their position regardless of any subsequent discussion. Some useful phrases:

   • "Well, let's not get locked into this just yet."

   • "Let's hear some more ideas before we commit to a specific action."

5. **KEEP THE DISCUSSION ON TRACK**. This is the hard part, because you are dealing with some people who want to dominate the discussion; some who want to introduce extraneous ideas; and some who do not want to contribute at all. Some of the comments in Chapter 9 .on group dynamics also apply here A certain amount of deviation from the subject is all right, maybe even helpful. Eventually, though, you must get the group back on the central issue.

- "Well, this is all interesting, but let's get back to the subject of . . . ." (Try calling on a new speaker at this point.)

Avoid letting the dominant personality in the group dominate the meeting. Don't let that person interrupt other speakers. Acknowledge the points made, then seek others.

- "I appreciate your ideas and I think we've got them down. Now let's hear from . . . . "

Insist that everyone gets a chance to contribute. Use your position as Chair to toss questions to the reticent members.

- "What do you think of those ideas?"

- "I'd like to hear your view of that."

6. **AVOID COMPROMISE**. If a particular idea is totally unacceptable to one member of the committee, there is no need to compromise or water the idea down to make it acceptable to that member just for the sake of unanimity. If that's the way things appear to be heading, then suggest that both sets of conclusions and supporting arguments be included in the minutes. This forces the minority member to clearly state a position for the record and it lets the group get on with the rest of the agenda.

7. **MOVE THROUGH THE AGENDA**. Take the agenda one step at a time. Take each agenda item one portion at a time. As you get consensus on a particular point, write that down and confirm that all agree to it, then go on to the next point. Don't let the committee keep returning to the points that have already been resolved. Use the same technique with each agenda item. Once you finish an item, close it and move on. Don't let the committee re-open those arguments. Summarize frequently and continually force the committee forward.

SUMMARY

A well run committee can do a lot for an aviation safety program and it can make its members proud to serve on it. A poorly run committee detracts from the program and is best abandoned - your choice.

DISCUSSION QUESTIONS

1. Your organization has an aviation safety committee. Here are some potential agenda items. Which would you put on the agenda and which would you omit? Why?

    A. Revision of vehicle traffic pattern on parking ramp.

B. Committee recommendations on a hazard report regarding rain-water leaking into a fuel pit on the parking ramp.

C. Anticipated problems and recommendations due to scheduled air field construction project.

D. Review of safety audits of dispersed flying operations.

E. Consideration of a new vendor for simulator instruction.

F. Review of actions taken following an incident involving an aircraft departing the runway during landing in wet conditions.

G. Proposal to hire an outside consultant for a company-wide aviation safety audit.

2. You are the Director of Safety. One member of the aviation safety committee seldom attends meetings, but always sends a representative whose instructions are to "take notes, but say nothing. Make no commitments." What are you going to do about this?

AVIATION SAFETY INSPECTION PROGRAMS

This is not a particularly popular aspect of aviation safety. In a small organization, it is probably unnecessary. Everyone knows what's going on anyway. In a large organization, though, the head of the organization is entitled to know whether the aviation safety policies are being followed and the operations and maintenance standards are being met. If there is uncertainty about this, someone should be a little concerned.

This is the part of management called "control" where the manager is constantly checking to make sure that results are conforming to expectations. In other words, are we doing what we think we are doing. There are many ways to do this, but, ultimately, someone has to go look and see what's going on.

Because we don't really like the term, "inspection," we've developed several euphemisms to make it sound better. Some of these are appraisal, assessment, audit, evaluation, inquiry, review, study, and survey. You can call it anything you like, but to keep the language in this book simple (and honest) we're going to call it "inspection." We're going to examine something and compare it with a set of standards. That's an inspection. If we don't do this occasionally, the news that our standards are not being followed is likely to come to us in an unpleasant manner.

Why are inspections so unpopular? That's easy! We've all met inspectors and they all tend to be professional fault finders who are dedicated to finding something wrong with our organization and either punishing us for it or embarrassing us with it. Inspections are not perceived as an aid to management, which in aviation safety they are — or should be.

INSPECTION PHILOSOPHY

As the Director of Safety, or aviation safety manager, you can't be a good guy most of the time and a bad guy some of the time without antagonizing the people you must work with. Fortunately, you don't have to do it that way. You can, but you don't have to.

Consider this. Going out and finding a list of aviation safety violations doesn't say much about your aviation safety program — except possibly that it's not working. You are not really trying to find things wrong; you are trying to verify that things are right. When you do find a problem, you are not interested in rubbing someone's nose in it; you are interested in helping correct it. Your point of view is that of the consultant who is trying to help the manager do a better job.

Some organizations actually hire outside consultants to conduct aviation safety inspections. This has some merit in terms of objectivity and experience, but this must be balanced against the cost and the need for the consultant to spend some time learning how the organization works. There is really no reason not to have an internal control or inspection system.

PURPOSE OF SAFETY INSPECTIONS

Safety inspections only serve two purposes: they determine the level of compliance with operations and maintenance standards and they validate the effectiveness of the aviation safety program. Any line manager ought to be interested in knowing the level of compliance and knowing that the aviation safety program is actually accomplishing something.

TYPES OF SAFETY INSPECTIONS

There are several different ways to approach this problem. Here are some of the common ones.

FORMAL INSPECTION

This is an extensive in-depth safety inspection of an organization, a location, or possibly a subject such as "airfield" or "fuel handling." It is usually conducted by the Director of Safety with technical help as needed. It results in a written report with recommendations and usually requires an answer.

INFORMAL, DAILY, OR SELF INSPECTIONS

These are the meat of the internal inspection program. If you operate an airfield or heliport, it has to be inspected at least daily. If you have a hangar, there are perhaps a dozen critical safety items that need to be checked daily. Other facilities may need a weekly or monthly safety check. Certain items in flight operations need to be checked regularly.

This is a line management responsibility and it should be done by someone in that organization. It usually doesn't generate a report (other than a checklist to show that it has been done), but it does identify minor safety problems and correct them. When the Director of Safety conducts a formal inspection, one key item should always be the effectiveness of the local informal or daily inspection program. If it is effective, then the formal inspection doesn't take long.

Part of the Director of Safety's program is to help the local organizations set up an effective internal safety inspection program. This provides the line manager at that level with direct knowledge of the degree of safety compliance and the opportunity to correct safety problems without waiting for the Director of Safety to identify them.

SPOT INSPECTIONS

These inspections are subject-oriented and are frequently reactive to a known or perceived problem. Question: Are we meeting our standards for crew duty time? Are our standards for aircraft fueling being followed? Answer: Go look. Those are spot inspections. They might be conducted by the Director of Safety or the line manager, or both. They may or may not generate a report.

INSPECTION PREPARATION

If you are going to spend a day or so examining part of your organization, you owe them a certain amount of preparation. Here are some steps to consider.

1. Know the organization's mission, structure, assets, and any current operational constraints. If, for example, there is a construction contract in progress, that might influence some parts of your inspection.

2. Review the organization's recent history of accidents, incidents, and hazard reports. Part of your inspection should be a review of the actions they have taken on these items.

3. Review the most recent safety inspection of that organization. Expect to verify that previous problems have been corrected.

4. If appropriate, review specific standards that apply to the area you intend to inspect. Bring copies if that would be helpful.

5. Develop checklists specific to that organization. With today's computer technology, this is not difficult. Scattered throughout this book are general checklists that don't apply to any particular organization.

If you had them in your computer, it would be easy to add or delete items to make them fit your company or any part of it. Then just save them under a different file and you suddenly have both a generic checklist and a specific checklist.

FORMAL INSPECTION PROCEDURES

1. Schedule and announce the inspections well in advance. No-notice inspections are very disruptive. You are not trying to sneak up on anyone and catch them doing something wrong. The act of announcing the inspection sometimes has a positive effect all by itself. The organization to be inspected tends to look around and clean up its house before you arrive. You show up and everything looks pretty good — which is exactly what you would like to find. If each organization or location has an effective informal, daily, or self-inspection program as discussed above, the formal inspection is mostly a matter of reviewing this local inspection program.

2. Tell them what you are looking for. If you are using a checklist, send them a copy of it. Let them build their own local inspection program out of your checklist. Let's face it. There are only so many things you can look at and there is no point in trying to keep them secret. If you have told them when you are coming and what you are going to look at — and they still don't clean it up, maybe they deserve a bad report.

3. Expect to be escorted. Insist on it. You want someone from that organization, probably the additional duty aviation safety specialist, to see what you see and hear what you hear. That will eliminate a lot of suspicion and controversy.

4. Start with a briefing or discussion with the line manager. Explain what you are doing, why you are doing it, how you are going to do it, and who is going to accompany you. Also, make an appointment for an informal meeting with the manager at the end of the inspection.

5. Don't worry about trivia. It is easy to find minor safety violations in any organization; any facility. Point them out to the additional duty aviation safety specialist and let them be corrected locally.

6. When you find a serious problem, look for the organizational or management deficiency that allows the problem to exist. Then, look for other possible results of the same deficiency. If, for example, you find ground support equipment unsecured or parked on the wrong place on the flight line, you first need to determine if that is common practice or an isolated incident. Assuming it is common practice, the basic problem might lie in the organization procedures, the enforcement of those procedures, or the training of flight line personnel. It

is also likely that the local inspection program could be expanded to regularly check that situation. In any case, your recommendation should help the line manager eliminate all such problems. This is really the difference between being an inspector and being a consultant; the difference between being a fault-finder and being helpful to management.

7. Validate your findings. When you find something wrong, discuss it with whoever is in charge of that operation and get their opinions and ideas. If it is really wrong, they will be forced to agree with you and you have at least relieved any anxiety about what you are likely to put in the report. On the other hand, they may point out to you a different interpretation of the situation, or even some facts that you did not know. This validation process can save you from putting something really stupid in your report. Suggestion. Always ask what they think can be done to correct the situation. If they have a reasonable solution and they are willing to do it, that's probably the one that belongs in the report as your recommendation. If you can agree on an action plan, putting that in the report adds some emphasis to it.

8. Before you leave, informally discuss your findings with the line manager. This is easy providing you have done a good job of validating your findings with the other supervisors. As a rule, don't discuss anything you haven't validated and don't put anything in the report you haven't covered in your informal briefing. This creates an atmosphere of honesty about the inspection and relieves a lot of tension and anxiety.

9. Take note of good things as well as bad things. If some aspect of aviation safety is working very well or is very effective, say so. Spread that news around to the other parts of the company.

AVIATION SAFETY PROGRAM EVALUATION

Along with evaluating the level of compliance with standards, it is important to take a serious look at your own safety program. This may be difficult to do objectively and it is helpful to have a line manager participate, or even an outside consultant. In safety, we tend to get involved in a lot of activities merely because they are a traditional part of safety programs. Safety bulletin boards are a good example. Do we ever evaluate the bulletin board in terms of its effectiveness? We should. If it is not effective, we should either make it effective or get rid of it.

An Aviation Safety Program should always meet two tests:

1. Is it doing what we want it to do?

2. Is it effective?

Merely having an Aviation Safety Committee, for example, doesn't mean much if it is not doing anything. The following guide provides some ideas on how to measure the effectiveness of the program and identify portions which are only given "lip service" and should be changed or eliminated.

AVIATION SAFETY PROGRAM EVALUATION GUIDE

1. MANAGEMENT SUPPORT

    A. Are the supervisors and managers visibly involved in and supporting the aviation safety program? How?

        - Attend safety committee meetings.

        - Review incident/hazard reports.

        - Review inspection reports.

        - Contribute to safety meetings/newsletters.

        - Action to resolve safety problems.

        - Other involvement.

    B. Does the aviation safety manager have direct access to management? At what level?

    C. Does the aviation safety manager regularly attend operational planning meetings and briefings? Staff meetings?

    D. Is the aviation safety manager kept advised of items and decisions involving safety?

2. AVIATION SAFETY STAFF

    A. Are all full time and additional duty aviation safety positions filled?

    B. Are the people filling these positions well qualified?

3. PROGRAM

    A. Is there a written statement of policy on aviation safety?

    B. Is there a written aviation safety program? Is it reviewed regularly? Has it been distributed? Does anyone but the aviation safety officer know what's in it?

    C. Is there a pre-accident plan? Has it been reviewed? Exercised? Is it current?

4. AVIATION SAFETY TRAINING

   A. What training is provided to aviation safety managers?

   B. What safety training is provided to other personnel?
      - How often?
      - What is covered?
      - Who gives the training?
      - What records are kept?

   C. Who has not received training?

   D. Is training provided to those specified in the safety program?

5. SAFETY OFFICE RELATIONSHIPS

   A. If there are additional duty aviation safety specialists at multiple levels, what is the relationship between them?
      - Do they meet regularly?
      - Do they communicate directly with each other?
      - What information is disseminated down?
      - What information is reported up?
      - What help does the higher safety office furnish the lower?

   B. What is the relationship between the additional duty aviation safety specialists and the aviation safety manager?

6. AVIATION SAFETY INSPECTION PROGRAM

   A. Does an aviation safety inspection program exist?

   B. Who conducts the inspections? How often?

   C. Are the inspection reports valid?

   D. Who acts on them?

   E. Is anything changed as a result of the inspections?

   F. Is there a system for follow up?

7. INVESTIGATIONS

   A. Are incidents investigated? By who?

   B. What is the quality and depth of the investigation?

   C. Is anything changed as a result of the investigation?

   D. Who reviews the investigation reports?

8. HAZARD REPORTING PROGRAM

   A. Does a hazard reporting program exist?

   B. Does anyone use it? How many recent reports?

   C. How are the reports processed?

   D. Is anything changed because of the reports?

   E. Is there feedback to the submitter?

   F. Who reviews the reports?

   G. Who reviews the changes generated by the reports?

9. DISTRIBUTION OF FLIGHT SAFETY INFORMATION

   A. How is safety information distributed?

   - Meetings?
   - Read Files?
   - Direct Distribution?
   - Dispatch System?
   - Bulletin Boards?
   - Bulletins/Newsletters?
   - Other?

   B. Is it getting to the people who need it?

10. AVIATION SAFETY COMMITTEE

    A. Is there an aviation safety committee?

    - How often does it meet?
    - Who chairs it?
    - Does it have an agenda?
    - Does it keep minutes?
    - Is anything accomplished by the committee?

    B. Is it effective?

11. ANALYSIS PROGRAM

    A. Is there an aviation safety analysis program?

    B. What data are analyzed?

    C. What use is made of the analysis?

    D. Is it effective?

12. MISCELLANEOUS

    A. Are the pilots and maintenance technicians familiar with the aviation safety program?

    B. Do they support it?

    C. Do they report hazards/incidents?

    D. Do they know who the Director of Safety or Aviation Safety Manager is?

    E. What is their opinion of the safety program?

INSPECTION CHECKLIST DEVELOPMENT

There are plenty of aviation safety checklists available and many of them can be tailored to your needs. It is also easy to develop a checklist to suit a specific situation. This is helpful if you want to examine and compare the same operation at several locations, or if you want different people to use the checklist and achieve consistent results. Here's how to do it.

1. Break the subject down into smaller components such as Operations; Maintenance; Fuel Handling; Airfield; etc. Guides for subjects to examine in these areas are found in this and other chapters in this book.

2. For each area, list the items that should be examined. For Operations, you might list Training, Currency, Crew Duty Limitations, and so on.

3. For each item, list the method to be used to determine the status of that item. Common methods are review of records, discussion with supervisor, discussion with pilots or maintenance technicians, personal observation, sampling of x number of records, and so on.

4. Also for each item, list the criteria, standard or reference that applies to that item.

5. Finally, leave a little room for the inspector to make notes and you have a checklist.

FLIGHT OPERATIONS SAFETY INSPECTION

This is a guide. It does not fit any particular type of organization and probably omits some items important to specialized organizations.

FLIGHT OPERATIONS SAFETY INSPECTION SUBJECTS

1. RECORD

   Flying hours last year by aircraft type

   Flying hours last three years

   Average flying hours per month

   Average flying hours per pilot per month

   Average flying hours per pilot per year

   Accident record

2. ORGANIZATION

   Operational chain of authority

   Clearly defined responsibilities

   Positions filled or vacant?

3. POLICY

   Published

   Delegation of authority to flight operations

   Operational standards

   Policy subjects

   - Accident prevention responsibility
   - Determination of standards compliance
   - Reporting of operational deviations
   - Reporting of incidents and hazards
   - Use of company aircraft
   - Outside flying (moonlighting)
   - Multiple currency
   - Crew duty time
   - Weather minimums
   - Crew minimums based on experience
   - Airport or heliport minimums
   - Substance (drug, alcohol) abuse

4. ADMINISTRATION

Certification

Scope of permitted operations

Standards agreed to during the certification process

Authority for flight approval

Authority for flight rejection

Flight crew scheduling

Flight crew standby duties

Dispatch

Distribution of essential information

5. EQUIPMENT

Aircraft types

Suitability

Specialized equipment availability

Maintenance and repair availability

Simulator availability

Vendor support

Fleet standardization

6. FLIGHT CREWS

Selection and testing

Experience of new hires

Experience level of qualified crew members

Personnel policies

Medical examinations

7. OPERATIONS MANUAL

Currency

Periodic review

Record of changes and amendments

Distribution

Logically organized

Contents

- General policies
- Duties and responsibilities of crewmembers
- Reference to applicable regulations
- Flight dispatch and flight following procedures
- Enroute flight, navigation and comm. procedures
- Type of route or flight authorized
- Type of operation authorized
- Airport information
- Weight limitations
- Passenger briefings
- Command and succession of command of aircraft
- Procedures for determining suitability of airports
- Procedures for operating in severe weather
- Training programs
- Instructions for maintenance and servicing
- Aircraft time limitations
- Procedures for refueling aircraft
- Airworthiness inspections
- Weight and balance procedures
- Pilot and dispatch route qualification procedures
- Accident notification procedures
- Hazardous materials handling
- Other safety information or instructions

8. FLIGHT OPERATIONS

Primary areas of operations

Operating certificates held

Insurance company restrictions

Flight request procedures

Flight approval procedures

Documentation and confirmation

Scheduling

Schedule changes

Flight crew assignment and notification

Flight crew limitations

- Individual experience, currency and proficiency
- Flight time
- Duty time
- Rest periods
- Days off
- Method of monitoring and recording limitations

Flight preparation

- Passenger manifest
- Cargo manifest
- Flight plan
- Weight and balance
- Weather
- NOTAMS
- Distribution of essential information
- Airworthiness of aircraft

Flight

- Appropriate publications aboard aircraft
- Emergency equipment aboard aircraft
- Use of checklists
- Crew coordination
- Flight following
- Recording of discrepancies
- Reporting of safety items

9. TRAINING

Training manual

Training records

Training record review

Availability of check airmen

Availability of instructors

Availability of aircraft flight hours for training

Conduct of training during operational missions

Integration of flight deck and cabin emergency training

Use of vendors for training

Types of operational training

- Initial new hire training
- Initial equipment training
- Transition training
- Upgrade training
- Recurrent training
- Requalification training

Contractor training

Cabin crew training

Dispatch training

Miscellaneous training

- Operations manual review
- Federal Air Regulation review
- Aeronautical Information Manual review
- Meteorology
- Performance
- Survival
- First aid, CPR
- Hazardous materials
- Fuel servicing
- Physiological training
- Crew resource management training
- Emergency training
  - Aircraft evacuation
  - Fire extinguisher use
  - Emergency equipment review

10. FACILITIES

Flight planning facilities

- Adequate equipment
- Access to weather information
- Appropriate publications
- NOTAMS
- Airport information
- Flight safety information

Flight scheduling and dispatch

- Adequacy
- Communications
- Records
- Crew rest accommodations

Company facilities at airports or contractor locations

11. PASSENGER SUPPORT

Passenger service manual

- Adequacy
- Used?

Cabin crew

- Qualifications
- Training

Passenger emplaning and deplaning

- Route
- Safety
- Carry-on luggage

Cabin incidents

- Policy
- Reporting
- Investigation

Cabin briefings

SAFETY INSPECTION REPORT FORMAT

This sample format is designed for a formal safety inspection of a large organization. As with any sample, you must modify it to suit the needs of your organization.

PART I — EXECUTIVE SUMMARY

This is written to let the line managers rapidly digest the "meat" of the report without reading all of it.

1. Introduction. Describe authority, purpose, and scope of the safety inspection.

2. Commendable Observations. In one paragraph, cover the good points.

3. Major Problem Areas. In one paragraph, summarize the problems observed.

PART II — FINDINGS

If necessary, sub-organize by area inspected. Number all findings consecutively.

1. FINDING: State your basic conclusion, good or bad.

   • Symptoms: List the facts that justify the finding. List the cause or management deficiency that allowed the situation to occur. Omit if not needed.

   • Impact: List the probable result if the situation remains uncorrected. Omit if not needed.

   • Recommendation: What management action would eliminate this problem?

   • Reference: If appropriate, cite the FAR or standard that applies.

2. FINDING: Use same format for all findings.

PART III — ADMINISTRATIVE DETAILS.

Cover what should be done about the report.

1. Reply Instructions: Identify, by number, those findings which deserve an answer and specify which agency/office should prepare the answer. Establish a suspense.

2. Distribution: Show who received the report. Make sure that each office tasked with responding to a finding gets a copy.

FOLLOW UP

It is pointless to have an inspection program that generates a lot of paperwork, but no action. On the key items, there has to be some method of ensuring that they have been corrected. In a well-run program, the line manager is expected to monitor correction. That is the person who should be most interested in it. This way, the aviation safety manager does not have to personally pursue each item. On subsequent inspections, of course, deficiencies noted on previous inspections should always be examined.

SUMMARY

Aviation safety inspections should be an asset to your program and they should give the head of the organization some degree of confidence in the safety of the operation. They do not have to be an unpleasant experience for anyone. Done correctly, they can provide positive assistance to the line managers.

DISCUSSION QUESTIONS

1. Your airline is certified to carry hazardous material (HAZMAT) as cargo. Lately, a number of pilots have rejected HAZMAT cargo due to improper manifesting, labeling, or compatibility. What kind of inspection program would you recommend to control this problem?

2. You are the Director of Safety. You have conducted a formal aviation safety inspection of one of your divisions. The vice president of that division has rejected your report and refused to respond to it. What are you going to do now?

AVIATION SAFETY EDUCATION AND TRAINING

You probably weren't expecting this, but education training is almost always a part of an aviation safety program. There are several reasons for this:

1. There are some mandated training programs (HAZMAT training, for example) that are usually considered part of the aviation safety program.

2. There will be a certain amount of turnover among your pilots and maintenance technicians. The new ones need to be brought into the organization safety program as soon as possible.

3. If you have developed a safety organization which includes additional duty aviation safety specialists at all levels (as recommended), someone has to teach them how to do their job.

4. There is always a need for recurring aviation safety training among the pilots and maintenance technicians.

5. If you are in charge of pre-accident planning, some degree of training will be necessary if you expect people to respond correctly.

6. New station managers, supervisors, and executives need to know something about the company aviation safety program. While this may not be considered training, you still need some organized method of getting this information to the people who need it.

PROVIDING THE TRAINING

There are any number of different methods of providing the training. It doesn't really make any difference how it is done as long as it is done well. In some cases, recurring training (hazardous materials handling, for example) will be provided as part of the regular operational training program. In other cases, some subjects you would want covered with new pilots or maintenance technicians will automatically be covered during their indoctrination. In still other cases, it might be best to set up a training program and let the additional duty aviation safety specialists actually conduct it. Occasionally, you may find it best to purchase the training from a vendor. First aid and CPR training might be something you would "outsource." If you are not conducting the training yourself, your role is that of monitoring the training program for content and quality.

Except for large organizations, training is probably not provided in a formal classroom setting. There aren't that many people who need the training at any one time. Assuming that most of the training will be done in batches of three or four people across a table, one easy way to do it is to use the notebook method. Organize a three ring notebook with dividers for each type of training. Within each divider, there is a teaching outline of the subjects, plus whatever visual aids are needed. If you want to get fancy, use a notebook with covers that will open 360 degrees and will stand up on the edges of the covers. Organize it so that the instructor sees the notes and the students see the visuals when the notebook is placed between them.

TRAINING RECORDS

It is a good idea to keep minimal records by name, date, and subject. In some cases, the record of training should be posted to the individual's master training record. In other cases, it is sufficient to keep a list of names and dates at the end of each divided section in the training notebook. These records eliminate future arguments over whether an individual was ever briefed on a certain subject or not. For that reason, it is probably a good idea to keep the records as long as the employee is with the company.

TYPES OF TRAINING

We can categorize all safety training as initial, specialized, or recurring. Initial training, as the name implies, is for the person new to the organization. Specialized training is training that only certain people need. Recurring training, of course, is merely a regular review of either initial or specialized training.

INITIAL TRAINING

In this category, we would list any training subjects that are new or are provided to people that are new. Included might be:

- Aviation safety training for new pilots and maintenance technicians

- Safety indoctrination for management personnel

- Aviation Safety Specialist training

- Pre-accident response training

SPECIALIZED TRAINING

This could include:

- HAZMAT Training

- First Aid and CPR for crewmembers and maintenance technicians

- Use of Fire Extinguishers

RECURRING AVIATION SAFETY TRAINING

As stated, this is a review and update of initial and specialized training.

TRAINING COURSE CONTENTS

This varies with the needs of the organization. You start by finding out what subjects are already being adequately covered (in employee indoctrination perhaps) and build your program from there. For any given subject or target audience, it is fairly easy to pick out the topics that need to be covered. What follows is a list of topics that might be appropriate. As with any suggested list, these must be modified to suit your needs.

NEW PILOTS

1. Company Aviation Safety Policy and Program. This is the time to make sure the new pilot understands how the boss feels about aviation safety and how the program works.

2. Operations and Maintenance Safety Standards. What rules do we follow?

3. Aviation Safety Record. Are we proud of it? What problems have we had in the past? Where are we going?

4. Aviation Safety Staff. It is important to introduce the new pilot to the aviation safety staff now; not after an incident or an accident.

5. Reporting Accidents, Incidents, Minor Injuries. What is an accident or incident? What should the pilot do?

6. Reporting Hazards. If the pilot sees something hazardous, how do you want it reported? What will happen?

7. Pilot Responsibility following an Aircraft Accident.

   A. Company Policy. Are we going to immediately remove the pilot from flying duties as many organizations do? Are we going to require toxicological testing? If so, now is the time to explain the policy.

   B. Investigation. How is the investigation going to be handled?

C. Pilot's Rights. Is the pilot entitled to representation? (Yes, if it is an NTSB investigation.) To what degree will the organization provide assistance?

8. Unique Operational Hazards.

9. Local Terrain/Airfield Hazards.

10. Local Weather Hazards.

11. Local Mid-Air Collision Potential.

12. Problems and hazards other pilots in the organization have encountered.

NEW MAINTENANCE TECHNICIANS

This is similar to the aviation safety training for new pilots, but adjusted for the needs of the maintenance technician.

1. Company Safety Policy and Program.

2. Company Safety Standards.

3. Aviation Safety Staff.

4. Reporting Accidents, Incidents and Injuries.

5. Reporting Hazards.

6. Unique Operational Hazards.

NEW ADDITIONAL DUTY AVIATION SAFETY SPECIALISTS

1. Company Safety Policy and Program.

2. Company Safety Standards.

3. Safety's Role in the Organization

4. Safety Staff Organization.

5. Line/Staff Relationships.

6. Distribution of Safety Information.

7. Aviation Safety Inspections and Audits. How often? What areas? Who conducts the inspections? What records/reports are kept?

8. Accidents and Incidents. Definitions. Reporting and investigation procedures.

9.   Hazard Reports. Processing and resolution.

10.   Aviation Safety Training. Requirements. Records.

11.   Aviation Safety Committee. Membership, meetings, and procdures.

12.   Safety Awards Program.

13.   Records, Reports, and Correspondence.

14.   Assistance Available from the Aviation Safety Manager.

HAZARDOUS MATERIALS HANDLING (HAZMAT) TRAINING

In the United States, this training is mandated as described in Department of Transportation Regulations, 49 CFR Parts 171-175. It is also addressed in ICAO Annex 18 and FAA Advisory Circular 121-21B. OSHA Standard 1910.1200 may also apply as OSHA sees an airplane parked on the ramp as another facility subject to OSHA rules. The training is both initial and annual recurrent, and must be FAA approved. All personnel involved in handling hazardous materials receive the training. Operators who do not accept or transport hazardous materials, still must provide minimum training so that their personnel can recognize hazardous materials.

The following list is suggested minimum training subjects. Since this is subject to change, the current regulations should always be consulted. In this list, the asterisked items are those suggested for operators who do not accept or transport hazardous materials.

*1.   Hazardous materials and classifications

 2.   Shipping paper and certificate requirements

*3.   Packaging, marking and labeling

 4.   Exemption authority

*5.   Exceptions from the regulations

 6.   Written notification of Pilot-in-Command

 7.   Keeping and replacement of lost or damaged labels

*8.   Reporting hazardous materials incidents/deficiencies

 9.   Loading, unloading and handling

10.   Specific regulations applicable according to classification of material

FIRE EXTINGUISHER TRAINING

This training should be provided on an initial and recurring basis to crewmembers and anyone involved in flight line operations. In many cases, the airport fire department will provide the training on request. As a minimum, it should cover:

1. Fire chemistry and extinguishing methods

2. Classification of fires

3. Classification of fire extinguishers and extinguishing agents

4. Types of extinguishers available

5. Use of extinguishers

6. Servicing of extinguishers

7. Notification of fire department

PRE-ACCIDENT PLANNING

It is of almost no value to develop a comprehensive plan for responding to an aircraft accident without providing training on how the plan is supposed to work. Consider these subjects.

1. Initial notification and verification of an accident or incident

2. Notification of other personnel

3. Response (location)

4. Transportation

5. Equipment

6. Accident response management and organization

7. Initial actions

8. Scene control

9. Government investigations

10. News media

11. Relatives, next of kin

12. Communications

13. Plan exercise

MISCELLANEOUS TRAINING

Depending on the nature of the operation, there may be a requirement for other types of training. In most cases, this will be an operations or a maintenance responsibility, but the aviation safety manager is frequently in the best position to identify the need for the training and help develop the program. Some common types of training are:

1. PASSENGER EMERGENCY TRAINING. If your organization is regularly carrying the same passengers, it makes sense to provide them with regular in-depth training on the aircraft and its emergency equipment. Thus when an emergency does occur, the passengers are much better prepared for it and can assist instead of hinder the situation.

2. MANAGEMENT TRAINING. One consistent complaint in small flying organizations is that they are working for people who don't understand airplanes. This is true in corporate flying, hospital EMS operations, law enforcement, oil company support, and a number of other operations. Even in airlines, senior management does not necessarily have an extensive background in aircraft operations. If that situation exists, then the only real solution is to teach the managers what they need to know about the flying business. This could involve subjects like flying regulations, licensing, weight and balance, aircraft limitations, crew limitations, and so on.

3. CUSTOMER-CONTRACTOR. It is not unusual for you, the aircraft operator, to depend on someone else to provide you with a helipad, fuel your aircraft, load it, whatever. If they don't know how to do this, you are going to have to train them to meet your standards. Airlines do this all the time as most of them depend on other agencies to handle their aircraft at various stations.

4. FLIGHT ATTENDANT AND/OR DISPATCHER TRAINING. If you use flight attendants or dispatchers, they need safety training, too. The methodology for developing courses for them is about the same as for pilots or maintenance technicians.

PROFESSIONAL EDUCATION

Finally, there is always a need for the aviation safety staff to obtain formal training and maintain currency in the aviation safety business. There are numerous courses offered through universities, professional organizations, and trade associations. You should have some training goals and keep yourself and the additional duty aviation safety specialists involved and current.

DISCUSSION QUESTIONS

1. You are a corporate operator. A group of company executives regularly fly as passengers on your aircraft. You plan to provide them with in-depth passenger safety and emergency training.

   A. What training methods could you use to do this?

   B. What subjects do you intend to cover?

2. The notebook method of conducting training for small groups was discussed in the chapter. Name some other methods and discuss their pros and cons.

AVIATION SAFETY AWARDS PROGRAMS

It is very difficult to develop and manage a good aviation safety awards program. The problem is that we are trying to reward a negative idea — no accidents. If we had a lot of accidents, it might be easier. We could tell who deserved an award. In aviation, though, we don't really have enough accidents to use that as a measuring device. Based strictly on mathematical probabilities, a flying organization should go for years without an accident. An individual pilot should never have one. A pilot will never fly enough hours to be mathematically entitled to one. Realistically, we can't reward someone for not having something that probably wouldn't have happened anyway.

Realizing this, we try to come up with some other scheme for measuring aviation safety so we can decide who gets the award. At best, these schemes may be perceived as phony and they can be "gamed." At worst, they actually take our safety program in the wrong direction. Some safety award programs, for example, count minor incidents as negative values. The predictable and inevitable result of this is that units will deliberately hide or just not report events that we would really like to know about. Other awards programs count submission of hazard reports as positive values. Because of that, I remember one organization which required its pilots to submit a minimum of two hazard reports per flight. It didn't take long for the Director of Safety to get tired of that program.

Other awards programs probably do more harm than good. If, for example, workers are given a monthly bonus for no lost-time injuries, they begin to expect it and treat it as part of their income. Removing that income (for reasons they could not control) is likely to be unpopular. Along the same lines, a program that punishes the entire work force for an accident or injury sustained by one individual will probably result in strong pressure to not report that accident or injury. Programs that award safe workers with extra draws in a monthly lottery are similarly flawed. Since lotteries are ultimately decided on the basis of luck, participation in the lottery is not perceived as much of an incentive to be safe. In one classic case, a worker sustaining an injury was removed from participation in the monthly lottery while the worker causing the injury was left in. There's something wrong there!

Some awards programs are based on skillful handling of emergencies. This has some dangers. Sometimes, a pilot's handling of an emergency absolutely deserves an award — no question. Occasionally, though, it turns out that the pilot was the one who created the emergency in the first place and we are actually rewarding stupidity. That won't enhance the program. The old saying that "A superior pilot is one who stays out of trouble by using superior judgment avoids having to use superior skill," contains a certain amount of truth.

The best approach is to reward something positive. The problem is that we can't predict what is going to happen that we might consider positive with respect to aviation safety. This means that the program must be somewhat open ended and loosely defined. Ideally, we want to be in a position to reward positive events as they occur.

AWARD CRITERIA

Here are some criteria that might be used as the basis for an award.

- Best safety article in the company safety publication. This would be a good one to let the safety committee judge. If you can get the crewmembers or other employees to submit articles for publication, you are gaining participation in the program.

- Best resolution or correction of a hazardous situation. (Not, of course, if they created the hazardous situation.)

- Achievement award for completing some advanced safety training activity. CPR Instructor or Water Safety Instructor, perhaps.

- Additional Duty Aviation Safety Manager of the Month award. Based on overall performance and safety activity.

- Best Safety Audit award. This would be a unit or organization award and it would involve a very consistent audit and scoring system. A better scheme might be to award any organization that does very well on a safety audit.

PURPOSE OF AWARDS

There are really only two reasons to have an awards program.

1. To reward positive activities or behavior.

2. To motivate others to act or behave in that same fashion.

Both of these reasons must be satisfied or there is something wrong with the program.

MANAGING AN AWARDS PROGRAM

1. RECIPIENT. Generally, it is always better to reward individuals rather than units or organizations. Another plaque or trophy on the headquarters wall doesn't necessarily reward or motivate individuals. The military services present a lot of group awards. The U.S. Air Force has a fairly elaborate safety award program. It is a mix of unit and individual awards and it works fairly well. An interesting phenomenon occurs with the USAF individual awards. They are so hard to win that the act of merely being nominated for one of them is an award in itself. Thus, an organization can get most of the benefits of the award by just nominating the individual and publicizing the nomination.

2. CRITERIA. The award criteria should be achievable and everyone who meets it should be rewarded. Many small awards are better than one big one.

3. TIMELINESS. The award should follow the event as soon as possible before everyone forgets what was done to earn it. If at all possible, the time lapse shouldn't exceed 30 days.

4. PRESENTATION. The presentation must be public, or at least publicized. If not, one of the two purposes of the program is lost.

5. POSSESSION. The individual should keep it and it should have some permanence. Awards that disappear, such as a free dinner for two, don't have much lasting effect. They will be forgotten as soon as the heartburn is gone. Actually, the free dinner can be turned into a positive award by taking a picture of the couple eating the dinner, giving them a copy, and using the picture as part of the award publicity.

6. DISPLAY. The best awards can be displayed and serve as constant reminders of the event. Thus, a nameplate that goes on a desk is better than a money clip that goes in the pocket. This means that a cash award is not as good as a tangible award.

7. PERSONALIZATION. People like to have something with their name on it. It is worth the extra time and cost.

8. VALUE. This is interesting. The value of an award is in what it is worth to the recipient; not in what it cost the giver. Thus some very good awards (pictures, certificates, letters of appreciation) can be very inexpensive.

EXAMPLE PROGRAM

This program was run successfully in a large aviation organization. The actual award was a ceramic coffee cup with the company logo, the words "Aviation Safety" and the individual's name, all fired into the cup.

The program was run through the line managers at the operating locations. The manager could nominate any individual the manager felt had made a significant contribution to the aviation safety program. This contribution could be in the form of some specific act which prevented damage or injury, or some other contribution in the form of a well-written hazard report, an investigation of an incident, service on the aviation safety committee, or anything else that the line manager considered significant. There were no limitations on what could be awarded or on how many awards could be given.

The nomination procedures were fairly simple. The line manager forwarded a one page memo to the senior manager describing the act. If the senior manager agreed, the nomination was forwarded to the Director of Safety. If the nomination was valid and met the criteria for the company aviation safety award program, the Director of Safety approved it. If the Aviation Safety Committee meets often enough, this might be a decision that they should make. The cup was made and delivered to the line manager for presentation to the individual.

This program satisfied all of the criteria listed above. The entire process took less than 30 days and the individual got a very good looking coffee cup which served as a permanent advertisement for the award program. More important, the award came from the individual's supervisor; not the safety department, although the Director of Safety usually attended the presentation. That increased participation in the aviation safety program and reinforced the idea that the program really belonged to the line managers; not the safety office.

Eventually, this program generated three or four awards per month. The program was essentially self-working as the line managers did all the work. The Director of Safety merely managed the program and furnished the coffee cups.

SUMMARY

An aviation safety awards program can enhance your program or detract from it. Pick one that enhances it. One that motivates people toward better safety behavior is a program enhancer.

DISCUSSION QUESTIONS

1. The company president wants to present a single monthly safety award to an individual and have the presentation publicized in the company newsletter. What criteria are you going to use to determine the monthly winner?

2. Considering the situation described above, what type of award are you going to recommend that the president give?

3. What are two disadvantages or pitfalls associated with this type of program?

ACCIDENT PREPARATION AND INVESTIGATION

This is not a book on aircraft accident investigation and no attempt will be made to cover the subject here. Consult the references in the Bibliography for more information.

Nevertheless, the aviation safety manager needs some understanding of the investigative process. When an aircraft accident occurs, everyone in the organization is going to look to the aviation safety manager as the person who knows what to do. Let's establish some basic ideas.

First, since the expectation of an aircraft accident is very low, few organizations are well prepared for one. They have no one on the payroll who is hired strictly to respond to aircraft accidents. They may have set aside some emergency funds somewhere, but they are usually not targeted exclusively for aircraft accidents. At best, they may have a plan and they may have set aside some equipment they think they will need. When the accident occurs, it is going to be very disruptive and they are going to respond to it with the people and the plans available at that time. The more they can learn about the process in advance, the better off they will be.

Second, although all accidents are different, the process of responding to them and investigating them is not. It may be unique to the organization that had the accident, but it is fairly routine to professional investigators. Even the confusion and disruption becomes predictable.

Third, the strength of the organization lies with its line managers. Although the aftermath of an aircraft accident may be new to them, it is their decision-making authority and management of resources that is going to determine the outcome. The pre-accident planning should take advantage of the existing management structure. This is the wrong time to set up a new organization.

Fourth, any aircraft accident is going to be investigated by some government agency. In the United States, of course, that only applies to accidents as defined by the NTSB. See Chapter 3. There is just no substitute for knowing the ground rules. The time to obtain copies of the applicable laws and regulations is now; not after the accident.

Keeping in mind that this book can only reflect procedures current at the time of publication, here is a short description of various aircraft accident investigation procedures.

INTERNATIONAL INVESTIGATIONS

When an aircraft operated by one country (or state) crashes in another, the procedural rules are covered in Annex 13 to the ICAO Convention. The title of this is *Aircraft Accident and Incident Investigation*. Here are the salient points.

1. For their mutual convenience, two countries (contracting states) can always agree to a procedure not specifically covered in Annex 13. Anything is possible.

2. In general, though, the state in which the accident occurs always has the right to appoint the Investigator-In-Charge (IIC); conduct the investigation; and prepare the report. If the accident occurs in international waters, this right reverts to the state of registry.

3. The state of registry has a right and an obligation. The obligation is to furnish to the tate of occurrence information on the aircraft, flight crew, and mission. The right is to send an "Accredited Representative" to participate in the investigation. This Accredited Representative represents the state and is authorized to bring advisors who may represent the aircraft operator, the manufacturer, the unions, and so on.

4. The state of manufacture or design can request the right to send an accredited representative whenever it is believed that this participation could be useful or result in increased safety. This determination, though, will be made by the state conducting the investigation and is, therefore, permissive.

5. Under certain circumstances, Annex 13 permits other states to send accredited representatives.

6. The accredited representative (and advisors) should be entitled to participate in the following manner:

   A. Visit the scene of the accident.

   B. Examine the wreckage.

   C. Obtain witness information and suggest areas of questioning.

   D. Have full access to all relevant evidence as soon as possible.

   E. Receive copies of all pertinent documents.

   F. Participate in readouts of recorded media.

G. Participate in off-scene investigative activities such as component examinations, technical briefings, tests, and simulations.

H. Participate in investigation progress meetings including deliberations related to analysis, findings, causes, and safety recommendations.

I. Make submissions in respect of the various elements of the investigation.

J. Receive a copy of the final report.

INTERNATIONAL INVESTIGATIONS — MILITARY

When a military aircraft crashes in another country, the procedures are somewhat different. If the two countries involved are both members of NATO, then Standard NATO Agreement 3531 (Aircraft Accidents) applies. This permits a single investigation by either country; a joint investigation; or two separate investigations. The most common practice is to allow the country operating the aircraft to conduct a single investigation.

If one of the countries is not a member of NATO, the NATO guidelines may still be followed as a matter of convenience. If not, there may exist a Status of Forces Agreement (SOFA) between the two countries. If so, one of the standard paragraphs in the SOFA deals with aircraft accidents. If a SOFA does not exist, then one or both countries may apply ICAO Annex 13. Even though this was not written to apply to military aircraft accidents, it may be the only document on the subject to which both countries have agreed.

If none of these solutions are applied, it becomes a matter of diplomatic negotiation between the two countries and there is no predicting how it will be resolved.

CIVIL INVESTIGATIONS — UNITED STATES

In the United States, all civil aircraft accidents are investigated by the National Transportation Safety Board (NTSB).

Here, we need to examine the difference between "civil" and "public" aircraft. This is a problem peculiar to the United States and it creates a lot of misunderstandings.

In the United States, there are only two types of aircraft; civil and public. A civil aircraft is any aircraft other than a public aircraft. A public aircraft is an aircraft used only in the service of a government, or a political sub-division. It does not include any government-owned aircraft engaged in carrying persons or property for commercial purposes. "Public" aircraft include all U.S. military aircraft and all aircraft owned and operated by or on long term charter or lease to any government agency at federal, state, county, or city level; providing they are not used for commercial purposes. By separate agreement, it does not include commercial airliners chartered by the government under CRAF or other charter programs. They are civil aircraft for accident investigation purposes.

A change to the rules in 1994 (effective in 1995) required that public aircraft be involved in certain specific operations such as fire fighting, law enforcement, or rescue at the time of the accident. If not, they would be considered civil aircraft for accident investigation purposes and the NTSB would be responsible for the investigation. The NTSB is not responsible for the investigation of public aircraft accidents. Aircraft operated by the military and United States intelligence services are always considered to be public aircraft regardless of what they are doing.

Misunderstandings occur because the NTSB is chartered only to investigate "civil" aircraft accidents. This is not a problem for the military, because they have always had strong internal investigation systems and they always investigate their own accidents. They are, in fact, the reason why the law (Air Commerce Act, 1926) was originally written to exclude them. At that time, they were the only operators of "public" aircraft. It is a problem for other operators of public aircraft as there is potential confusion over the aircraft's status at the time of the accident, and (therefore) who is going to investigate it.

Some operators of public aircraft, mostly at the federal government level, have an agreement with the NTSB for the conduct of all accident investigations involving their aircraft. This is not entirely satisfactory as the NTSB is not manned for this workload and it is unlikely that the resulting report will satisfy the operating agency's need to take internal preventive action. The best advice for any operator of public aircraft in the United States is to be prepared to conduct an internal investigation regardless of what the NTSB does.

Back to an explanation of the NTSB. The NTSB, or "The Board" as it is called, is composed of five presidential appointed members who are confirmed by the Senate. The Board is a multi-modal operation in that it is charged with the investigation of railroad, marine, pipeline, and highway accidents in addition to civil aircraft accidents. The Board's total strength is less than 400 people at the Washington headquarters and the Regional Offices. The Board is totally independent and is responsible only to the President and the Congress.

The size of an NTSB investigation is adjusted to fit the size of the accident. An air carrier accident will generate the "Go" team from Washington with an Investigator-In-Charge and a dozen or more working groups each headed by an NTSB investigator as Group Chairman. A small accident (aircraft operated under Part 135 or Part 91, for example) will usually be investigated by a single investigator from a regional office with the assistance of one or more "parties" (see below). A really small accident (fender-bender) may be investigated by having the operator fill out and mail in the report forms. Some accidents, usually agricultural aircraft accidents and accidents involving home built experimental aircraft, may be delegated to the FAA, but this is becoming less and less common. In these cases, the FAA investigator is satisfying the needs of the FAA and also acting on behalf of the NTSB. It is still an NTSB investigation. The factual information collected is forwarded to the NTSB for determination of probable cause or causes. You should realize that the FAA investigator is wearing both an enforcement hat and a safety hat. The information collected can be used for any purpose.

NTSB procedures follow those recommended by ICAO Annex 13 very closely. One procedure unique to the United States (and Australia) is the use of "parties to the Investigation." Because of the Board's small size, they are very dependent on the assistance of industry for the collection of factual evidence during the investigation.

The criteria for acceptance as a party to the investigation is; the organization's employees, functions, activities, or products were involved in the accident, and the organization can provide suitable qualified technical personnel to actively assist in the field investigation.

Except for the FAA, acceptance as a party is not automatic. It is permissive and it can be withdrawn for non-compliance with NTSB procedures. Parties to the field investigation are commonly the FAA, the aircraft operator, the airframe manufacturer, the engine manufacturer, and any involved unions. Parties to the investigation fully participate in the gathering of facts and the development of the factual report(s) of the investigation. They do not participate in the analysis or cause determination.

If the investigation results in a public hearing, which is common only for air carrier accidents, there are also parties to the hearing who serve under the same general ground rules.

Following the public hearing, if held, the Board, on the basis of all the information it has available, makes a determination of probable cause (or causes) and issues a report. The report may be in one of several formats and the process may take eight months or longer from the date of the accident.

CIVIL INVESTIGATIONS — OTHER COUNTRIES

We cannot, of course, cover the laws and procedures of all the contracting states (currently 188) of ICAO. The ICAO Aircraft Accident Investigation Manual and ICAO Annex 13 are good places to start learning the investigative structure of most other countries. The following general statements will apply in most cases.

1. Most countries are well aware of and expect to follow ICAO Annex 13.

2. Most countries expect and accept accredited representatives. Few of them have anything resembling the United States system of "parties to the investigation."

3. Most countries have a staff of investigators trained in either the United States or the United Kingdom. Thus they all share some common knowledge, techniques and procedures.

4. Many countries, notably Canada, United Kingdom, Australia, New Zealand, Sweden, Switzerland, and others have established independent agencies to conduct their investigations.

5. Most countries are familiar with each other's capabilities and draw freely on each other for laboratory and technical assistance. The mutual quest for aviation safety cuts across a lot of borders. The system works better than you might think.

Considering everything said so far, an aircraft operator, particularly in the United States, would be wise to prepare for participation in any investigation of accidents involving the operator's aircraft. Many operators do not participate because they either don't understand the rules or they are unable to furnish suitably qualified technical personnel. Obviously, if they don't participate, they are not going to know what's going on until the report is published.

In addition to participating in the NTSB investigation, you should seriously consider conducting a concurrent internal investigation. There are at least two reasons for this.

1. It allows you to investigate incidents and other events which will not attract the attention of the NTSB.

2. It gives you a report on which to base corrective actions immediately. You don't have to wait for the NTSB report.

Procedurally, this is not difficult to do. If you participated in the NTSB investigation, you'll get a copy of the factual report. Starting with that, you can put together your own group to analyze it, develop conclusions and recommendations, and write your own report. This will work best if you specify the procedures before the accident. These should include:

1. At what level will the internal investigation be managed? Place the investigative authority at least one level above the section that had the accident.

2. Who will participate? Generally, you can do a good job with a chairman, an experienced pilot, someone from maintenance, and the aviation safety manager. The chairman should definitely be a line manager. Accident investigation is a line responsibility.

3. What will be their authority? Can they interview witnesses? Under what conditions? Do they have full access to records?

4. What is the purpose of the investigation? Prevention? Blame? Resolution of loss? Stick with prevention. Any other purpose divorces the investigation from aviation safety.

5. What kind of report should be written? Keep it simple. Facts, Analysis, Conclusions, Recommendations, Exhibits (if any.)

6. What happens to the report? Who reviews it? Who acts on it?

MILITARY INVESTIGATIONS — UNITED STATES

The U. S. military has investigation procedures that go all the way back to the invention of the airplane. Although they differ somewhat from service to service, the investigations are generally conducted by an appointed board of officers which is responsible for both the conduct of the investigation and the preparation of the report. In the military, there is nothing comparable to the civil public hearing. The factual portions of a military safety investigation are available for release, but the non-factual portions are normally withheld.

The U. S. military may also convene an entirely separate investigation to determine the facts of the mishap and satisfy all legal requirements other than prevention of accidents. This investigation is conducted through the military services judge advocate office; not the aviation safety office. The full report of this investigation is available for release.

One exception to the foregoing is the case of a civil-military accident. These are usually mid-air collisions between a military and a civil aircraft, but there are other ways to have one. When this happens, the accident becomes a civil accident and the primary investigative agency is the NTSB. Like the FAA, the military is guaranteed participation as a "party" and they are always well advised to participate fully. Beyond that, the military may (and usually will) choose to conduct its own independent investigation.

PRE-ACCIDENT PLANNING

It should be obvious by now that you are going to need a plan. If your company has an aircraft accident, a lot of things will need to be done rather quickly and you better have the procedures written down someplace. Some considerations:

1. WHAT'S THE SCOPE OF THE PLAN?

You can make it as big as you like. My approach is to not duplicate any existing plans and not attempt to cover each and every eventuality. At some point, we must depend on our organizational structure to take over and address the problems as they come up. My idea of a workable plan is one that will carry us through the first several hours until we have our senior line managers in place and functioning and the government investigators start taking over. On the front end, there is no point in trying to duplicate existing city or airport emergency plans. We should have copies of them and write ours in harmony with them. On the other end, there is no point in trying to write our own manual of accident investigation. We can buy one, and as the co-author of one of them, I recommend that. See Bibliography.

2. WHO IS GOING TO USE IT?

This is important. Who are we likely to have on duty at the time and place where an accident may occur? Having a group of qualified operations and maintenance personnel is one thing. Having a group of reservations clerks and baggage handlers is something else. We have to write our plan to suit the needs of the people who we will have available at the time of the accident.

3. HOW IS IT GOING TO BE ORGANIZED?

There are many ways of doing this. My preference is for a plan that has immediately useful things (like checklists) in the front and amplified instructions in the back — neatly organized by subject. I also like plans that are written workbook style. Places to take notes and copy down information are built into the plan.

4. WHERE DO WE START?

Start with the mandatory requirements of law. Certain records must be preserved. The wreckage must be secured. There are procedures for handling mail and diplomatic pouches. The NTSB will want to know how many people were on board and what cargo was carried. An accurate crew and passenger list is essential. Begin collecting copies of existing airport emergency plans. Know what actions and notifications are going to occur, then move into other obvious post accident events. Organize this logically and assign responsibilities to appropriate line managers.

PLAN CONTENTS

Regardless of the format, the plan may need to cover some or all of these items, although not necessarily in this order.

1. **GOVERNING LAWS AND REGULATIONS.** Summarize both the applicable laws and company directives applying to aircraft accidents.

2. **COMPANY POLICY AND PRIORITIES.** Normally, the priorities are to protect life, reduce injuries, protect property, and restore operations.

3. **NOTIFICATION.** Who, within the company, is to be notified of an accident and by what means? Who will make outside notifications (NTSB, FAA, Insurance Carrier, etc.)

4. **RESPONSE.** Who, within the company, is expected to respond to the scene of the accident? Cover how they will travel and what they should bring (company identification, flight records, etc.)

5. **WRECKAGE SECURITY.** Cover the obligation of the first company representative on the scene to secure and preserve the wreckage.

6. **PHOTOGRAPHY.** List photography requirements.

7. **NEWS MEDIA.** State how queries from the news media are to be handled. Specify who, within the company, is authorized to speak on behalf of the company. Caution against premature speculation as to cause. What information can be released? What should not be released? What announcements should employees at or near the scene make?

8. **RECORDS.** Cover the requirement for impounding and securing records relevant to the aircraft, the flight crew, and the mission.

9. **INVESTIGATION.** Describe in general terms how the investigation will proceed. Cover how the company's portion of the investigation will be organized. Specify report requirements.

10. **COMPANY RESPONSE ORGANIZATION.** Usually, you will need company representatives at the company office nearest to the scene, the scene itself, and company headquarters. Deciding who goes where and who is in charge takes a bit of planning.

11. **COMMUNICATIONS**. How will the response organization communicate internally? Don't expect your listed telephone numbers to be useful. They will be overloaded with incoming calls.

12. **MANAGEMENT OF PASSENGERS**. Uninjured, injured and fatalities.

13. **MANAGEMENT OF AIRCRAFT CONTENTS**. Cargo, baggage, mail, and personal effects.

14. **NEXT OF KIN (NOK) NOTIFICATION**. Verification of passenger list. Records. Dealing with NOK.

15. **DAMAGED AIRCRAFT RECOVERY**. Many airlines share recovery equipment and major airports usually cover this in their emergency plans.

16. **FUNDS AND ACCOUNTING**. Who is authorized to commit company funds. What accounting records need to be kept?

This list is far from complete, but it is a good start.

PRE-ACCIDENT PLAN TRAINING AND EXERCISE

Just writing and publishing the plan is rarely good enough. The people who will need it must understand it. At a minimum this should require some sort of briefing or training session when the plan is first published. From then on, portions of it can be exercised selectively. The notification system, for example, can be exercised regularly with a simple test message. If a full scale exercise is desired, try working it in conjunction with a required airport emergency plan exercise. A "table top exercise" can be effective. In this type of exercise, the entire accident response team gathers around a conference table and works their way through an accident scenario. One benefit to an exercise is that it exposes glitches in the plan and allows them to be corrected before there is an accident.

SUMMARY

An aircraft accident is a traumatic event and it is probably not possible for an operator to respond to it in a manner that makes everyone happy. Those that have had the best response are those that have the best plan and have practiced it. Those without a good plan make serious mistakes early in the response process. This not only generates bad publicity and future legal problems, but it makes it difficult for the company to restore operations and get back in business. In extreme cases, an operator may be unable to get back in business. Good preparation can help avoid this.

DISCUSSION QUESTIONS

1. Develop a checklist format for one member of your accident response team.

2. Referring to both this chapter and chapter 15, develop an outline of topics for pre-accident plan training.

ANALYTICAL TECHNIQUES

The word "Analysis" is one of those buzzwords that sounds good, but has many different meanings. There are a lot of different approaches to aviation safety analysis and very few standard techniques.

For our purposes, we're going to define "analysis" in two different ways. First, we'll use it as a means of organizing numerical data for the purpose of measuring something or determining trends. Second, we'll look at some analytical techniques to be used for problem solving or cause resolution. Let's start with the numbers.

RATES

You need to understand basic rate calculations and their limitations. You have heard or read statements to the effect that, "The accident rate last year in XXX organization was such and such." So what? Where did that come from? What does it mean? What good is it? Those are good questions.

A rate is the number of events divided by the exposure to those events. The only reason for calculating a rate is to account for differences in exposure. If the exposure was constant, there would be no point in calculating a rate. We could just use the number of events that occurred and that would be perfectly accurate. To put that in simpler terms, the number of accidents we have is obviously related to how much we use the airplane. If we used the plane exactly the same amount each month (or year) we could just use the number of accidents for our analysis. We don't do that, though. Our flying hours vary and we know that an increase in accidents doesn't mean much if the flying also increased.

As an aside, this relationship between total flying and total accidents leads to something I call the "Chicken Little Syndrome." You may recall that Chicken Little was hit on the head by something and immediately jumped to the conclusion that the sky was falling. He spread this rumor at the top of his lungs and got many of the other animals to believe it. This started a mild panic in the barnyard. Same thing happens in aviation.

Deregulation in the United States spawned a remarkable growth in aviation. With more flying, there were more accidents. The news media interpreted this as an indication that the sky was falling and passed that bit of news on to the public. This ignored the fact that the rate of accidents was actually decreasing even though the total number of accidents was increasing. Explaining that to the news media had almost no effect. It was a classic case of looking at only the total numbers and not accounting for the exposure.

Back to our discussion of accident rates; we don't use the total numbers of accidents. We calculate the number of accidents per something; usually per flying hour or departures. Suppose our organization flies 4000 hours in a given year and has one accident. Our accident rate per flying hour is:

$$\frac{1}{4000} = 0.00025$$

That is not a very handy number to talk about, so we multiply it by a constant to get rid of the decimal point. If we multiply it by 10,000 we get a rate of 2.5 accidents per 10,000 hours. If we use 100,000, which is fairly standard in our industry, we get a rate of 25 accidents per 100,000 hours. Now our equation reads:

$$(\frac{1}{4000}) \times 100,000 = 25.0$$

That's our aircraft accident rate per 100,000 hours. There are two points to be made here. The actual rate per hour is always a very small number, and the 100,000 is just a mathematical constant. It has no particular significance. We commonly use 100,000 because that converts most rates to a whole number. The rate for scheduled air carriers is a decimal, so they would need to use 1,000,000 (or more) to get a whole number. As we will see, we use whatever constant we need to suit our calculation.

The problem with this rate calculation is that it only considers two things; accidents and flying hours. Mathematically, it assumes that each additional flying hour is an equal increment of exposure. That doesn't make sense. We know that flying an airplane for five hours is not five times as dangerous as flying it for one hour — but that's what the rate calculation says. The rate calculation assumes that the accidents are evenly distributed throughout the exposure. That may be true of (say) railroad accidents, but it is not true of aircraft accidents. Something like 65% of our accidents occur in the takeoff/departure or approach/landing phases. The rest of the flight is fairly benign.

If we use flying hours as an index of exposure, the calculation always favors the type of flying that produces lots of hours in relation to the number of flights. That means that the scheduled air carriers are always going to have the lowest rate and general aviation is always going to have the highest. Trying to compare the two on the basis of accident rate just doesn't work. As a matter of fact, if you were given a description of the type of flying done by several organizations, you could list them in their proper order by rate without ever knowing what the rates are. Just put the ones flying the long range missions on the bottom and the ones flying short hops on top.

Suppose we change our exposure element and calculate the rate in terms of sorties, missions, or departures. Does that change anything? Certainly. Now each departure is assumed to be an equal increment of exposure and the calculation favors the organization with the most total departures. For air transport flying, this is probably more accurate than the flying hour calculation; but it is still a poor method of comparison, because it gives no credit for the length of the flights.

The real problem is that the rate calculation does not consider differences in equipment, mission, or environment. Because of that, it is impossible to accurately compare organizations on the basis of accident rate if their mission, equipment or operating environment is different. The military services can sometimes do this because they may have several units doing essentially the same thing with the same equipment. Certain types of flying can be separated out (hospital EMS helicopter operations, for example) and some comparisons made. Generally, though, the rate calculation isn't useful as a comparative device.

What is it good for? Well, it can be used to compare an organization to itself. By plotting the rate over a period of time, we can see whether the unit is getting better or worse. This works providing we know what we are doing when we plot the data (see below) and providing there hasn't been any significant change in equipment, mission, or environment during that time. Obviously, if we switch from a fixed wing to a rotary wing operation (or vice versa), our historical rates aren't going to mean much.

Another use of rates is to put our safety record in perspective and bring us back down to earth. For example, let's suppose that we are running an air taxi operation and we fly about 4,000 hours per year. We've been accident-free for the past four years and we are proud of our record. Should we be proud?

Maybe. The air taxi accident rate per 100,000 hours has been hovering around 4.0 for the last few years. That means that one accident occurs about every 25,000 hours. Dividing our 4,000 hours into that shows us that we ought to have an accident every 6.25 years if we are just average. Thus our four year accident-free record is a good start, but it does not necessarily mean that we've got a super wonderful safety program and we can sit back and relax.

That points out a problem in this business. As an industry, we have really done a good job in preventing aircraft accidents. The rates are very low and safety managers in other industries and other forms of transportation would kill for those rates.

They are so low, in fact, that we have trouble using them as a measure of progress. The accident rate calculation is just not particularly useful outside of very large flying organizations. Furthermore, the small numbers involved create problems. Take the scheduled air carrier fatal accident rate. This goes up and down a little, but it has been around 0.05 for several years. This translates into one fatal accident every 2,000,000 hours, or, based on average flying hours in the United States, an average of five per year. That's not very many accidents. The problem is that we don't actually have five per year because small numbers don't distribute themselves evenly. They bunch up. We will have some years when we have seven or eight fatal accidents and we refer to that as a terrible year. We'll have other years when we have only two or three (or maybe none) and we spend a lot of time congratulating ourselves on how safe we are.

Actually, we are not that bad in the bad years and not that good in the good years. We create this false impression of progress (or lack of it) because we don't really understand the rate calculations. In the case of air carriers, we could correct this by looking at the record over a longer period of time, perhaps five years instead of one year.

All of this aside, rate calculations can be useful in individual organizations as long as we understand what we are doing. In a fairly extensive study of aviation safety, the U. S. Congressional Office of Technology Assessment concluded that attempting to measure safety by considering only accident data was not effective. Nonaccident data (meaning incidents) had to be used for short-term safety analyses. In the same study, they also pointed out that incident data was difficult to collect reliably because of the imprecise definition of an aircraft incident. That was the point made in Chapter 11. We are free to define incidents in any manner that suits our needs and build our own analysis system.

We can pick any event that is meaningful to our program and calculate a rate based on whatever exposure is appropriate. Suppose, for example, we are interested in the number of high speed (above 100 kts) aborts occurring in our operation. We would logically use the number of takeoffs or departures as the exposure index. It would make no sense to calculate runway aborts per flying hour. We might find that we need to multiply by a constant of 1,000 to get rid of the decimal point. Now we have a rate we can use to spot trends in takeoff aborts. In a large operation, there is probably a takeoff abort rate which would be considered normal.

If we watch the rate for a few months, we'll discover what that "normal" rate is and we can start putting limits on our chart, perhaps by calculating standard deviations. If the rate goes significantly above normal, that's where we need to focus our attention and find out why. If the rate dips well below normal, there must be a reason for that, too. Maybe there has been a procedural change which has reduced the number of aborts or maybe they are just not being reported accurately. If we have a computer, we can let the computer monitor any number of events for us. All we have to do is enter the fact that the event occurred and keep the exposure numbers up to date. The computer can be programmed to automatically flag events that are occurring at a greater than expected rate. Now we have a proactive prevention program. We're not just sitting around waiting for an accident and reacting to it.

DATA PORTRAYAL

Now that we have rates, what do we do with them? There are three common methods of handling the data. None of them are perfect.

MONTHLY RATES

Here, you calculate a monthly rate by dividing that month's events by that month's exposure. This will work all right if you have a lot of events. If not, it creates a chart with wild swings between the peaks and valleys and it is very difficult to see any trend.

CUMULATIVE RATES

This is by far the most common method used for safety statistics, and it is also one of the most deceptive. You start your chart in January (or the beginning of the fiscal year, if you like) and divide January's events by January's exposure. February's rate is the sum of both January and February events divided by the total exposure for both months. You keep going like this through December, which is an entire year's worth of events divided by the total exposure for the year. On December 31st, you get a new chart and start out at zero again.

This method has several problems. First, each event stays in all subsequent calculations. If, for example, you have an accident in January, all of your calculations for the rest of the year will still be influenced by January's accident. It is possible, if you know how many hours you are going to fly that year, to calculate exactly what your end-of-year accident rate is going to be if you have no more accidents. Second, it really doesn't make much sense to turn the rate back to zero at the end of the year. This almost eliminates this as a method for determining trends. Third, the effect of a single event is influenced by the time of year in which it occurs. January's accident produces a large rate, because there hasn't been much exposure so far. The same accident occurring in December produces a much smaller change in the rate. Fourth, as more and more exposure is accumulated, the rate eventually flattens out and the effect of a single accident is hardly noticeable.

MOVING WINDOW OR MOVING AVERAGE RATES

This is the best of the methods, but the least used. In effect, the rate calculation for each month is really the cumulative rate for the preceding three months — or six months, or whatever. Each month, you add in the new events and exposure, then subtract the earliest month's worth. You ignore the end of the year and just keep right on going. The result is a graph that is a much more realistic portrayal of your present situation. January's accident will eventually drop out of the calculation and, if your record is good, the chart will reflect it. This is the best of the methods for determining trends. Depending on the size of the window you pick, the chart will show you the trend for that period of time. Twelve months seems to work well. It is long enough to see trends and short enough to manage.

To illustrate the differences among these methods of rate portrayal, consider Figures 18-1 and 18-2. In our organization, we are trying to make some sense out of a particular event that involves our aircraft and occurs regularly. We haven't defined the event, so you can assume any equipment failure or procedural activity that you might want to analyze.

Figure 18-1 shows the number of events per month and a running total (cumulative) number of events. It also shows the number of hours we flew each month and the cumulative hours.

In the rate section, the monthly rate is just the monthly events divided by the monthly hours. We multiply this by 1,000 to put the decimal point in a better place. Thus the rates are per 1,000 hours; not per hour. The cumulative rate is the cumulative events divided by the cumulative hours. The three-month average rate is the sum of the last three months' events divided by the sum of the last three months' hours.

Figure 18-2 shows these three rates plotted on the same chart. It is hard to believe that all three of these curves were generated by the same events and hours, but they were. An analysis of that chart would go something like this.

| EVENTS, EXPOSURE AND RATES | | | | | | |
| EVENTS | | EXPOSURE | | RATES | | |
MONTH	MONTHLY	CUMULATIVE	MONTHLY	CUMULATIVE	MONTHLY	CUMULATIVE	3 MONTH AVERAGE
JAN	2.0	2.0	600.0	600.0	3.3	3.3	
FEB	2.0	4.0	700.0	1300.0	2.9	3.1	
MAR	8.0	12.0	700.0	2000.0	11.4	6.0	6.0
APR	7.0	19.0	900.0	2900.0	7.8	6.6	7.4
MAY	6.0	25.0	1100.0	4000.0	5.5	6.3	7.8
JUN	6.0	31.0	1300.0	5300.0	4.6	5.8	5.8
JUL	3.0	34.0	1000.0	6300.0	3.0	5.4	4.4
AUG	5.0	39.0	700.0	7000.0	7.1	5.6	4.7
SEP	6.0	45.0	700.0	7700.0	8.6	5.8	5.8
OCT	5.0	50.0	600.0	8300.0	8.3	6.0	8.0
NOV	4.0	54.0	700.0	9000.0	5.7	6.0	7.5
DEC	7.0	61.0	1000.0	10000.0	7.0	6.1	7.0

Figure 18-1. Events, Exposure and Rates

In January, the monthly rate and the cumulative rate start out the same because they are the same. The monthly curve is characterized by wild variations because the exposure is always just one month's worth of flying. A single event has a large effect on the curve. March was so bad that the monthly curve makes April look good. Actually, April wasn't very good at all. We can ignore the monthly curve as a method of determining trends.

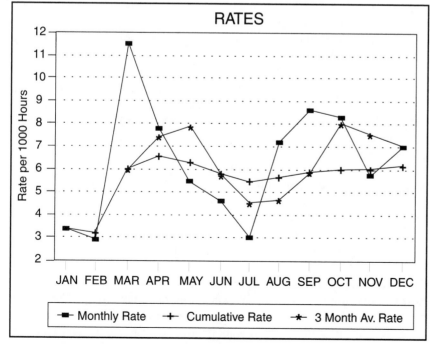

Figure 18-2. Rates from Figure 18-1 Plotted

To be honest, it shouldn't be displayed as a line graph at all. Connecting the points together creates a false sense of gain or loss. It would be better displayed as a bar graph.

In March, the three-month average begins. This is the first time we've had three months of data to plot.

Looking at the cumulative curve, it starts out fairly wild but smooths out. This is because we are accumulating more and more exposure and a single event has less and less effect on the curve. If you look at Figure 18-1 and the cumulative curve in October-December (Figure 18-2), the rates are changing but they are not reflected in the curve. That's because the cumulative method always carries the history of events and exposure for the whole year. The longer we use this method, the less it reflects reality.

The three month average curve never smooths out like the cumulative curve. The reason is that it never considers more than three months worth of exposure, so a single event has a definite effect on the curve. It gives us the most accurate picture of what's happening now and what the trend is for the last three months.

If you were asked to predict what is going to happen in January of next year, you would be wise to disregard the monthly curve altogether. If you believe the cumulative curve, the trend has been slightly up over the past six months. If you believe the three-month average curve, the trend is definitely down over the past three months.

In actual practice, the cumulative curve normally goes to zero in January of next year and we start over. We might as well. That curve can only get flatter. The three month average curve should keep right on going and continue to tell us the three month trend.

By now, you've probably decided that basing decisions solely on rate curves might not be a good idea. That's true. Using Figure 18-2, we could go either way. Yes, we have a problem and it's getting worse; or no, our problem is getting better and we can ignore it. As mentioned earlier, the rate calculation only considers events and exposure. It tells us nothing about the influence of equipment, mission or environment.

One thing a rate curve can do is to alert us to the possibility of a problem. How bad the problem is or why it exists is going to take some effort. Why, for example, was March (Figure 18-2) such a bad month? What happened? Why did June and July suddenly get good? Have there been any changes in the equipment or its use during this period? Are the events being consistently reported? Have we changed vendors? Is there any correlation between events and mission? Airport? Weather? Flightcrew? Aircraft tail number? If we really have a problem here, we've got more work to do. We can't just sit at the desk and make decisions based on the rate charts.

PIE CHARTS

Pie charts or circle charts are worth mentioning because they are so commonly used in safety. Actually, they are very deceptive and should be viewed with skepticism.

The problem is that pie charts are based on percentages and the percentages always have to add up to 100 percent. That means that if one factor on the chart changes, all the other factors must automatically change to keep the total at 100. Actually, the other factors may not have changed at all — or they may have changed in the opposite direction. Their percentage of the total, though, is influenced by the total itself and the changes of the other factors; neither of which are accurately displayed on the pie chart. To be strictly accurate, the size of the pie chart should change to reflect a different total number of events, but you never see that done.

COST BENEFIT ANALYSIS

This is a method of helping management determine whether a particular change or proposal is worth the cost. In its simplest form, all costs of a particular change are compared with the expected benefits of the change over a given time period. This makes sense as long as the benefits can be calculated or predicted with reasonable accuracy. It is a very difficult method to use in aviation safety because of the difficulty in projecting a reduction in accidents and in calculating what that would be worth. It can be done on what we might call an industry-wide basis where we have enough data to do it with some accuracy. We have, for example, done this type of analysis for various pieces of safety equipment on airliners. How many lives could we reasonably expect to save with life rafts? Smoke masks? Oxygen masks? Sometimes the data is shown in terms of how much it will cost to save one life considering each of several options. This shows which of several possible safety modifications would be the most effective. While the results of these calculations aren't necessarily popular with everyone, they do allow us to spend our money where it is likely to do the most good.

One way to deal with the benefit side of the analysis is to use the published accident rate for your type of flying and, based on your annual flying hours, calculate the number of accidents you expect over the time period covered by the analysis. Then, using a breakdown of accidents by type, calculate how many of those accidents would reasonably be prevented by the safety equipment you are considering. Using average values of destroyed aircraft and average costs of fatalities and injuries, you come up with a benefit number that can be compared to the cost of the equipment over the same time period. As you can see, this is not wonderfully accurate. If you are a fairly small organization whose accident expectancy over the given time period is zero, you are wasting your time with this type of calculation. If you can find other benefits, such as reduced insurance premiums or better aircraft performance, then the calculation may be worthwhile.

RISK ANALYSIS

This is a method of quantifying risk. It is used in system safety engineering and in aircraft design to determine critical failure modes and trade-offs in various methods of correction. Risk is basically the probability or chance that a particular event or result will occur. For our purposes, we will assume that there are three components of risk; probability of a single occurrence, exposure, and severity. In some calculations, probability and exposure are considered together and severity is ignored. That's fine as long as you understand what you are doing.

There are methods for calculating (or sometimes estimating) the probability of a single event. If, for example, we are flipping coins, the probability of either of us flipping a head is 1/2 or 0.5. The probability of both of us coming up heads is the product of our individual probabilities or 0.25. Thus once every four times, we should both get heads. If we invite a third player, the probability of all three of us getting heads is 0.125, or once every eight times.

The exposure is the number of opportunities for that single event to occur. In many cases (as stated above), single event probability times exposure equals risk. In the case of three people flipping coins, the single event probability of three heads (0.125) seems low, but that is for only one coin flip. If we expose ourselves to that probability eight or more times, the risk becomes very high indeed.

Severity is a subjective assessment of how bad it is going to be if the event does occur. If the results are going to be negligible, we would just use the basic risk calculation. If the results are almost always going to be fatal, we would multiply the calculated risk by some constant that reflected that severity.

By understanding how the calculation works, it is sometimes possible to use the logic without actually doing the calculations. In considering redundant systems, for example, we don't really have to know the single system failure probability in order to know the effect of adding a second system. It is going to be the single system probability squared — whatever that is. Also if we have high exposure in a particular situation, we can predict the effect of that exposure on the probability. Suppose, for example, we notice that a six inch lip has developed on the landing edge of our runway. Now the probability of any one plane touching down short of the runway is low, but the exposure is the amount of landing traffic, which may be quite high on that runway. Without knowing the probability of a short landing, we can say that the chance of substantial damage (risk) to an aircraft is quite high due to the traffic count (exposure). If we can reasonably say that the damage is probably going to be severe, we can make a pretty good argument for some sort of corrective action.

We can also approach this subjectively by accepting some recognized definitions of probability and severity. In this case, the probability definitions include both single event probability and exposure. Figure 18-3 shows a comparison of the most common methods of assessing probability. These are plotted against the corresponding quantitative probabilities. In these definitions, exposure is included.

Figure 18-4 compares the common methods of assigning a severity classification.

In both figures 18-3 and 18-4, the standards most commonly used are those listed for Military Standard 882, which is the standard for system safety program requirements. The definitions of those terms are shown in figure 18-5.

Assigning categories with Roman numerals and letters is common, but not particularly useful for our purposes. The table in figure 18-6 shows a risk assessment matrix similar to the one in Chapter 11, except that this one has more categories and uses numbers from one to eight.

The actual numbers used are not considered as important as the criteria assigned to them. In figure 18-6, we might use the following criteria:

- 1, 2 or 3. Unacceptable.

- 4. Undesirable. Management Decision Required.

- 5, 6. Acceptable, Management Review Required.

- 7, 8. Acceptable.

HAZARD ANALYSIS

This is one of a number of analytical techniques that can be used to analyze a particular task or operation and examine the hazards or risk

COMPARISON OF EVENT PROBABILITY SYSTEMS

QUALITATIVE PROBABILITY	PROBABLE		IMPROBABLE		EXTREMELY IMPROBABLE
FAA	FREQUENT	REASONABLY PROBABLE	REMOTE	EXTREMELY REMOTE	EXTREMELY IMPROBABLE
JAA	FREQUENT	PROBABLE	OCCASIONAL	REMOTE	IMPROBABLE
MIL-STD-882	FREQUENT				
QUANTITATIVE PROBABILITY	1×10^{-1} 10^{-2} 10^{-3}	10^{-4}	10^{-5} 10^{-6}	10^{-7} 10^{-8}	10^{-9}

Figure 18-3. Comparison of Event Probability Systems

COMPARISON OF AIRCRAFT HAZARD SEVERITY SYSTEMS

SEVERITY OF FAILURE AND EFFECT ON AIRCRAFT AND OCCUPANTS					
COMMERCIAL	NORMAL	NUISANCE OR OPERATION LIMITING	SIGNIFICANT REDUCTION IN SAFETY MARGIN. SOME INJURIES	LARGE REDUCTION IN SAFETY MARGIN. SERIOUS INJURIES, SOME DEATHS	CANNOT CONTINUE SAFE FLIGHT AND LANDING
MILITARY	LESS THAN MINOR INJURY OR OCCUPATIONAL ILLNESS LESS THAN MINOR SYSTEM OR ENVIRONMENTAL DAMAGE	MINOR INJURY OR OCCUPATIONAL ILLNESS OR MINOR SYSTEM OR ENVIRONMENTAL DAMAGE	SEVERE INJURY OR OCCUPATIONAL ILLNESS OR MAJOR SYSTEM OR ENVIRONMENTAL DAMAGE	DEATH, SYSTEM LOSS OR SEVERE ENVIRONMENTAL DAMAGE	

HAZARD CLASSIFICATION OF FAILURE CONDITIONS				
FAA	MINOR	MAJOR	SEVERE MAJOR	CATASTROPHIC
JAA	MINOR	MAJOR	HAZARDOUS	CATASTROPHIC
MIL-STD-882	NEGLIGIBLE	MARGINAL	CRITICAL	CATASTROPHIC

Figure 18-4. Comparison of Aircraft Hazard Severity Systems

RISK PROBABILITY AND SEVERITY	
PROBABILITY DEFINITIONS	
A. FREQUENT	LIKELY TO OCCUR FREQUENTLY.
B. PROBABLE	WILL OCCUR SEVERAL TIMES IN THE LIFE OF AN OPERATION.
C. OCCASIONAL	LIKELY TO OCCUR SOMETIME IN THE LIFE OF AN OPERATION.
D. REMOTE	UNLIKELY, BUT POSSIBLE, TO OCCUR IN THE LIFE OF AN OPERATION.
E. IMPROBABLE	SO UNLIKELY, IT CAN BE ASSUMED OCCURRENCE MAY NOT BE EXPERIENCED.
SEVERITY DEFINITIONS	
I. CATASTROPHIC	DEATH. LOSS OF EQUIPMENT.
II. CRITICAL	SEVERE INJURY. MAJOR DAMAGE TO EQUIPMENT.
III. MARGINAL	MINOR INJURY. MINOR DAMAGE TO EQUIPMENT.
IV. NEGLIGIBLE	NO INJURY. NO DAMAGE TO EQUIPMENT.

Figure 18-5. Risk Probability and Severity

involved. It is sometimes known by other names, such as Job Hazard Analysis (OSHA) or Job Safety Analysis (Industrial Safety). The technique works well when done by a small group, and it can be used as a means of achieving participation in the aviation safety program. Although it can be applied to anything, it tends to generate a lot of paperwork and is best applied selectively. Try applying it to operations or tasks which are new to your organization, or to those activities which are obviously high risk and deserve extra attention.

The basic procedures are:

1. Break the task or operation into small steps; the smaller the better.

2. For each step, identify all possible hazards.

3. For each hazard, make some assessment of the level of risk. This can be done using a hazard prioritization or assessment matrix (Chapter 11 or figure 18-6 in this chapter), a subjective assessment of the hazard as high or low (Chapter 6), or the method discussed earlier in this chapter under Risk Analysis.

RISK ASSESSMENT				
FREQUENCY OF OCCURRENCE	HAZARD CATEGORIES			
	CATASTROPHIC 1	CRITICAL 2	MARGINAL 3	NEGLIGIBLE 4
FREQUENT 0	1	2	3	4
PROBABLE 1	2	3	4	5
OCCASIONAL 2	3	4	5	6
REMOTE 3	4	5	6	7
IMPROBABLE 4	5	6	7	8

Figure 18-6. Risk Assessment

4. For each hazard (or risk) that is unacceptable, list the most practical way to eliminate or reduce the risk.

Start with a large piece of paper and divide it into five vertical columns labeled STEPS, HAZARDS, R/A (for risk assessment) CONTROLS, and REVIEW. The last column provides for validation and approval of the analysis.

To illustrate how this works, let's suppose that we want to taxi a transport-size aircraft into a very restricted area and park it without damaging anything; particularly the aircraft. We break the task into two steps:

1. Taxi into the parking area.

2. Taxi into the parking space.

We take each of these separately and consider all of the possible hazards for the first step before moving on to the second step. Our analysis might look like the one shown in figure 18-7.

This technique forces you (and your group) to think logically about what can go wrong, how bad it will be, and what should be done about it. Done correctly, this is also an excellent training device. The new pilot can be taken step by step through an operation; shown exactly where the hazards lurk; and shown what is to be done to eliminate or reduce those hazards.

HAZARD (OR JOB SAFETY) ANALYSIS				
STEPS	**HAZARDS**	**RISK**	**CONTROLS**	**REVIEW**
1. TAXI INTO PARKING AREA	BLOCKED BY ANOTHER AIRCRAFT	7	RADIO COORDINATION	
	PILOT MAY TAXI IN WRONG PLACE	4	PAINT TAXI LINE	
	OBSTRUCTIONS IN TAXI AREA	4	PAINT OBSTRUCTION CLEARANCE LINES	
2. TAXI INTO PARKING PLACE	PILOT MAY NOT BE LINED UP CORRECTLY	4	USE MARSHALLER	
	PILOT MAY NOT SEE MARSHALLER	5	USE LIGHTED WANDS AND RADIO CONTACT	
	BRAKES MAY FAIL	2	PREPOSITION CHOCKS	

Figure 18-7. Hazard Analysis

OPINION SURVEYS

This is a form of analysis where a group of pilots or maintenance technicians are asked to respond with their opinions on various questions. The classic survey contained two questions:

1. What do you think will cause the next aircraft accident in this organization?

2. What should be done to prevent it?

Some other questions that could prove useful:

• What do you think about our aviation safety program? Is it effective?

• Is our flying operation as safe, safer, or less safe than it was a year ago? If it has changed, what contributed to that change?

• Do you see any unsatisfactory trends developing that could affect aviation safety?

• Are all of our standards and procedures being followed? If not, which are consistently ignored?

The ICAO Accident Prevention Manual recommends a structured questionnaire which asks the respondent to complete various sentences.

FINISH EACH SENTENCE.

1. Safety training in my department . . .

2. My knowledge of accident prevention . . .

3. My boss's view on safety . . .

4. The best part of our safety program is . . .

5. I think we can improve our safety program by . . .

These techniques work only if the anonymity of replies is guaranteed. They should not be used too often as people get tired of surveys and start ignoring them. The big problem is in analyzing the responses. Since the questions are broad and open ended, there tends to be a wide variation in responses. What you are hoping for is an obvious trend in the responses that identifies a problem worth your attention.

CRITICAL INCIDENT TECHNIQUE

A variant of this is called the Critical Incident Technique which can be used to collect ideas on a particular operation or task. While it is normally done with interviews, it can also be done with a questionnaire similar to the following:

- "Assume that we have hired a new pilot who is going to start flying the _____ mission. We are going to assign the new pilot to you and we want you to cover the dangerous or hazardous parts of this mission; the situations where a new pilot can really get into trouble. List as many of these as you like and please rank them starting with the worst first."

Done correctly, this usually gets a pretty good response. The pilots are being asked for help and they don't mind that. What happens, of course, is that each pilot lists the factors in the mission that involved close calls from that pilot's experience. Since they are ranked by severity, most of the scoring is done for you. By combining all of the responses and constructing a master list ordered by frequency of response, you should get a pretty good idea of where the problems are in that particular mission.

ACCIDENT CAUSATION MODEL

This is an analytical tool developed and refined by the U.S. Army. They started with William Heinrich's basic causation model and expanded it to include the concept of system defects. The diagram shown in Figure 18-8 is a variant of the U.S. Army model.

As an analytical tool, the model is useful in that it requires an examination of the systemic weaknesses which ultimately contributed to the result. It is worth noting that the result (Figure 18-8) is entirely unpredictable. It may be a serious accident or, more likely, it will be a no damage-no injury incident. Perhaps it will go unnoticed. This is consistent with ideas expressed in Chapter 2.

An explanation of each of the blocks in the causation model should be beneficial.

CORPORATE GOALS AND MISSION. If aviation safety is not incorporated into the basic purposes for corporate existence, this may be the origin of the problem. As stated in Chapter 2, safety may not be a primary goal, but it is certainly one of the considerations in any flying operation.

MANAGEMENT ERROR. This refers to failure to support the organization's aviation safety program; failure to allocate adequate resources to accident prevention; failure to fully implement corporate goals and mission, etc.

AVIATION SAFETY PROGRAM DEFECT. This is failure on the part of the safety program to identify a particular weakness or failure to adequately inform management of the nature of the weakness.

SYSTEM DEFECT. This refers to any weakness in the total system which includes errors or defects traceable to corporate goals and mission; decisions of senior management; and weaknesses in the aviation safety program.

SUPERVISOR ERROR. There are really three types of supervisor errors: those resulting from system defects, those resulting from improper managerial actions at the supervisory level, and those directly resulting from flawed personal characteristics.

OPERATOR ERROR. There are likewise three types of operator errors: those mandated by the system (through the supervisor), those generated by the operator because of misunderstanding or lack of experience, and those resulting from personal characteristics.

PERSONAL CHARACTERISTICS. These can affect judgment and decision making at any level, but they are most noticeable (and correctable) at the supervisor or operator level. The five personal characteristics most commonly cited as causal in aircraft accidents are anti-authority, impulsivity, invulnerability, machoism, and resignation. These characteristics

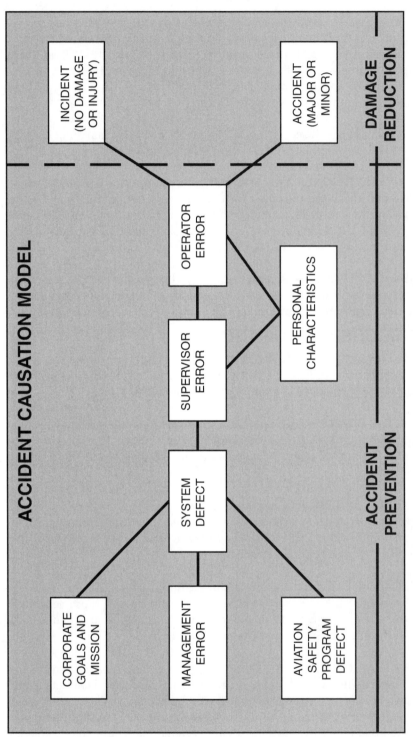

Figure 18-8. Accident Causation Model

were discussed briefly in Chapter 7. Recognition of these characteristics is considered to be the responsibility of the supervisor and (as we get more involved in human factors training) the operator.

In using the model, it is best to start with "Operator Error" and work backwards. While it may be true that nothing can be done about personal characteristics, a lot can be done about system defects — if the analysis stretches to the basic causes.

SUMMARY

As stated at the beginning of this chapter, there are many different forms and methods of analysis. It is impossible to cover them all and it is difficult to get them all in one place in a book. Chapter 6, for example, contains an analytical method that applies risk management logic to accident analysis. Chapter 11 contains a simple method of risk assessment. The best analysis methods are those that suit your immediate needs and produce meaningful results in your organization.

DISCUSSION QUESTIONS

1. Excluding aircraft accidents, list as many possible uses for rate calculations in your organization as you can. List the different types or categories of exposure you might use.

2. If you have analyzed an operation (or part of it) and an accident occurs, does that invalidate your analysis? Discuss the steps you would take to review your analytical methods.

3. Describe how you would use one of the analysis techniques discussed in this chapter to improve your organization's safety program. Be specific.

AVIATION SAFETY OFFICE MANAGEMENT

Along with the job of aviation safety manager or director of safety, you get a certain amount of administrative paperwork. Sometimes you get some administrative help with this, but many times you do not. We make this business work with additional duty safety managers, but we seldom see additional duty secretaries.

This chapter doesn't have much to do with aviation safety except that if you can't keep the office humming along, you won't have much time to work on aviation safety. You'll be up to your ears in paperwork.

Aviation safety managers seem particularly vulnerable in this area. I think it's because most of them spent a dozen or more years learning the craft of flying. That was certainly a lot of fun and a good investment, but it also represents a dozen or more years spent not learning the craft of office management. Now they are in a job that requires some paper shuffling skills that they don't have and don't particularly want.

Cheer up. It happened to all of us and the situation is far from hopeless. Keep a few key points in mind.

1. Your company probably already has some policies or procedures on various administrative subjects. It would be wise to learn these before you begin operating in conflict with them. Typically, these might include:

   - Office Standards

   - Forms and Publications

   - Unions

   - Personnel Policies

   - Signature Authority

   - Coordination Requirements

   - Budgeting and Accounting

   - Key Management and Staff Meetings

   - Mail and Document Distribution

   - Document Control — Files

   - Office Supplies and Equipment

2. Whatever office management problem you have, someone, and probably someone within your own organization, has already had that problem and already solved it. There is no need to reinvent the wheel. All you have to do is find the person who can help you.

3. You need to keep things in perspective. Some of the paperwork that crosses your desk is important, but little of it is life-threatening. There are no fire warning lights in the office and very few desks actually crash.

OFFICE PROCEDURES

Let's attack this problem logically. Your office probably isn't big enough to afford inefficiency. You need to take advantage of every known method of simplifying and automating your office procedures. Here are some basic ideas that will work.

1. FILES

As a rule, don't file company paperwork that you didn't originate. If someone else originated it, let them keep the master file on it. If you want to know more about it, go to their office. Obviously, there are exceptions to this. For instance, it might pay to keep a document originated by someone else in a file you are keeping on a specific subject. If you don't have a filing system and your company doesn't specify one, use the one in figure 19-1 to start with.

2. DISTRIBUTION

Your company most likely has some sort of internal or routing system. This may involve office symbols, stamps, routing slips, fax, e-mail or some other method. Learn it and take full advantage of it. To the extent that you know what type of information will be coming into your office, you should be able to predict how it ought to be distributed. If you are organized, probably 80% of your incoming correspondence can be automatically routed to the units that can benefit from it. This can save you a lot of time.

3. SUSPENSE SYSTEM

This is sometimes called a tickler file. You really need to track two types of suspense; those you must do and those you have asked others to do.

One of the simplest is a card file with dividers numbered 1 to 31. Whenever something is supposed to happen such as a report due, meeting scheduled, whatever, you stick a reminder in the file about three days ahead of the deadline. Each day, you train yourself to look at the reminder notes for that day. If they apply to next month or next year, you leave them

---

1. OFFICE ADMINISTRATION

1.1 FILE PLAN
1.2 COMPANY POLICY FILE
1.3 OFFICE PERSONNEL
   1.3.1 Position Descriptions
   1.3.2 Employment History
1.4 OFFICE SUPPLIES AND EQUIPMENT
1.5 BUDGET AND FINANCE
1.6 SECURITY

---

2. CORRESPONDENCE

2.1 – 2.12 Outgoing Correspondence (Filed by month)

---

3. ACCIDENT/INCIDENT REPORTS

3.1 REPORT LOG
3.2 ACCIDENT REPORTS (Filed by report number)
3.3 INCIDENT REPORTS (Filed by report number)

---

4. HAZARD REPORTS

4.1 REPORT LOG
4.2 HAZARD REPORTS (Filed by report number)

---

5. AVIATION SAFETY AUDITS

5.1 AUDIT SCHEDULE
5.2 AUDIT CHECKLISTS
5.3 AUDIT REPORTS (Filed by location or activity)

---

6. AVIATION SAFETY COMMITTEE

6.1 COMMITTEE CHARTER
6.2 COMMITTEE MEMBERS
6.3 AGENDAS
6.4 MINUTES

---

7. AVIATION SAFETY TRAINING

7.1 TRAINING COURSES
7.2 TRAINING OUTLINES
7.3 TRAINING RECORDS

---

8. PRE-ACCIDENT PLANNING

8.1 PRE-ACCIDENT PLAN
8.2 TRAINING AND EXERCISES

---

9. MISC. AVIATION SAFETY PROGRAMS

9.1 FOREIGN OBJECT DAMAGE
9.2 DROPPED OBJECTS
9.3 BIRD STRIKES – HAZARDS
9.4 AIRPORT HAZARDS
9.5 AVIATION SAFETY AWARDS
9.6 FLIGHT LINE SAFETY
9.7 BULLETINS AND NEWSLETTERS

Figure 19-1. Aviation Safety Filing System

in the file. If they apply to this month, you've got three days to get ready. If the suspense is really on someone else, you can give that person a three-day reminder on what is due.

This system has been around a long time in various versions. The same thing can be done on a large calendar. Now that we all have computers, we can use the calendar or reminder program to do it, The basic suspense file system is simple and it works very well.

4. TO DO LIST

Before you quit each night, make a list of things that you want to do tomorrow. This should include all the mandatory meetings and reports due plus all the projects you really want to work on. Start the morning with a review of this list and let that set your priorities for the day. If you don't finish everything, either forget it or carry it forward to the next day.

5. WORKING FILES

Most desks are equipped with a drawer big enough to hold files, but few people use them for that purpose. This is supposed to be your "working file" drawer and you can save yourself a lot of time if you use it that way.

Let's (for example) set up the following files:

- Aviation Safety Meetings

- Aviation Safety Committee

- Inspection Items

- Bulletin Board Material

- Newsletter Items

- Personal Items

Now, when something comes across your desk that ought to be brought up at a future safety meeting — or added to the safety committee agenda, open your working file drawer, stick it in the appropriate file and close the drawer. When the time comes to prepare the agenda for the next safety committee meeting, pull that file. Most of what you need is right there. If there is nothing in the file, cancel the meeting.

The last item listed above (Personal Items) may have some value to you. This is where you put a copy of everything you have written, received or done that you are proud of. If someone ever asks what you have done to justify your job, you can answer that very quickly.

6. PERSONAL FILES

These are technical reference files of information related to aviation safety programs and their management. The information comes from seminars, conventions, trade magazines, professional journals, or maybe from other aviation safety offices or other organizations. Every time you read something that might have some future use in your program, clip it out and file it alphabetically in a file box. These are not part of the office correspondence files and they are not working files. These are your personal technical reference files and they belong to you. Within a very short time, you'll be able to go to your own files and find information on almost any aviation safety subject.

BUDGET

Aviation safety programs are not particularly expensive, but they do require some funds to operate and you will need to plan and justify your expenditures about a year ahead. As a general rule, you should budget for the cost of running the program. Don't ask for any funds to correct safety deficiencies; those should come out of a line manager's budget. In organizations where the Director of Safety controls funds for the correction of safety deficiencies, the prevention program then belongs to the Director of Safety, not the line manager. This doesn't work well and goes against much of what we've said in this book about prevention responsibilities.

As an aside, you should be watching the budget or fund allocation process to make sure the line managers are budgeting for the correction of deficiencies they have agreed to correct. The excuse, "Sorry, I'd like to correct that, but there is no money," should only work through one budget cycle. You should also be watching the process to see if "Aviation Safety" has been added to the justification for a particular project in order to obtain a higher priority for funding. A good rule to establish is that if safety is to be used to justify an expense; then the safety office should review it and verify that safety will, in fact, be enhanced.

Here are some items you should consider building into your budget.

1. Subscriptions to technical publications.

2. Purchase of technical reference books. (See Bibliography.)

3. Safety incentives and awards.

4. Professional society membership (corporate or individual).

5. Meetings and conferences. If you have a dispersed operation, you may want to bring the additional duty aviation safety specialists together occasionally and that costs money.

6.   Travel.

7.   Professional seminars and conventions.

8.   Professional education and training courses.

9.   Office expenses (supplies, computers, copier, software programs, etc.).

10. Purchase/Rental of films and video tapes.

11. Safety equipment (camera, video camera, investigation equipment, etc.).

12. Printing (newsletters, etc.).

COMPUTERS

The use of a computer will aid your program and save you personally a lot of time. If you are not presently into computers, consider putting a computer into your budget along with a training course on how to use it. The chances are that e-mail is a principle method of communication within your company and if you can't transfer documents, files and comments via e-mail, you are falling behind.

At this writing there are some specialized software programs available in some safety areas. There is nothing, however, specifically tailored to an aviation safety program. One reason is that basic aviation safety program needs are not that exotic. Most of them can be met with a word processing program, a spreadsheet program and a data base program. Here are some possible uses of a computer in an aviation safety program.

1.   Word Processing. Plan on learning and using the word processing system used by your company.

2.   Reference. You can maintain a lot of important reference material on CD-ROM and save the cost of purchasing and updating hard copies of many manuals and regulations. You can, for example, purchase a CD-ROM containing a complete set of Federal Aviation Regulations, Advisory Circulars, applicable HAZMAT regulations, NTSB regulations, the Aeronautical Information Manual, and other documents. See Bibliography.

3.   Incident Reports. Using a data base program, you can enter the basic facts of the incident (date, location, aircraft, damage, description, causes, actions, status, etc.) in a four or five line data block and then selectively retrieve the information by combinations of parameters such as type of incident, causes, status, type of aircraft, and so on. One airline lets the computer print out the status of all open incidents for publication in the quarterly safety bulletin.

4. Material Safety Data Sheets (MSDS.) These go with industrial safety and industrial hygiene, but sometimes the aviation safety manager has to maintain them. The easiest way to do this is to purchase a commercial software program that maintains the sheets for you and provides regular updates.

5. Hazard Reports. With a data base program, hazard reports can be tracked just like incident reports.

6. Training Records. Although the computer cannot totally replace hard copy training records, a data base program can help keep track of what training has been given and what training is due.

7. Aviation Safety Inspection Program. Inspection checklists should be kept in a word processing program and the record of inspections can be kept in a data base program by organization inspected or by subject.

8. Bulletin/Newsletter Formats. You can publish a very satisfactory newsletter by writing it on a word processor and printing it on colored paper with an aviation safety title and logo. If you want to get fancy, get a desktop publishing program.

9. Suspense and Follow-up. You can let the computer keep track of your calendar and your suspense.

10. Distribution Addresses. There is no point in repetitively writing addresses of people or offices you regularly correspond with if you have a computer. Most word processing programs can merge addresses with letters and envelopes and can maintain mailing lists for you. If the word processing program won't do what you need, there are data base programs that will.

11. Statistical Analysis. This requires a spreadsheet program, preferably one that will also draw graphs for you. Some of the possibilities of this were discussed in Chapter 18. This type of analysis is well within the capability of the most popular spreadsheet programs.

THE NOTEBOOK OFFICE MANAGEMENT SYSTEM

Ok, so you don't even have an office, much less a computer or a secretary. Furthermore, the additional duty aviation safety specialists in your company don't have one either. Now what do you do?

Actually, you can run a pretty good program out of a large three-ring notebook. If you are the aviation safety manager in a fairly large organization, this is a good system to set up for your additional duty aviation safety

---

TAB 1. COMPANY DIRECTIVES
AVIATION SAFETY POLICY STATEMENT
AVIATION SAFETY PROGRAM DOCUMENT
PRE-ACCIDENT PLAN

TAB 2. ACCIDENTS/INCIDENTS
REPORTING INSTRUCTIONS
FILE COPIES OF REPORTS
BLANK REPORTING FORMS

TAB 3. HAZARD REPORTS
HAZARD REPORT LOG
FILE COPIES OF REPORTS
BLANK HAZARD REPORT FORMS

TAB 4. AVIATION SAFETY AUDITS
LAST AUDIT REPORT ON YOUR ORGANIZATION
AUDIT SCHEDULE
FILE COPIES OF YOUR AUDIT REPORTS
AUDIT CHECKLISTS

TAB 5. AVIATION SAFETY TRAINING
TRAINING OUTLINES
TRAINING RECORDS

TAB 6. AVIATION SAFETY COMMITTEE
MEMBERSHIP
FILE COPIES OF AGENDAS AND MINUTES

TAB 7. AVIATION SAFETY MEETINGS
DATE/SUBJECTS COVERED
ATTENDANCE

TAB 8. MISCELLANEOUS CORRESPONDENCE

Figure 19-2. Notebook Management System

specialists. You need to organize it to suit your own needs, of course, but figure 19-2 shows a sample notebook safety program.

SUMMARY

Under safety office management, we could certainly talk about some other subjects, but these will get you started. As one final bit of advice, here is an all purpose solution to office problems. It's called SELECTIVE NEGLECT and it works quite well. It is based on the idea that there is always more that you could do than you have time to do. SELECTIVE NEGLECT requires you to take a few minutes each day to examine your workload and toss out the part of it that eats up a lot of time and has a very low payoff in terms of aviation safety. If you don't do this (or something like it) you will inevitably waste your time on things that are of no real value. Worse, you will miss the opportunity to work on the really important things.

DISCUSSION QUESTIONS

1. When something happens in your company that involves aviation safety, you or your staff need to know that it happened in time to advise management on the proper response. Set up a system that ensures that:

    A. Your office is notified.

    B. The notification gets to you or someone who can respond to it.

2. Considering the filing system and notebook management system suggested in this chapter, what items would you add to better reflect the needs of your company?

A SAMPLE AVIATION SAFETY PROGRAM

This chapter incorporates many of the ideas discussed in earlier chapters. The sample program offered is probably more extensive than any single organization needs. As was stated in Chapter 1, you build the aviation safety program to suit your organization. You can't copy the sample directly from this book and expect it to work. This will only help you get started.

PROGRAM DEVELOPMENT

First, you need to make some decisions on what kind of a program you want. Copy this section and use it as a worksheet.

DEVELOPING AN AVIATION SAFETY PROGRAM

1. AVIATION SAFETY GOALS AND OBJECTIVES

    • List the goals and objectives of your aviation safety program.

2. AVIATION SAFETY POLICY

    • List subjects to be covered in your aviation safety policy statement.

3. MANAGEMENT

    • Where will you place the aviation safety department?

    • Who will the aviation safety manager report to?

    • Will the aviation safety manager be full time or additional duty?

    • What staff assistance will be provided?

    • Will there be additional duty aviation safety specialists at other levels or locations?

4. AUTHORITY AND RESPONSIBILITY

    • Who, in the organization, will be held responsible for aircraft accident prevention?

    • What will be the authority of the aviation safety manager?

    • What will be the responsibilities of the aviation safety manager?

5. AVIATION SAFETY PROGRAM ELEMENTS

A. Internal Reporting System.

• What events will be reported as incidents?

• Who will be responsible for reporting them?

• What records will be kept?

• Do you need a hazard reporting program?

• How will it be managed?

• Who will act on the reports?

• What records will be kept?

B. Information Distribution.

• How will critical information be distributed?

• How will routine information be distributed?

C. Aviation Safety Committee.

• Do you need an aviation safety committee?

• Who will chair it?

• Who will serve on it?

• What is the purpose of the committee?

• How often will it meet?

• What authority will it have?

• What records will be kept?

D. Aviation Safety Audits and Inspections

• Do you need an aviation safety audit or inspection program?

• What areas?

• How often?

• Who will conduct the inspections?

• What reports will be prepared?

• What action will be taken?

• What records will be kept?

E. Safety Education and Training.

• Do you need aviation safety training?

• What group(s) should be trained?

- Who conducts the training?
- What records will be kept?

F. Aviation Safety Awards.

- Do you need an aviation safety awards program?
- What will be the award criteria?
- What awards will be given?

G. Accident Investigation.

- Do you need a pre-accident plan?
- Who will be responsible for it?
- Who will investigate incidents?
- What reports will be prepared?
- What records will be kept?

H. Analysis.

- Do you need an aviation safety analysis program?
- What do you expect it to do?

I. Other Program Elements.

- Are there other elements you want in your program such as flight safety meetings, newsletters, participation in professional associations, etc.?

As you can see, the answers to these questions are fundamental to the development of your aviation safety program.

SAMPLE PROGRAM

Here is the aviation safety program for a mythical aviation company, Avsafe Aviation. It generally follows the preceding worksheet. Obviously, this requires some assumptions about the size and organization of Avsafe Aviation. Let's assume that Avsafe Aviation operates about 50 aircraft at various locations and employs about 800 people. The company is run by a President and has Vice Presidents for Flight Operations and Aircraft Maintenance. We will also assume that in scope, the program is limited to aviation safety. That, after all, is the title of the book. Actually, we're talking about an orderly method of program development; not a specific program. This same method can be applied to a program encompassing other safety activities.

Here's the sample program.

COVER/TITLE PAGE

REVIEW/REVISION RECORD

TABLE OF CONTENTS

1. STATEMENT OF POLICY

Avsafe Aviation intends to provide a safe and healthful working environment free of all recognized hazards for its employees. Avsafe Aviation also intends to provide the safest possible aerial transportation to its customers. In pursuing these goals, Avsafe Aviation will maintain an active aviation safety program and all company personnel are expected to participate in the program and take an active role in the identification, reduction, and elimination of hazards. This document constitutes the Avsafe Aviation Company Aviation Safety Program.

Signed:_____, President, Avsafe Aviation

2. ORGANIZATION

The position of Director of Safety (or Aviation Safety Manager) will be a full time position reporting directly to the President. The Vice Presidents for Flight Operations and Aircraft Maintenance will appoint an additional duty aviation safety specialist to report directly to them. They will also appoint additional duty aviation safety specialists at each operating location under their control.

3. AUTHORITY AND RESPONSIBILITY

Managers and supervisors at all levels are responsible for accident prevention and the implementation of this program.

The Director of Safety has the authority to:

1. Develop the necessary forms and instructions for implementing the aviation safety program.

2. Require the reporting of any aviation safety-related event.

3. Conduct an investigation of any aviation safety-related event.

4. Conduct aviation safety audits of any Avsafe Aviation operation or facility.

5. Represent Avsafe Aviation regarding aviation safety matters in dealing with government agencies and professional organizations.

6. Approve expenditures of up to XXXX dollars to support the safety program.

The Director of Safety is responsible for:

1. Maintenance, review, and revision of this program.

2. Providing timely advice and assistance on aviation safety matters to line managers at all levels.

3. Maintaining a reporting system for accidents, incidents and hazards.

4. Distributing aviation safety information.

5. Acting as recorder on aviation safety committees.

6. Conducting regular aviation safety audits.

7. Providing aviation safety training to new personnel.

8. Maintaining an aviation safety awards program.

9. Developing and maintaining a pre-accident plan.

10. Conducting accident and incident investigations.

11. Maintaining an aviation safety analysis program.

12. Submitting an annual budget to support the safety program.

4. REPORTING OF ACCIDENTS, INCIDENTS, AND HAZARDS

*   **ACCIDENTS.** All accidental damage to Avsafe Aviation aircraft; injury to Avsafe Aviation personnel or customers resulting from aircraft operation; or damage to non-Avsafe Aviation property or injury to other personnel resulting from Avsafe Aviation operations will be reported to the company control center by telephone. The company control center will notify the appropriate company officials and the Director of Safety.

*   **INCIDENTS.** The following aircraft incidents will be reported to the company control center by radio or telephone: (See Chapter 11 for list.)

The following aircraft incidents need not be reported to the control center, but will be logged on the captain's trip report. (See Chapter 11 for list.)

- HAZARDS. Any employee observing a hazardous situation that could affect aviation safety is encouraged to report it to the Director of Safety or to an aviation safety specialist by any available means. The Director of Safety will provide hazard reporting forms which may be used for this purpose. Anonymous reports will be accepted.

On receipt of a hazard report, the Director of Safety (or aviation safety specialist) will verify the existence of the hazard, assign a priority to the hazard, and route it to the appropriate line manager for investigation and resolution. Under normal circumstances, the line manager will have ten days to provide the Director of Safety with results of the investigation and action taken or contemplated. The Director of Safety will maintain a log reflecting the status of all hazard reports.

5. DISTRIBUTION OF AVIATION SAFETY INFORMATION

The Director of Safety is responsible for obtaining and distributing pertinent aviation safety information. Critical information will be distributed through the company dispatch system. Non-critical information will be distributed to the additional duty aviation safety specialists with instructions on how it is to be sub-distributed.

6. AVIATION SAFETY COMMITTEES

There will be two aviation safety committees; one in flight operations and one in aircraft maintenance. The committee chairs will be line managers. Both the chair and the membership will be appointed by the respective vice presidents. The Director of Safety will serve as recorder to both committees and will prepare agendas and minutes in cooperation with the chairs.

The committees will meet at the call of the chair, but no less than quarterly. The committees will serve the following purposes:

1. Review of status of current accidents and incidents. Review of actions taken.

2. Review of status of hazard reports. Review of actions taken.

3. Review of aviation safety audit reports. Review and approval of audit response and actions taken.

    - NOTE: Each of these items will be reviewed by the most appropriate committee; not both committees.

4. Review and resolution of any aviation safety matters that may be brought before the committee.

The committees may approve, reject, or recommend action on any matter brought before them. Review of the minutes and signature by the appropriate vice president constitutes approval and the minutes then become directive.

Aviation safety committee records will be maintained by the Director of Safety. Agendas and minutes will be destroyed after two years.

7. AVIATION SAFETY AUDITS

Avsafe Aviation will maintain an aviation safety audit program to verify compliance with safety standards and determine the effectiveness of the overall aviation safety program.

Each functional area within flight operations maintenance will receive a safety audit at least annually. The audits will be conducted by the Director of Safety using other specialist team members as appropriate. The Director of Safety will maintain checklists to be used during the audits and will make the checklists available through the additional duty aviation safety specialists.

Reports will be prepared and will be routed to the appropriate line manager and vice president. Items requiring action or response will be identified along with the office expected to take action.

Reports and responses will be reviewed by the appropriate aviation safety committee for adequacy.

Records will be kept by the Director of Safety and only the current audit reports will be retained; although items from previous reports may be extracted for use in the aviation safety analysis system.

Additional duty aviation safety specialists will conduct daily or weekly audits of selected subjects within their areas as appropriate. Reports and records will be as directed by the line manager of that area. Review of the effectiveness of these audits will be conducted by the Director of Safety during the annual aviation safety audit.

8. AVIATION SAFETY TRAINING

The Director of Safety will develop a training program to indoctrinate all new personnel into the company aviation safety program. This training may either be incorporated into existing indoctrination programs or given separately by the Director of Safety or the additional duty aviation safety specialists. Records reflecting dates, names and subjects covered will be maintained.

In addition, the Director of Safety will provide aviation safety training to additional duty aviation safety specialists appointed by the vice presidents or line managers.

9. AVIATION SAFETY AWARDS

Individuals who contribute significantly to the company aviation safety program will be recognized. The contribution may be a single act which prevented damage or injury or it may be in the form of an investigation, hazard resolution, service on a safety committee, or anything that significantly enhances the safety program.

Nominations for the award will be initiated by the line manager in the form of a one page memo to the appropriate vice president. If the vice president agrees, the nomination will be forwarded to the Director of Safety for final review. If the nomination is consistent with intent and purposes of the awards program, the Director of Safety will provide the award to the vice president for presentation to the individual. The Director of Safety will also provide for appropriate company-wide publicity.

10. AIRCRAFT ACCIDENT INVESTIGATION

The Director of Safety will develop and maintain a pre-accident plan as a separate document from this aviation safety program. This plan will be coordinated with other company disaster control procedures and will be exercised or reviewed at least annually.

In the event of an aircraft accident, the Director of Safety will ensure that the FAA and NTSB are notified and will coordinate company participation in the NTSB investigation. To facilitate this, the Director of Safety will maintain a roster of personnel in both flight operations and aircraft maintenance who are qualified to participate in an investigation.

In addition, there will always be an internal company investigation of any aircraft accident and selected aircraft incidents. This investigation serves two purposes: it establishes the facts of the matter and it provides recommendations on what should be done to prevent that accident (or incident) in the future. The person in charge of the investigation will be designated by the President and the investigation team will include the Director of Safety. If there was an NTSB investigation, company personnel participating in that investigation may expect to continue as part of the internal investigation.

The company investigation is authorized access to any company records relevant to the accident and can interview any personnel with knowledge of the accident. At the request of the person being interviewed, the results of the interview may be held in confidence and destroyed when the report is completed.

The report will be addressed to the President and will include a summary of the facts and the investigating team's analysis, conclusions, and recommendations. Dissenting members of the investigating team may prepare a minority report stating their disagreement.

Management of the investigation and preparation of the report will be done through the Director of Safety's office.

11. AVIATION SAFETY ANALYSIS

The Director of Safety will maintain an analysis system using data derived from company accident and incident reports. The purpose of the analysis program is to identify trends and areas requiring management action. Results of the analysis program will be made available to management at least monthly.

12. REVIEW AND REVISION

This aviation safety program document is maintained by the Director of Safety. It will be reviewed annually and suggestions for revision should be forwarded to the Director of Safety.

Signed: _____, President, Avsafe Aviation

USE OF THE SAMPLE PROGRAM

Although this book is copyrighted, you have the author's permission to use any portion of the sample program (and the preceding program development worksheet) in any manner that suits your needs. Remember, though, you can't just copy the program and expect it to work. You have to build it to suit your organization and your organization has to agree to implement it and make it work.

INTRODUCTION TO SECTION 4

SPECIALIZED AVIATION SAFETY SUBJECTS

We're done with the program development and management part. This section examines some special subjects that don't fit elsewhere in the book. First, we're going to examine customer-contractor problems as they relate to aviation safety. Many of us are either a provider of aviation services to a customer or a purchaser of aviation services from a contractor. The question of how the two safety programs are related can be an important one.

Next, we'll examine the role of aviation safety in aircraft maintenance operations and the flight line. We'll look at airports and heliports. Regardless of our organization, we all have some interest in the airports and heliports that we use.

Finally, we'll introduce the subject of environmental safety. Aviation operations generate a certain amount of waste. Control and disposal of that waste is something we need to understand.

- Chapter 21   CUSTOMER-CONTRACTOR RELATIONSHIPS

- Chapter 22   AIRCRAFT MAINTENANCE SAFETY

- Chapter 23   FLIGHT LINE SAFETY

- Chapter 24   AIRPORTS AND HELIPORTS

- Chapter 25   ENVIRONMENTAL SAFETY

CUSTOMER-CONTRACTOR RELATIONSHIPS

Most aviation safety programs tend to be internally oriented. They are concerned with preserving the organization's equipment, personnel, and facilities. One potential weakness in this program is that there is no obvious need to protect the assets and people who are outside the organization nor is there an obvious need to involve ourselves in the management of some other organization. From the point of view of the Director of Safety, there is plenty to do without worrying about the safety problems of someone else.

Aviation is basically a service industry. There is almost always some interaction between the people flying and maintaining the airplanes and those using them. In hospital EMS helicopter operations, for example, the helicopter operator is usually a contractor. The hospital is a customer. They both have a legitimate interest in each other's safety, particularly since each must use facilities and equipment supplied and maintained by the other. The same is true of oil industry support, charter and air taxi operations, and government/industry contractor operations. Taken further, a corporate flying operation's customers are the company executives they transport. An airline's customers are its passengers.

Sometimes this concern for the safety of others goes in one direction only. The airline passenger, for example, is not furnishing anything (except money) to the airline and is in no position to assess the quality of the airline safety program. The airline, on the other hand, has an obligation to the passenger and must (or should) include the passenger in their overall safety program.

Frequently, though, this problem goes both ways. An oil company is planning to contract with a helicopter company for off-shore oil rig support. Does the oil company have an interest in the helicopter company's safety program? Absolutely! Since the oil company is furnishing and maintaining the helipads, does the helicopter company have an interest in the oil company's safety program? Certainly! Each must be aware of the other's safety program and each must expand its own safety program to include the other.

In some situations, there seems to be a reluctance to discuss safety for fear of scaring the customer or the passenger. This is probably a mistake. There is always a certain level of concern about aviation safety and the fact that the customer doesn't bring it up doesn't mean it doesn't exist. An aircraft operator with a good safety program ought to be proud of it and ought to use it as a selling point to people who want to purchase those services. Furthermore, the time to teach the customers their role in an emergency situation is before the situation occurs. The time to relieve fear and anxiety is before they develop.

RESPONSIBILITY

Who, within an organization, should be responsible for customer safety? We're really talking about here is the quality of the product (transportation, in this case) that we are furnishing our customer. From that point of view, customer safety should be part of the line manager's responsibilities; not something to be left to the safety department. That's true, but as a practical matter it is usually the safety department that identifies the need for customer safety and advises the line manager on how to apply it to customer relationships. That's a legitimate function of aviation safety.

Looking at the other end of the problem, who within an organization should be responsible for assessing contractor safety? Logically, the line manager with authority to contract for aviation services from another company should be responsible for ensuring that the contractor has an acceptable aviation safety program. Again, the procedures and the methodology for doing this usually come from the aviation safety department.

CONTRACTORS

These days, most aircraft operators contract out (outsource) some of their aircraft maintenance activities. They do this for convenience or cost control. It hardly pays a small organization to do its own heavy maintenance when it can contract for that service at less cost.

There has been an assumption that if the contractor is an FAA-approved repair facility and had all the correct certificates, it was all right to use them without further concern. The company had no need (or right) to examine the contractor's actual safety and quality standards.

This has never been true. The company always has a right to know if the product it is buying meets the company's standards. The contractor, if he wants the contract, has no choice but to permit the company to examine his operation. As discussed in Chapter 5, mere compliance with the Federal Aviation Regulations only means that the contractor is meeting minimum standards — which are not your standards. If we accept the contractor's standards without review, we are merely transferring our management responsibility to the FAA — and that doesn't work. This problem was brought home to us rather forcibly after a 1996 airline crash in the Florida Everglades. If we intend to "outsource" our maintenance, oversight responsibility is ours; not the FAA's.

Actually, major oil companies have figured this out some time ago. They all contract for a lot of aviation services and most of them have a separate office for contract oversight. Before they sign a contract, a team from this office does a complete safety audit of the contractor and they visit him regularly thereafter. The oil companies exchange contractor information with each other and they have developed excellent safety audit checklists. There is no comparable program among air transport operators. If there were, we would almost certainly see an upgrading of safety standards among contractors. That's exactly what has happened among oil industry contractors.

Here are some ideas on what should be examined in either a customer or a contractor relationship. The first checklist would be used by an aviation organization which is furnishing aviation services to a customer. The second would be used by an organization which is contracting for aviation services from another company. As with any checklists, these are not all-inclusive and are only meant to suggest areas where further examination may be required.

CUSTOMER SAFETY

1. Is the customer familiar with our safety program?

2. Does the customer know our safety standards?

3. Do we retain final authority on mission safety? (Of course we do, but does the customer know it?)

4. If there is a safety problem involving the customer, do we know who to call to discuss it?

5. If the customer has a safety problem with us, does the customer know who to call to discuss it? (These last two items can avert a lot of problems.)

6. Are we prepared to explain to the customer the limitations of our aircraft? (See Chapter 15.)

7. Does customer-furnished ground support meet our standards?

8. Are we prepared to train the customer's ground support personnel?

9. Does the customer manifesting of cargo meet our safety standards?

10. Are we prepared to train the customer on proper cargo manifesting?

11. Does the customer-furnished helipad meet our standards?

12. Does customer-furnished equipment meet our standards?

13. Do we have adequate procedures for safely emplaning and deplaning passengers?

14. Are our passenger briefings adequate?

15. Is our emergency equipment adequate?

16. Are our flight crews adequately trained in passenger emergency procedures and passenger safety?

17. Do we have a plan for handling passenger injuries?

18. Do we have a reporting system for potential safety problems affecting the customer?

CONTRACTOR SAFETY

1. What is the contractor's safety record?

2. Does the contractor have an aviation safety program?

3. What are the qualifications of the people running the aviation safety program?

4. What are the qualifications and experience of the contractor's pilots?

5. Does the contractor have an operations manual?

6. Is the operations manual adequate?

7. How does the contractor manifest passengers and cargo and control weight and balance?

8. Are the contractor's aircraft operated within their limitations?

9. What safety standards is the contractor meeting?

10. What is the contractor's training program?

11. Does the contractor have adequate emergency equipment?

12. Is the contractor providing adequate passenger briefings?

13. Does the contractor control fuel quality?

14. Does the contractor handle and store fuel safely?

15. Are the contractor hangar and maintenance facilities adequate?

16. Does the contractor have a maintenance plan?

17. What are the qualifications of the contractor's maintenance personnel?

18. Does the contractor have adequate maintenance manuals and technical documents?

19. If we notify the contractor of a hazardous situation, what action will be taken?

20. Does the contractor have a pre-accident plan?

21. What is the overall condition of the contractor's equipment?

ESTABLISHING CUSTOMER-CONTRACTOR RELATIONSHIPS

Customer and contractor relationships should be established before the contract is signed. Afterwards, it's a little late. Amending contracts tends to be expensive and trying to retroactively add safety to the program is seldom popular. This means that the Director of Safety must stay ahead of these relationships. The safety office should routinely review any proposed contracts for safety implications.

For those contracts involving flying or aircraft maintenance, it is entirely reasonable to ask the contractor to furnish information about his safety program and safety record. It also means that the Director of Safety must monitor the contracts on a regular basis to catch the little problems before they become big ones. As mentioned, this is what major oil companies do very well. It is fair to say that they have upgraded the level of safety in oil field aviation support world wide. If a contractor is reluctant to discuss his aviation safety program with you, there is probably a reason, and it is usually negative.

On the other hand, if you are the contractor, you may be asked to reduce your safety standards if you want the contract. Take hospital helicopter EMS operations. Few hospitals were built with helipads and it is not unusual to find a hospital helipad in use that does not meet anyone's standards in terms of size, obstruction clearance, lighting, and so on. Why is it being used?

Simple. This is an economic problem (Chapter 1) and the helicopter contractor is willing to reduce his standards in order to get the contract. One of two things should happen. The contractor should tell the hospital what his minimum helipad standards are and stick to them. The hospital should realize that they are exposing their own doctors, nurses, and patients to risk and they should decline to do business with a contractor who has no standards or is willing to lower the ones he has.

Bottom line. You cannot let the customer set your safety standards for you; nor can you accept services from a contractor whose standards don't meet yours.

Another actual example involved a corporate operator who flew his planes out of several locations. At all but one, the planes were maintained through the company maintenance program. At one location, though, all maintenance was outsourced for reasons of convenience. This created problems in that the contractor's standard of maintenance didn't meet that of the company. In one situation, the company did not like the level of training of the contractor's maintenance technicians. They were not factory-trained on the company's airframes or engines. The company finally negotiated an arrangement whereby they would pay the training costs if the contractor would dedicate those trained technicians to working on the company's airplanes. That was an expensive solution, but it points out how seriously one company took another's standards.

So far, we've only been talking about two types of relationships; our customers and our aircraft maintenance contractors. Actually, there are other contract relationships that may deserve the same approach. If, for example, we contract for some repairs to our parking ramp and we intend to keep using it during the repairs, we better have a firm agreement on how safety will be maintained. Contractors tend to have a low appreciation for things like aircraft right-of-way, FOD prevention, obstruction marking, and so on.

Likewise, if we contract for fuel we should never forget that the airplane still belongs to us. The safety standards in use should be ours. It is a little disappointing to see a pair of corporate pilots park their million dollar jet and head for the coffee shop without even a glance at how their plane is being serviced or who's servicing it. Airlines seldom keep maintenance personnel at all of their stations and they regularly contract for servicing with another airline or sometimes an FBO. When they do this, the better airlines will send in a training team to make sure that their planes will be serviced to their standards.

In the occupational safety and health arena, anytime we permit an outside contractor to operate in our facility, that facility becomes the contractor's workplace and we have an obligation to make sure that it meets the appropriate safety standards. Technically, anyone entering our facility deserves a certain amount of protection. If you don't believe that, wait and see what happens when someone gets hurt in your facility.

Speaking of injuries, a significant number of airline passengers are injured each year by falling carry-on luggage, runaway beverage carts, turbulence, and a host of other things. We are not sure how many because they are not considered employees (of the airline) and there is no mandatory reporting unless the injuries are serious enough for classification as an aircraft accident. Some airlines do not know there has been an injury until the claim or lawsuit is filed. They are in the position of trying to retroactively figure out what happened and defend themselves. Other airlines have excellent programs for immediately responding to the situation and collecting all available information about the event. In most cases, that system comes from the safety department; another example of customer-contractor relationships.

SUMMARY

Safety involving customer-contractor relationships tends to be weak in any industry. We are reluctant to involve ourselves in some activity that is not ours. It is helpful to remember that if our airplanes or personnel are at risk, we certainly should be involved in any activity that increases that risk.

DISCUSSION QUESTIONS

1. Your company operates aircraft and carries passengers. You are going to develop a passenger safety program. List the topics you would cover in your program.

2. A passenger on one of your aircraft has been injured during turbulence. What kind of investigation are you going to conduct and what questions are you going to ask?

AIRCRAFT MAINTENANCE SAFETY

Aircraft maintenance organizations actually have (or should have) two safety programs. One is an internal one where the primary concern is the protection of the employees, facilities and equipment. The emphasis in this program is largely on industrial safety and industrial hygiene and it will only be mentioned briefly here. The other program is an external one where the concern is for the safety of the product being furnished the customer. In this case, the product is an airworthy aircraft and the customer is flight operations. It is this program, or lack of it, that has an impact on our aviation safety program.

The quality of aircraft maintenance is commonly overseen by a quality control or quality assurance function and it is here that the aviation safety manager can find the answers to most maintenance safety problems. What follows is a discussion of some of the areas or subjects in maintenance which should be of concern to both quality control and the aviation safety manager.

AIRCRAFT DISCREPANCIES

The manner in which aircraft discrepancies are identified and corrected is fundamental to the health of any maintenance organization. On the one hand, the pilots must enter the discrepancies correctly and completely. Maintenance obviously cannot fix that which they cannot find. If the entering of the discrepancies is not adequate, the aviation safety manager is in a good position to identify the problem and recommend some corrections. On the other hand, the system for correcting the discrepancies should include some sort of feedback so that the pilots know what was done to fix the plane. Granted, this isn't absolutely essential from the point of view of maintenance, but in organizations where this is not done, there is almost always disharmony between operations and maintenance. The pilot, after all, is responsible for determining whether the aircraft is in condition for safe flight; not the maintenance technician.

DELAYED OR DEFERRED DISCREPANCIES

These are officially frowned on. The plane is either fixed or it isn't. Realistically, though, there are some things that cannot be immediately corrected and are allowable under the minimum equipment list. The question is, how many of these delayed discrepancies are there and how are they handled? In some organizations, these are discouraged to the point where the pilots are not entering discrepancies in the log book and are carrying them as "hip pocket" discrepancies and passing them on verbally to other pilots. This is no way to run a flying operation.

TRAINING

By regulation, pilots are required to have a certain amount of training every time they transition to a new aircraft or change seats in the cockpit. They also get regular check rides and annual refresher training. There are no comparable requirements for a maintenance technician and there is wide variation in the industry on the amount and quality of training furnished the licensed maintenance technician. This is a holdover from the days when aircraft and engines were relatively simple and a technician could fix any of them. We have moved quite a distance from that situation and a maintenance organization whose maintenance technicians have not been factory-trained on the airframe or engine should cause some concern in the aviation safety department. Also, there are some obvious types of training that ought to be provided to the technician on a regular basis. These include fire prevention, use of fire extinguishers, fuel handling, disaster response, hazardous materials, hazardous waste control and so on.

CONFIGURATION CONTROL

In some flying operations, there are several different ways to configure the aircraft or helicopter. This needs to be tightly controlled and supervised by qualified maintenance personnel because it affects both weight and balance and aviation safety if the equipment is not correctly installed.

MAINTENANCE ENGINE RUNS AND TAXIING

Should maintenance personnel run aircraft engines or even taxi the aircraft? How about running helicopter engines where the rotor system cannot be decoupled from the engine? Actually, FAR Part 43 requires that the person certifying piston and turbine engines after an annual or 100 hour inspection actually run the engine(s). Thus, there is already a requirement for maintenance personnel to run engines under certain conditions.

This generates some risk, but it is a manageable risk. Obviously, the safest thing to do is to leave engine running and taxiing to the pilots. This is not practical in all organizations and there is really no reason why the maintenance technician can't be trained to do this safely. If it is necessary to do this, then the technician should be given the same training on running engines or taxiing that the pilot is given. This means that the burden of conducting the training and giving the checks really belongs in flight operations and it should be done using the same instructors, checklists, simulators, or procedures trainers that are used for pilots.

Also, the maintenance technician who has been trained to taxi aircraft, for example, should do it routinely; not just when they can't find a pilot to do it. It is important to keep the technician current and proficient.

MAINTENANCE TEST FLIGHTS

Occasionally it is necessary to fly the plane and expose it to air loads in order to verify a repair that cannot be checked on the ground. This is obviously done by a pilot from flight operations. During the test flight, though, the pilot is actually working for the chief of maintenance as a maintenance inspector. That's all a maintenance test flight is. It is a maintenance inspection and it needs to be taken as seriously as any other maintenance inspection. The aviation safety manager is usually in a good position to know whether the test flights are adequate.

MAINTENANCE ANALYSIS

Some aviation safety problems are equipment related. Maintenance ought to have some method of logging and analyzing equipment failures if only to know how many new parts to buy. An understanding of the maintenance data collection and analysis system is important to the aviation safety manager.

TOOL CONTROL

This is a touchy subject among maintenance technicians. The fact is that modern turbine-powered aircraft are intolerant of the misplaced tool. Organizations that do not have tool control programs usually develop them as soon as they destroy their first engine. This problem is of some interest to the aviation safety manager as there is a good chance that the errant tool will be discovered in an undesirable manner during flight. The solution to the problem depends on whether the tools are company-owned or employee-owned. Company-owned tools are fairly easy to control. It's just a matter of spending the money and doing it. Employee-owned tools are not so easy. Here, the solution depends on what the maintenance technicians are willing to accept. As professional maintenance technicians, they are probably very much aware of the problem. This is a good subject for discussion by a maintenance safety committee.

HAZARDOUS WASTE DISPOSAL

Maintenance generates a certain amount of hazardous waste in the form of solvents, paints, oils, hydraulic fluids, etc. The handling of this is largely an industrial safety problem, but sometimes there are some flight safety aspects. Fuel spills, for example, sometimes occur during ramp operations with the flight crew involved. The days when we called out the fire trucks to wash the spilled fuel into the sewers are gone — at least in the United States. Maintenance is expected to have on hand the necessary equipment to contain and collect spilled fuel or anything else they can reasonably foresee. This subject is discussed at greater length in Chapter 25.

BOGUS PARTS

This is a serious problem throughout the industry. The truth is that bogus parts are almost impossible to detect at the user level. The only real protection against them is in the reputation and certification procedures of the parts supplier. Company policy on purchase of parts should be an item of interest to the aviation safety manager.

TECHNICAL DATA

Modern aircraft and engines cannot be adequately maintained without current manuals and technical data. There must be a system for ensuring that Airworthiness Directives (ADs) and Service Bulletins (SBs) are reviewed for applicability. These days, the technical data for many aircraft and engines are provided on microfiche with regular updates and revisions. If the microfiche reader has a printout capability, this provides some advantages to the maintenance technician as the appropriate page can be printed and taken to the aircraft for reference. There is at least one disadvantage to this system. When hard copy revisions are received, a technician usually reviews them for important changes as they are posted to the manual. Microfiche revisions can be (and usually are) filed without review.

The wide spread use of computers for storage and retrieval of technical data is also common. Many manufacturers are providing maintenance manuals and parts catalogs on CD-ROM disks. In the corporate world, some aircraft carry only a notebook computer and CD-ROM disks. They don't carry a library of manuals.

MAINTENANCE INSPECTIONS

A fundamental principle of aircraft maintenance is that the maintenance technician performing the work is not allowed to perform any required inspection of that work. Even when inspection is not required, it is not unusual for professional technicians to rely on each other for a quick check of the work area before the panels are buttoned up. In a dispersed operation with only a single maintenance technician available, the advantages of this system are lost. Under certain circumstances, the pilot can perform certain maintenance functions and having the pilot look over the shoulder of the technician is certainly better than nothing.

FLIGHT LINE PRACTICES

Flight operations and maintenance come together on the parking ramp. There must be some harmony regarding parking, chocking, engine starts, push-backs, fueling, and so on. If not, we can expect accidents and damage to the aircraft. We have learned, for example, that a large aircraft cannot be maneuvered safely in a confined area unless there is direct interphone communication between the cockpit and ground. Hand signals are not adequate. To the extent that we need hand signals, though, we should all be using the standard ones.

MAINTENANCE SAFETY PROGRAM

As stated earlier, the aircraft maintenance function really has two safety programs and sometimes the line between them is blurred. If a strong internal safety program already exists in maintenance, then aviation safety items can be added to it. If such a program does not exist, there is no reason why a maintenance aviation safety program can't be developed. Existing maintenance safety programs tend to be more oriented toward internal safety problems involving industrial safety and industrial hygiene. The aviation safety manager can contribute significantly to both the internal maintenance safety program and to the development of a companion program to examine aviation safety aspects. The program elements discussed in this book can work very well in maintenance.

This book is not meant to be a definitive guide to all aircraft maintenance safety practices. For that, a review of the occupational safety and health standards (OSHA) is necessary. Nevertheless, there are certain maintenance subjects or areas that are somewhat unique to aviation. An introduction to these areas may be helpful to the Director of Safety.

HANGAR SAFETY

An aircraft hangar is a fairly unique work environment. The potential for injury to personnel or damage to aircraft is very high. Basically, we're dealing with a work situation that never looks the same. Aircraft are not always spotted in the same location. The maintenance being performed varies from day to day. It is difficult to organize all these variables into an effective hangar safety program.

1. ELECTRICAL SYSTEMS

It is possible that the hangar needs different electrical currents. If so, the receptacles should be clearly marked as to the voltage available at that receptacle. There should be a central circuit breaker (cb) panel within the hangar and there should be a lockout system where some lines can be locked out at the cb panel while they are being worked on. The type of receptacle used for various voltages should be consistent throughout the hangar.

2. AIR PRESSURE SYSTEMS

If possible, the compressor should be located outside of the hangar. The pressure should be reduced to that needed for normal maintenance and the outlet lines should be marked with the maximum available pressure. Except for special applications, 15 psi is adequate for most maintenance activities, although some air-driven tools require more. The maximum pressure used should be 30 psi or less.

3. CORDS AND LINES

The electrical and pressure lines must be run from the source to the aircraft where they are needed. This means the cords and hoses must be trailed across the floor. Wooden channels should be constructed to protect the cords and hoses from damage and eliminate tripping hazards to personnel.

4. EQUIPMENT RACKS

Much of hangar maintenance involves removing panels from aircraft. They have to be put somewhere. Equipment racks should be provided so the panels are not set on the floor of the hangar where they become a hazard to personnel and are vulnerable to damage.

5. HANGAR WORKSTANDS

Hangar workstands should be equipped with wheel brakes and safety rails around the perimeter of the work stand. If the workstand is designed to be raised or lowered, there should be a mechanical locking device to prevent inadvertent collapse of the stand.

6. HEATERS

Combustion heaters installed in the aircraft will not be operated in the hangar. Portable heaters may be used if they are attended and approved for use in hangars. Obviously, there are work situations where there is risk of flammable vapors where the portable heaters should not be used. Portable heaters should be placed as far from the aircraft as the ducting will permit.

7. HANGAR SAFETY EQUIPMENT

Each hangar should be equipped with eye wash fountains, deluge showers, and first-aid kits. These should be positioned in easily accessible locations close to major work areas.

8. FIRE PROTECTION

Hangars may or may not have built-in fire extinguishing systems. If so, there should be procedures for regular testing and inspection and clear instructions on how the system is to be used.

If not, the hangar is dependent upon portable extinguishing equipment and notification of the fire department. In this case, there should be an adequate number of fire extinguishers available at clearly marked and accessible locations around the perimeter of the hangar. In addition, a dedicated telephone line or alarm system to the fire department should be installed, clearly marked and regularly tested.

9. GENERAL HOUSEKEEPING

The most important aspect of hangar fire prevention is probably house-keeping. Work areas should be clean and free of debris and waste materials. Proper receptacles for waste materials should be available and spills of fuel or hydraulic fluid should be cleaned up immediately. Additionally, good housekeeping practices will provide a safe workplace.

10. HANGAR FLOOR

The floor should be painted with a light colored paint that is specifically designed for hangars. It should have a skid-resistant surface and be easy to clean. In addition, it should reflect light. This has the effect of improving the lighting of the entire hangar and improving aircraft maintenance.

Equipment for cleaning up minor fluid spills should be readily available. If the hangar incorporates a drainage system, the grates should be removable and the drain should empty into a suitable holding tank for future disposal.

11. HANGAR DOOR

Improper operation of hangar doors is responsible for a significant number of personnel injuries and aircraft damage. Regardless of how the door works, it is a large piece of moving structure. Once it is set in motion, it is difficult to stop.

Hangar door systems should incorporate a warning horn or buzzer that sounds at least five seconds before the door actually starts to move. The door switches should incorporate a deadman switch which requires someone to hold the switch in the open or close position whenever the door is in motion. With this type of switch, it is not possible to set the door in motion and walk away from the switch. Also, the door can be stopped by merely releasing the switch.

Closing the door is more of a hazard than opening it. Some door switches have guards to prevent the door from being accidentally closed. Others have door closed lockouts wherein the door cannot be closed unless the lockout is removed. Anytime the door is opened, it should be opened at least ten feet. This is so that anyone in the opening when the door is closed will have a few seconds to escape.

MAINTENANCE SHOP SAFETY

Aircraft maintenance shops are less unique than other flight line operations and tend to resemble activities found in many industries. Thus, OSHA standards are applicable to all maintenance shops. We will concentrate primarily on aircraft-unique activities which require additional safety precautions.

Good safety practices start with the layout of the shops. There should be adequate lighting and ventilation. There should be ample workspace so that people working on one machine (or workbench) do not interfere with another. Aisles should be marked and kept free of debris and obstructions. Exits should be marked and accessible.

The number of workers permitted in a shop should be limited to the number necessary for the job. Shops should not be used as break rooms or lunch rooms. Administrative offices should be separated from the shops.

All machinery should be anchored to the floor (or workbench) and electrical machinery should be grounded. Appropriate personal protective equipment (PPE) should be available at each machine. Machinery with moving parts should have suitable mechanical guards installed. Portable power tools should be centrally stored and regularly inspected. Personal power tools should not be permitted.

1. COMPRESSED AIR SYSTEMS

Air pressure should be limited to 30 psi (except for the tire shop or air-driven tools that require greater pressure) and should be reduced to 15 psi if used for general cleaning. Air nozzles should incorporate a spring-loaded finger switch or "deadman" switch. Face shields or goggles should be worn when compressed air is used for cleaning. Compressed air should never be used to clean chips or dirt off personal clothing.

2. COMPRESSED GAS STORAGE

Compressed gas cylinders should be stored upright and secured to the wall unless stored in carts designed for that purpose. Cylinder caps should be installed except for the cylinder currently in use. Gas cylinders should be stored by compatibility groups. Cylinders of flammable gasses should be stored separately. Oxygen cylinders should be stored away from flammable gas cylinders and away from petroleum products.

3. FLAMMABLE STORAGE

The storage of flammables (paints, hydraulic fluids, etc.) should be limited to that immediately needed in the shop area and they should be stored in suitably marked cabinets approved for flammable storage. Bulk storage of flammables should be in a separate building designed for that purpose. Maximum quantities for shop and bulk storage are found in OSHA standards 1926.152 and 1910.

4. SOLVENTS

Operations requiring the use of solvents should be ventilated and isolated from other activities. The choice of solvents should always consider toxicity and the nature of the waste created. As with any chemical, Material Safety Data Sheets (MSDS) on the solvent should be available to the workers. If needed, aprons, gloves and face shields should be available along with eye wash fountains and deluge showers.

5. ELECTRICAL SHOPS AND ELECTRICAL MAINTENANCE

By OSHA regulation electrical systems need to be de-energized using tag-out and lock-out devices. These are devices wherein technicians, using their own padlocks, can have positive assurance that a circuit cannot be energized while it is being worked on. If a machine uses other forms of energy besides electricity (hydraulic or gravity) these should also be de-energized. If a circuit breaker opens during electrical maintenance, it should not be reset until the reason it opened is determined.

Electrical and avionics shops should have grounded workbenches and non-conductive floor mats. They should also have extra safety equipment in the form of wooden canes, poles, and ropes that can be used to rescue a person who has become part of an electrical circuit. These are usually maintained on an electrical safety board accessible to all personnel.

6. BATTERY MAINTENANCE

All aircraft batteries outgas hydrogen and can be a fire hazard. Most aircraft battery compartments are designed for inflight ventilation only and their batteries should be charged in the shop; not on the aircraft.

Battery shops should be separated from all other maintenance activity and the shop area should be well ventilated. The ventilation system should include an automatic cutoff of the charging system if the ventilation blower or fan fails.

7. AIRCRAFT PAINT SHOPS

Painting operations are high hazard activities. Chemical paint strippers and aircraft paints are toxic. Thus, the paint shop (or hangar) must be separated from other maintenance activities and must be well ventilated. Protective garments and breathing equipment are necessary. In addition, used paint stripping chemicals become toxic waste and must be collected and either recycled or disposed of. Painting and stripping operations both fall under OSHA and EPA regulations.

AIRCRAFT JACKING

Aircraft jacking is a specialized activity that has high risks of both personnel injury and aircraft damage. All aircraft maintenance manuals specify procedures to be used in jacking that aircraft. These, of course, take precedence over this book.

1. JACKING AREA

The area selected for jacking should be free of all equipment not directly involved in the jacking operation or the maintenance to be performed after the aircraft is on jacks. There is always some reason for the aircraft to be on jacks and, as a general rule, other maintenance activities should not be permitted while the aircraft is on jacks. The area should be marked with rope stanchions or, at the very least, signs identifying an aircraft jacking operation. Only those people directly involved in the aircraft jacking or subsequent maintenance should be permitted in the area.

2. OUTSIDE JACKING

If the aircraft must be jacked outside, consider the wind limitations. These are usually found in the maintenance manuals for the aircraft to be jacked. If none are specified, a maximum surface wind of 15 mph is normally used. If the wind is higher than the maximum permitted, it may be possible to select another area that is sheltered from the wind.

3. INSIDE JACKING

It is almost always better to jack an airplane inside a hangar or maintenance dock. This eliminates the wind problems and allows better control of the area. One consideration is the type of engine or pump used to provide pressure to the jacks. It should be of a type approved for use in a hangar and it should be grounded and positioned a minimum of 25 feet from the aircraft.

AIRCRAFT TIRE SERVICING

An aircraft tire should be treated as a pressurized container. Its failure mode always involves release of that pressure and, in the flight line environment, this presents a considerable hazard to personnel. Modern aircraft tire pressures can be well over 200 psi, which is lethal as far as human beings are concerned. Every year, there are fatalities related to aircraft tire servicing; all of them unnecessary.

The most common type of accident occurs when the technician attempts to demount the tire while it is still inflated. Unless the tire is on the aircraft and under a load, it is impossible to look at the tire (or kick it) and tell whether it is inflated or not. Since most aircraft wheels are of the split rim design, the two halves of the wheel are unbolted to demount the tire. As the bolts are removed, the pressure from the inflated tire fails the rest of the bolts and the resulting explosion can be fatal to anyone in the vicinity.

Because of this problem, a general safety rule is that tires are always deflated before they are removed from the aircraft and sent to the tire shop. Tires are always inflated in the tire shop (in an inflation cage) and delivered to the aircraft at the correct inflation pressure. An exception to this rule is when a tire is removed to facilitate other maintenance and it is to be immediately be put back on the aircraft and not taken to the tire shop. If this basic rule is followed, personnel in the tire shop are never exposed to pressure hazards as they demount the tire. Personnel on the flight line are never exposed to the hazards of completely inflating a tire. They only service it to bring its pressure up to the required pressure.

1. INFLATION PRESSURE MEASUREMENT

Before doing anything to a tire, it is always a good idea to check for hot brakes or an overheated wheel assembly. Not only will this affect any pressure measurement, but it can be a hazard in itself. It usually takes several minutes to achieve peak wheel temperatures after a heavy braking situation.

Tire manufacturers define underinflation as anything less than 95% of the required inflation pressure. This means that the inflation pressure can only be accurately measured using a precision pressure gage that has been correctly calibrated. The date of current calibration should be on the gage itself.

2. INFLATION GAS

The gas of choice for aircraft tires is dry nitrogen. The reason is that the oxygen in compressed air reacts with the rubber in tires at high pressure and temperatures. Aside from tire deterioration, this can actually produce a combustible gas within the tire and lead to an explosion.

The nitrogen used should be a Class 1 oil-free nitrogen commonly called "water-pumped" nitrogen. Class 2 "oil pumped" nitrogen should not be used as the oils will also react with the rubber and produce the same result.

AIRCRAFT DEICING OPERATIONS

Aircraft deicing poses three hazards in flight line operations. First, the deicing equipment must operate close to the aircraft and there is always risk that it will damage the aircraft. Second, there is risk that deicing fluid will be applied to areas of the aircraft where it should not be applied. Third, the deicing fluid itself poses some degree of hazard to the deicing crew and to the environment. Appropriate personal protective equipment (PPE) should be used.

1. DEICING EQUIPMENT

Positioning the deicing equipment should follow the same guidelines listed in Chapter 23 for Flight Line Vehicle Operation. The boom or basket should only be operated by trained personnel. If a basket is used, the operator should be secured to the basket with a safety harness. The protection of the aircraft from damage and personnel safety should be primary considerations.

2. USE OF DEICING FLUID

Deicing fluids are classified as Type I or Type II Freezing Point Depressant (FPD) fluids. The actual application of the fluids should be as specified in appropriate Federal Aviation Regulations, Advisory Circulars, and aircraft manufacturer's handbooks. Type I fluids are primarily used for deicing, although they do provide limited anti-ice capability. Type II fluids are thicker and adhere to surfaces longer. They are used for anti-icing after the aircraft has been deiced.

In general, Type II fluids should never be applied to the following:

- Pitot heads

- Static ports

- Angle of attack sensors

- Control surface cavities

- Cockpit windows and fuselage nose

- Lower portion of fuselage underneath nose or radome

- Air inlets

- Engines

Type I fluids may be applied to some of these areas, depending on the aircraft manufacturer's recommended procedures, but never to the pitot heads or static ports.

3. HEALTH HAZARDS OF ANTI-ICE AND DEICING FLUIDS

Detailed health hazard information should be found on the Material Safety Data Sheet (MSDS) for the fluid in use. In general, the following information will usually apply.

FPD fluids are only moderately toxic. The vapors or aerosols of any FPD fluid may cause transitory irritation of the eyes. Exposure to vapors may cause nose and throat irritations, headaches, nausea, vomiting, and dizziness. Respirators are recommended for personnel exposed to vapors. Passengers and flight crew should be shielded from the vapors by turning off all cabin air intakes during the deicing process. Outside of the aircraft, the vapors are usually dispersed and not a serious problem. Skin irritation from contact with FPD fluids is considered minimal, but protective clothing is recommended.

If ingested, FPD fluids can cause abdominal discomfort and pain, dizziness, and effects on the central nervous system and kidneys. Because the fluids are considerably diluted with water, it is unlikely that deicing personnel would ingest anything close to a lethal amount (3 to 4 ounces) of pure glycol.

MAINTENANCE SAFETY INSPECTION

For reasons stated above, a safety inspection of aircraft maintenance activities really looks at two aspects of maintenance; how well the work is being done and how safely it is being done. These two aspects are largely inseparable. It is very difficult to look at one without looking at the other. The following guide for maintenance safety inspection subjects lists both. Other applicable guides are in Chapters 14 and 23.

MAINTENANCE SAFETY INSPECTION SUBJECTS

1. RECORD

   - Number of aircraft maintained
   - Number of licensed maintenance technicians
   - Number of unlicensed personnel
   - Number of Inspection Authorized technicians
   - FAA repair station or service center
   - Level of maintenance performed
   - Types of maintenance contracted out

2. ORGANIZATION

   - Adequacy
   - Direct supervision
   - Quality Assurance
   - Inspection separated from maintenance
   - Personnel
   - Qualifications
   - Vacancies

3. POLICIES

   - Standard of maintenance
   - Safety
   - Separation of inspection and maintenance
   - Correction of discrepancies
   - Delayed/deferred discrepancies
   - Outside (contracted) maintenance
   - Configuration control
   - Cannibalization

4. MANUALS AND TECHNICAL DATA

   - Maintenance manual
     - Current
     - Distribution
     - Use

- Minimum Equipment Lists
- Organization description
- Policies
- Maintenance plan
- Quality Assurance
- Safety
- Designation of inspectors
- Outside maintenance
- Approved maintenance contractors
- Analysis system
- Maintenance test flights
- Reporting of accidents, incidents and hazards
- Foreign Object Damage
- Tools and equipment
- Engine runs
- Taxiing aircraft
- Manufacturer's manuals
  - Hard copy or microfiche
  - Currency
  - Use
- Airworthiness directives and service bulletins
- Federal Air Regulations
- Advisory Circulars

5. TRAINING
  - Records
  - Initial qualifications
  - Certificates
  - Training received
  - Training due
  - Manufacturer's school
    - Airframe
    - Engine
    - Components

- Miscellaneous training
  - FAR Review
  - Inspector Authorization Review
  - Hazardous materials
  - First Aid/CPR
  - Fire extinguisher use
  - Fueling safety/procedures
  - Running engines
  - Taxiing aircraft
- Training methods
- Training effectiveness
- Training adequacy

6. AIRCRAFT RECORDS
  - Log books
    - Airframe
    - Engines
  - Configuration control
  - Weight and balance
  - Delayed/deferred discrepancy records

7. QUALITY ASSURANCE
  - Inspection program
  - List of designated inspectors
  - List of approved contractors
  - Separation of inspection and maintenance
  - Use of Q/A inspectors
  - Maintenance flight test
  - Maintenance analysis data base and methods

8. PARTS AND SPARES
  - Storage area housekeeping
  - Aisle and door clearance
  - Stacking (load, height)

- Flammable storage
  - Paints
  - Solvents
  - POL products
- Sprinklers and fire extinguishers
- Parts certification
- Inspection of incoming parts
- Inventory control
- Control of shelf-life limited items
- Separation of serviceable and unserviceable items

9. TOOLS AND EQUIPMENT

- Tool control
- Calibration of precision tools
- Availability of specialized tools
- Equipment
  - Condition
  - Brakes
  - Railings
  - Locking devices
  - Adequacy
  - Storage

10. FACILITIES

- Overall condition of maintenance area
- Sufficient fire extinguishers
- Adequate utility outlets
- Lighting
- Heating and ventilation
- Exits

11. MAINTENANCE SAFETY PROGRAM

- Organization of maintenance safety program

- Program elements
  - Distribution of Information
    - Meetings, briefings
    - Direct distribution
    - Material Safety Data Sheets
  - Internal safety inspection program
    - Frequency
    - Effectiveness
  - Safety committee effectiveness
  - Reporting of accidents, incidents and hazards
  - Investigation and resolution of incidents
  - Investigation and resolution of hazards
  - Other program elements

12. MAINTENANCE SAFETY

- General workplace safety
- Housekeeping
- Aisles and exits clear
- Fire prevention
  - Fire plan
  - Adequate fire extinguishers
  - Free access to fire extinguishers
  - Fire department notification
- Flammables
  - Adequate storage
  - Minimum quantities on hand
  - Oily rags separated
  - Oxygen tanks separated from POL products
  - Control of smoking
- Personnel protection
  - First aid kits
  - Showers, eyewash fountains
  - Hearing protection

- Eye protection
- Finger rings, jewelry restricted
- Fall protection
- Lockout/tagout procedures
- Respiratory protection
- Equipment (general)
  - Brakes
  - Locking devices
  - Railings
  - Capacities marked
  - Security
- Flight line
  - Regular inspection
  - Condition of pavement
  - Vehicle control
  - Security of loose equipment
  - Fire extinguishers
  - Lights
  - Power outlets
  - Grounding points
  - Tie-downs
  - Flight line markings, painted lines
  - Foreign Object Damage control
  - Control of smoking
- Flight line procedures
  - Marshaling aircraft
  - Taxiing aircraft
  - Towing aircraft
  - Parking aircraft
  - Hearing protection
  - Propeller/rotor safety
  - Passenger emplaning/deplaning safety
  - Cargo/baggage handling safety

- Hangar
  - General housekeeping
  - Control of vehicles
  - Fire protection
  - Hangar facilities
    - Power outlets marked with voltage
    - Electrical cutoff switches available
    - Pressure lines marked with pressure
    - Hoists load limit marked
    - Pressure vessels protected, inspected
    - Gas cylinders properly stored and capped
    - Ladders, stands and jacks
  - Hangar door
    - Opening/closing procedures
    - Warning device
  - Hangar floor
    - Condition
    - Drips and spills
  - Hangared aircraft
    - Chocked and grounded
    - Access for emergency removal
- Maintenance shops
  - Machine shop
    - Containers for oily rags
    - Containers for metal scrap
    - Machine tools securely mounted
    - Machine tools grounded
    - Eye protection available, used
    - Grinding wheels tool rest 1/8"
    - Power transmission points (belts, shafts) guarded
    - Electrical hand tools — condition
    - Extension cords — condition
    - Machine safety devices installed, used
  - Tire shop
    - Inflation cage

- Tires deflated before maintenance
- Pressure measuring devices calibrated
- Battery shop
  - Separate area for lead-acid and nicad batteries
  - Separate tools for lead-acid and nicad batteries
  - Ventilation
  - Electrical fixtures explosion proof
  - Control of smoking
  - Deluge shower
  - Protective goggles, gloves and aprons
  - Acid-resistant floors and storage racks
  - Separated from other maintenance
- Avionics shop
  - Power outlets marked with voltage
  - Worktables grounded
  - Electrical first aid and safety devices available
- Paint shop
  - Separated from other maintenance areas
  - Ventilation
  - Filters to trap paint and overspray
  - Free of fire hazards
  - Personnel protection equipment used
  - Air pressure regulator and gage available
  - Air hoses and couplings — condition
  - Storage of paint, flammables
  - Awareness of health hazards
  - Restrictions on food and drink in area
- Hazardous Materials
- Compressed gas
  - Protective caps on cylinders when not in use
  - Cylinders stored upright, secure
  - Cylinders separated and marked by type of gas
  - Cylinders protected from heat
  - Suitable trucks, carts used to move cylinders
  - Regulators, hoses, fittings — condition

- Separate plumbing for oxygen cylinders
- Oxygen cylinders separated from POL products
- Chemicals
    - Hazard communications procedures
    - Storage, separation, security
    - Personnel awareness (Material Safety Data Sheets)
    - Reactive chemicals separated
    - Deluge shower and eyewash fountains available
    - Ventilation of storage area
    - Control of smoking
- Radioactive materials identification
- Control of hazardous waste
    - Procedures
    - Equipment
    - Disposal

SUMMARY

Aircraft maintenance is an important part of an aviation safety program. The Director of Safety should make every effort to include it in the overall aviation safety program.

DISCUSSION QUESTIONS

1. It has been stated that any aircraft maintenance operation should have two safety programs. Why? What are their different areas of responsibility?

2. Some of the pilots in your organization have complained that some of their safety-related aircraft write-ups were not properly corrected. How are you going to handle this situation?

CHAPTER 23

FLIGHT LINE SAFETY

In aviation, we separate accidents into "flight" and "ground." Those occurring in flight are well reported and investigated. Those occurring on the ground are seldom reported outside of the company unless they involve serious injury or death. They may or may not be investigated.

Regardless, they represent a serious problem to the aviation industry. Estimates of the costs of aviation ground accidents run from several million to well over a billion dollars per year. Worse, they are almost chronic. While flight accidents are fairly rare events, ground accidents are not. They occur daily and they represent a substantial cost to any aircraft operator. Flight line safety is an effort to control these costs by reducing both accidents and injuries that occur during aircraft ground operations.

As discussed in Chapter 4 under scope of the safety program, flight line safety (or ground safety) may or may not be part of the program. It is the author's opinion that it should be. This chapter is included to support that opinion.

THE PROBLEM

An aircraft flight line is a high risk area. The flight line is full of high energy sources that can produce disaster if uncontrolled. Some of these energy sources include propellers, tail rotors, jet blast, fuels, oxygen, chemicals, electricity, high pressure air, and pressurized containers.

If airplanes were designed to be worked on safely, they probably would not include things like sharp static discharge wicks, blade antennas, pitot tubes, and propellers. They would come equipped with hand rails and non-skid surfaces on the wings and a fuselage high enough to walk under without bumping your head. They would be nice to work on, but no one would care because they would never fly.

All things considered, the potential for accidents and injuries in the flight line environment is very high and reducing that potential requires the efforts of everyone out there.

THE CAUSES

Based on a lot of accumulated experience with both industrial safety and aviation safety, we can make some general statements about the causes of flight line accidents.

1. **THE MAIN PROBLEM IS NOT WITH THE EQUIPMENT; IT'S THE WAY WE USE THE EQUIPMENT.** In other words, this is mainly a "people" problem, not a "thing" problem. Granted, the propeller of an airplane is inherently hazardous, but we know that and we can't do much about it. We can, however, avoid becoming personally involved with it.

2. **THE FLIGHT LINE IS A DYNAMIC ENVIRONMENT WHERE MANY THINGS ARE IN CONSTANT MOTION.** Aircraft are moving. Vehicles and equipment are moving. People are moving. Unlike the industrial environment where the machinery doesn't move much, the place on the flight line where it was safe to walk five minutes ago has suddenly become a very bad place to be.

3. **FLIGHT LINE OPERATIONS ARE AFFECTED BY THE WEATHER.** Most of what we do to an airplane takes place outdoors. This means that we do it in heat, cold, rain, snow, ice, and wind; not to mention darkness. This not only increases the difficulty of the task, but it increases our exposure to injury.

4. **SAFETY TRAINING AND EXPOSURE TO HAZARDS ARE NOT ALWAYS RELATED.** There is sometimes, in fact, an inverse relationship between training given and training needed. We tend to provide the best training to the people most technically qualified to work on the airplanes. They, after all, are our most valued employees. Unfortunately, the people most often exposed to the hazards and in a position to create the most damage tend to be the least technically qualified and (sometimes) the least trained. They drive the trucks, park the planes, service them and handle the baggage. They are on the front end of this problem and it is their activities that give us the most trouble.

5. **ALL FLIGHT LINE ACCIDENTS INVOLVE HUMAN FACTORS.** These can cover the entire range of human factors including stress, distraction, pressure (time or peer), haste, physical condition, complacency, ignorance, and fatigue.

THE SOLUTIONS

1. **THE LAYOUT OF THE FLIGHT LINE MUST BE DESIGNED WITH SAFETY IN MIND.** Our basic scheme for painting lines on the pavement should aid us in separating incompatible vehicles, equipment and aircraft.

2. **WE NEED A PLAN FOR CONTROLLING THE MOVEMENT OF BOTH AIRCRAFT AND VEHICLES**. Our plan must reduce movement hazards as much as possible and still allow us to get the job done.

3. **PERSONNEL WHO WORK IN THE FLIGHT LINE ENVIRONMENT MUST BE FULLY TRAINED IN BOTH THEIR JOB AND IN THE SAFETY PRECAUTIONS NECESSARY FOR THEIR JOB**. There is no job on the flight line that does not require some level of safety training.

4. **OUR FIRE PREVENTION PROGRAM SHOULD BE AIMED AT REDUCING FIRE HAZARDS**. There is more to fire prevention than just having a fire department and an alarm system.

5. **ALL PERSONNEL ON THE FLIGHT LINE SHOULD HAVE A BASIC UNDERSTANDING OF PERSONAL SAFETY PRACTICES AND THE USE OF PROTECTIVE EQUIPMENT**. Noise, for example, is both ubiquitous and non-discriminatory. None of us are immune to its effects.

FLIGHT LINE VEHICLE OPERATIONS

In any aircraft flight line operation, we need vehicles. The bigger the flight line and the bigger the aircraft, the more vehicles we need. We can't do the job without them.

Unfortunately, aircraft and vehicles are a poor mix. They can get in each other's way and do enormous damage to each other if they collide. In one classic case, a lavatory servicing vehicle was being backed toward a jet aircraft. For some reason, the accelerator stuck and the vehicle hit the aircraft and penetrated about a foot into the fuselage. The total tab was $375,000 for damage to the aircraft; $474,000 for lease of a replacement aircraft while repairs were made; and $1,300,000 for loss of revenue until a leased aircraft could be obtained and permanent loss of value to the damaged aircraft. Grand total: $2,149,000. The risk of something like that happening is always present on any flight line.

The basic problem is that the flight line is designed for aircraft; not vehicles. Most of the signs and markings are for the airplanes. The needs of the vehicle are given, at best, a low priority and on some flight lines, none at all. If there is no organized control of the vehicle traffic, a large flight line is a confusing place to drive regardless of driver qualifications. Let's bring some order to this confusion and discuss some proven methods of vehicle control.

GENERAL PROCEDURES

The general approach to flight line vehicle safety involves five steps.

1. **VEHICLE CONTROL PLAN.** This plan is usually developed by the airport authority and applies to all flight line areas and all vehicles operated on them. All airport tenants are expected to know and follow this plan.

2. **VEHICLE OPERATING STANDARDS.** These are the basic ground rules for how vehicles will be operated on that airport. They are normally developed by the airport authority, perhaps with the advice and assistance of the major tenants.

3. **VEHICLE LIMITATIONS.** A basic rule is to limit the number of vehicles on the flight line to the minimum number needed to do the job. Each vehicle has to be justified. All vehicles should be company-owned; no privately owned vehicles.

4. **VEHICLE OPERATOR TRAINING.** Another basic rule is that drivers must have some sort of training before they are allowed to operate vehicles on the flight line. This program may be administered by the airport authority or by the major tenants using airport authority guidelines.

5. **ENFORCEMENT.** Obviously, none of this will work unless the tenants and the drivers comply with the plan and the standards.

VEHICLE CONTROL PLAN

The vehicle control plan establishes vehicle flow, designates areas where vehicles are or are not permitted, and specifies pavement markings and control devices for vehicles.

1. **VEHICLE FLOW.** Ideally, the majority of vehicles are kept to the perimeter of the aircraft parking area. This is done through a system of marked roadways. Most maintenance vehicles, supervisory vehicles and personnel vehicles can be confined to these roadways. If this is done, then the only points of conflict are where the roadways cross a taxiway.

   Some vehicles, such as catering trucks or fuel trucks, must be permitted to operate outside of these roadways in the vicinity of the aircraft. This should be kept to a minimum and they should use the roadways most of the time.

   Some emergency vehicles must also be permitted to operate outside the roadways if an emergency is in progress. If so, they should be equipped with distinctive flashing lights to use during an emergency.

Vehicles permitted to operate outside of the roadways on the taxiway and runway complex should be radio-equipped, have a flashing light and have a specific reason to be there.

No vehicles, except possibly fire trucks responding to an emergency, should be permitted to operate off the paved surfaces. This will reduce foreign object damage (FOD) problems.

2. **MARKINGS**. It is always best to mark roadways using the same markings the drivers have become familiar with in that community. This includes lane edges, lane dividers, turn arrows, stop lines and so on. This is really a problem in traffic engineering and a large airport should have one available for consultation. Like all other pavement markings, these need to be repainted occasionally and this should be part of the regular airfield maintenance program.

3. **CONTROL DEVICES**. Vehicles can be controlled by the same signs and traffic lights used in the community. If lights are used, they are usually controlled from the control tower or from the ground movement control tower if there is one. One possible problem is that signs and lights must either be far enough from the aircraft movement area or close enough to the ground so that they are not obstructions to taxiing aircraft.

Other methods involve radios and control tower light gun signals. The use of radios for control should be limited to emergency vehicles and vehicles requiring access to the taxiways and runways. Light gun signals are not particularly reliable as the vehicle driver is seldom looking directly at the control tower. Vehicles subject to control by light signals should have a decal on their dashboard listing the signals and their meaning.

STANDARDS

The Vehicle Control Plan should establish the general standards for all vehicles. The following are suggested standards.

1. **SPEED LIMITS**. On designated vehicle roadways, the speed limit should be appropriate for the conditions. The posted speed limits could vary depending on proximity to the aircraft movement area.

- Aircraft parking area. Normally 15 mph and 5 mph within 25 feet of an aircraft.

- Vehicle parking area. 5 mph.

- Taxiways and Runways. As appropriate for conditions.

- Congested areas. 15 mph.

- Towing speeds:
  - Aircraft – 5 mph
  - Equipment – Single-towed – 10 mph
  - Equipment – Multiple-towed – 5 mph
  - Baggage trains – Normally 10 mph
  - Ground power equipment – 15 mph

To provide a frame of reference, 5 mph is equivalent to a brisk walk.

2. **PROXIMITY TO AIRCRAFT.** Some special purpose vehicles are specifically designed to operate close to, against, or under aircraft. Other vehicles should adhere to these safety standards.

- Do not operate the vehicle closer than 25 feet to any part of the aircraft.

- Do not approach the aircraft from such an angle so that if the brakes failed or the accelerator stuck, the vehicle would hit the aircraft.

- Do not permit vehicles to park in such a manner that the emergency movement of the aircraft would be impeded.

- Do not operate a vehicle closer than 200 feet behind a turbine-powered aircraft with the engines running.

3. **VEHICLE MARKINGS.** In addition to their identification, vehicles should be marked with reflective tape so they can be seen at night with their lights out. It is generally desirable to limit flashing or rotating lights to emergency vehicles as flashing lights are both blinding and confusing to pilots.

   All vehicles should be identified by company logo and, if possible, a number readable through binoculars from the control tower or an observation point.

4. **VEHICLE PARKING.** Vehicles should be parked only in designated areas with the engine off and the brakes set. Vehicles parked temporarily in close proximity to an aircraft should have the brakes set, the engine off and the key in the ignition. This would permit rapid movement of the vehicle in an emergency. If the vehicle must be parked so that it could roll into an aircraft (catering trucks, for example), the vehicle should be chocked.

5. **VEHICLE PASSENGERS**. Passengers should only be permitted to ride on vehicles equipped with seats specifically designed for passengers. Passengers should not ride on any part of the vehicle not intended for passengers.

6. **MOTORCYCLES AND BICYCLES**. These vehicles should follow the same general rules as other vehicles. They should be equipped with lights, brakes and reflective tape markings.

7. **RIGHT OF WAY**. Regardless of the vehicle control plan, an aircraft taxiing, or under tow has the right of way over any vehicle.

VEHICLE LIMITATIONS

The airport authority should exercise control over how many vehicles operate on the flight line and who owns them. Tenants wishing to use a vehicle on the flight line should file an application stating the identification of the vehicle, its purpose and the justification for permitting it on the flight line. If approved, the vehicle should be issued a numbered decal which not only identifies the vehicle but aids in security access control. The vehicle owner should be advised of any special marking requirements, such as reflectorized tape, at this time.

VEHICLE OPERATOR TRAINING

Airport tenants apply for training and certification of the drivers they need to operate on the flight line. Application should include verification of driver's license and review of driving record. A sample lesson plan for flight line driver training is shown here.

1. **TRAINING LESSON PLAN** (Sample).

- Airport Vehicle Flow Plan

- Authorized Driving Routes

- Areas not Authorized for Vehicles

- Vehicle Control
  - Pavement Markings
  - Control Signs and Lights
  - Radios
  - Control Tower Light Signals

- Vehicle Operating Standards
  - Speed Limits
  - Right of Way of Aircraft
  - Operating in Proximity to Aircraft
- Vehicle Parking
- Passengers
- Towing Operations
- Actions if an Accident Occurs
- Local Hazards
- Local Driving Regulations
- Examination

2. **LICENSE**. The license to operate a vehicle on the flight line should be a controlled document. One way to do this is to annotate the employee's security access credentials with information on driving privileges.

3. **REVIEW**. As a general rule, review or recertification should not be necessary as long as the employee maintains a state driving license and has a good flight line driving record.

ENFORCEMENT

The principal enforcement of flight line driving standards must be through the supervision provided by the individual tenants. They, after all, have a high stake in the safety of flight line operations. If one tenant is consistently violating the standards, the quality of that supervision must be questioned.

Beyond that, it is not realistic to expect airport security police to run traffic patrols of the flight line. They have other things to do. Since the flight line and the vehicle roadways are not public roads, it is usually possible to assign enforcement responsibility to the airport manager and the airport staff. They can be authorized to identify violators and issue citations. Acceptance of this arrangement should be part of the tenant's application to drive out there in the first place.

Some major airports have established a schedule of fines for driving violations which is almost beyond the financial capability of the individual driver. This, in effect, charges the tenant for the driver's violations. This puts the supervisory and enforcement burden where it belongs.

The ultimate penalty, of course, is revocation of flight line driving privileges. In some cases, that would cost the employee a job and in the extreme case would put the tenant or the contractor out of business.

Control of vehicle traffic on the flight line is an administrative procedure belonging to the airport authority; not a criminal procedure belonging to the local police or court system. Because of this, there are some powerful incentives available to the airport authority that should ensure compliance with vehicle operating standards.

AIRCRAFT TAXIING, TOWING AND PARKING

This is a general discussion of basic taxiing, towing, and parking safety procedures. Where there is a conflict with the aircraft manufacturer's taxiing or towing instructions, the manufacturer's instructions should prevail.

Good taxiing and towing safety practices start with the layout of the flight line and the manner in which the lines are painted. Ideally, aircraft of the same general size are always parked in exactly the same position on the flight line or at the gate. Taxi lines should keep taxiing aircraft on exactly the same route. Clearance lines at the wingtips mark areas where parked vehicles and equipment are not allowed.

If the flight line is laid out in this manner, then it should only be necessary to ensure that no equipment or vehicles are within the clearance lines and the aircraft is on the taxi line. If this is done, it is difficult to see how an accident could ever occur.

They do occur, of course. Other aircraft, vehicles and equipment are not always parked where they should be. When we push back an aircraft, we don't always push it back on the taxi line. Considering the size of the aircraft involved, darkness, weather and time pressure, it is easy to overlook some simple parking or towing preparation procedure that leads to an accident. The safety practices suggested in this chapter were all born of accident experience.

PERSONNEL QUALIFIED TO TAXI

Pilots are obviously qualified to taxi aircraft although some them have been known to taxi a wee bit fast. Almost all aircraft flight manuals specify a maximum speed of 5 mph or less in congested areas. That's brisk walking speed.

In some organizations, maintenance personnel are allowed to taxi aircraft. There is nothing wrong with this providing they have received the same training and use the same checklists that the pilots use. If the airplane requires two people to fly it, then it also requires two people to taxi it. If one of the two people is a qualified pilot, then the other can be a person who is not taxi qualified.

COMMUNICATIONS. As a rule, aircraft do not move on the airport complex without radio contact with and permission of the control tower. Even in situations where radio contact is not required, the radio should be in use as it is the fastest method of obtaining emergency response in the event of an accident. Thus the people taxiing the aircraft must also know how to use the radios.

ENGINE POWER. All taxiing should be done with full consideration of what is behind the aircraft. Engine power used should be the absolute minimum necessary to move the plane.

WING WALKERS. If the taxi path is obstructed (vehicles or equipment within the clearance lines) wing walkers should be used. They should also be used anytime the aircraft is to be taxied within 25 feet of an obstruction. An exception to this is when the aircraft is on the taxi line and there are no obstructions within the clearance lines even though they may be closer than 25 feet to the wingtips. If the obstruction is within 10 feet of the wingtip, wing walkers should always be used.

MARSHALLING SIGNALS. Final parking of the aircraft is usually done with marshalling signals. It is important that everyone use the internationally accepted marshalling signals.

PREPARATION FOR TAXIING

Windows and windshields should be clean and doors and hatches should be closed. Aircraft navigation lights and rotating beacons should be on. Strobe lights and landing lights should be off. Taxi lights may be used if installed.

AIRCRAFT TOWING

QUALIFIED PERSONNEL. The safe towing of a large aircraft in a congested area may require as many as six people.

TOWING SUPERVISOR. The towing supervisor is in complete command of the operation. The supervisor has a checklist covering all towing procedures and is in a position, usually at the nose, to see the towing team members at the wingtips and tail and signal directly to the tow vehicle operator. If possible, the supervisor is in direct radio or interphone contact with the tow vehicle operator and the brakeman in the cockpit.

TOW VEHICLE OPERATOR. The tow vehicle operator is qualified to operate that vehicle. The operator is in direct interphone contact with the brakeman in the cockpit and can see the signals of the towing supervisor.

WING AND TAIL WALKERS. These individuals are positioned at the wingtips and tail and are responsible for the vertical and horizontal clearance of the wings and tail from any obstruction. Ideally, they are in radio contact with the towing supervisor. Clearances may be very critical when hangaring an aircraft and the towing operation should be stopped when there is any doubt.

BRAKEMAN IN COCKPIT. A person should be in the pilot's seat with the seat properly adjusted to reach the brake pedals. The brakeman should be in direct interphone contact with the tow vehicle operator and should be able to see the signals of the towing supervisor. The brakeman should know how to maintain hydraulic brake pressure and should notify the tow vehicle operator if hydraulic pressure drops below safe operating limits. If the aircraft has a steerable nose gear, the brakeman should be cautioned not to use it while under tow. Finally, the brakeman should know how to use the aircraft parking brake and the emergency braking system if one is installed.

PERSONNEL NEEDED. Obviously, the number of tow team personnel actually needed depends on the aircraft and the route. Wing walkers are not needed if there are no obstructions within 25 feet of the aircraft. There will be cases where only one wing walker is needed as only one wing is vulnerable to obstructions. Except for hangaring, the tail walker is only needed if the plane is being moved backwards. In the case of small general aviation aircraft, a brakeman in the cockpit is probably not necessary as the tow vehicle can stop the aircraft. These are all decisions to be made by the towing supervisor. If some members of the team are temporarily not needed, they should not ride on any part of the aircraft or on the tow vehicle unless seats are provided for that purpose.

CHOCKS. The tow team should always have a set of chocks available. The chocks should be the correct size for the aircraft and should be used on the main landing gear.

RADIO CONTACT. If the tow is to use the taxiways, radio contact with the control tower will be necessary. Ideally, the towing supervisor should have the contact. If this is not practical, the brakeman in the cockpit should maintain contact using the aircraft radios.

TOWING SPEEDS. Five mph maximum.

TOWING SIGNALS. Ideally, all tow team members should be in radio or interphone contact, particularly when towing a large aircraft. Visual signals have not proved to be entirely effective. The problem is that a large plane has a certain amount of inertia and it cannot be stopped in an instant. When a wing walker realizes that clearance is in doubt, the wingtip is already within a few feet of the obstruction. By the time the wing walker's signal gets to the towing supervisor and is relayed to the tow vehicle operator and the brakeman, the accident has already occurred. If visual signals must be used, the standard luminous or fluorescent wands are probably best. In some non-noisy environments, whistles or horns powered by air pressure have been used successfully.

TOWING PREPARATION. Consult aircraft handbooks for specific instructions. In general, aircraft navigation lights and rotating beacons should be on and all doors and hatches should be closed. On some aircraft, the nose wheel steering system should be disconnected for towing.

PARKING. Specific aircraft parking procedures should be covered in the aircraft handbook. The following procedures are generally applicable, although not to all aircraft.

CHOCKS. Installed fore and aft on both main gear. Leave a small amount of space between the chock and the tire to permit the aircraft to settle during refueling without binding the chocks.

AIRCRAFT BRAKES. Released.

TIE-DOWNS AND MOORING LINES. If the aircraft has tie-down points, the tail and both wings should be tied down using standard mooring procedures.

TAIL STANDS. If the aircraft has a tail stand to keep it from tipping backwards onto its tail, it should be installed.

WING SPOILERS. This applies primarily to general aviation aircraft. If high winds are anticipated, spoilers should be installed on the top surface of the wings just behind the leading edges.

GROUNDING WIRE. Although not required in all cases, the aircraft should be grounded if there is a grounding point available.

DOORS AND HATCHES. Closed.

INTAKE COVERS AND PITOT COVERS. Installed.

LANDING GEAR SAFETY PINS. Installed if available.

REMOVE BEFORE FLIGHT STREAMERS. If wing spoilers, intake covers, landing gear pins or pitot covers are installed, they should be clearly marked REMOVE BEFORE FLIGHT with streamers or some other warning device.

SUMMARY

As mentioned in the introduction to this chapter, a well organized flight line with properly painted taxi lines, clearance lines and vehicle road-ways can solve a lot of flight line problems. If everything is where it is supposed to be, the chances of an accident are significantly reduced.

DISCUSSION QUESTIONS

1. Ground vehicles, when used around aircraft, are a common source of hazards on the flight line. How can the potential for accidents involving ground vehicles be reduced?

2. Imagine that you as the Director of Safety for an airline observe the driver of a contract fuel truck driving at excessive speed on the flight line. How do you handle this situation?

CHAPTER 24

AIRPORTS AND HELIPORTS

There are three situations that commonly occur in aviation safety that involve airports or heliports.

1. You are a tenant on someone else's airport. The management structure of the airport depends on whether it is a Part 139 (Title 14 CFR Part 139) airport serving air carriers. Most airports are not, but the larger ones should still have about the same management structure as a Part 139 airport. There is (or there should be) an airport safety committee. If there is, you, the aviation safety manager for your organization, are the logical member. In this case, you need to be familiar with the airport certification manual and emergency plan. As a tenant, you are in a position to recommend or influence change.

2. It's your airport (or heliport). All of its safety problems are your safety problems. Here, the airport operations manual is prepared by your organization and you are very interested in its contents. Furthermore, your organization is responsible for regular inspections of the airport and knowledge of airfield criteria is essential.

3. You use a lot of different airports (or heliports) belonging to other agencies. Part of your aviation safety program is a regular survey of these facilities so that you can warn your flight crews of hazards and, in the extreme case, decide whether you want to continue using those facilities. Among major airlines, this is usually a two step process. Prior to using an airport (and regularly thereafter) a team including someone from the aviation safety department examines the airport and documents its hazards. On a regular basis, flight crews using the airport are asked to fill out checklists designed to update current airport information and identify new hazards. This process can work quite well. It extends the reach of the aviation safety department and secures flight crew participation in the program.

In any case, the aviation safety manager tends to learn a lot about airports and heliports, regardless of who actually owns them. What follows are some basic ideas about how to approach common airport and heliport safety problems.

AIRPORT CERTIFICATION MANUAL

If the airport is located in the United States and serves air carriers, it must have an Airport Operating Certificate granted under Part 139 and it must maintain an Airport Certification Manual. Even if the airport is not a Part 139 airport, it should still have an airport operations manual. Although a manual is not technically required in this case, it is difficult to imagine how a busy airport can be safely operated without one. Understanding how the airport operates starts with understanding the manual. Listed below (paraphrased) are the general manual contents derived from FAR Part 139.

AIRPORT CERTIFICATION MANUAL CONTENTS

1. Airport operational responsibility.

2. Current exemptions to FAR Part 139.

3. Limitations imposed by FAA Administrator.

4. Airport grid map.

5. System of runway and taxiway identification.

6. Location of lighted or marked obstructions.

7. Description of aircraft movement areas.

8. Procedures for:

   • Interruption during construction work.

   • Maintenance of paved and unpaved areas.

   • Maintenance of safety areas.

   • Maintenance of marking and lighting systems.

   • Maintenance of traffic and wind indicators.

   • Complying with hazardous materials requirements.

   • Conducting a self-inspection program.

   • Controlling ground vehicles.

   • Protection of NAVAIDS.

   • Airport condition reporting.

   • Identifying, marking, and reporting unserviceable areas.

9.   Rescue and fire fighting equipment and procedures.

10.   Snow and ice control plan.

11.   Public protection.

12.   Wildlife hazard management plan.

13.   Airport Emergency Plan (see below).

AIRPORT EMERGENCY PLAN

The Airport Emergency Plan is part of the Airport Certification Manual although the plan is sometimes published and distributed separately. Each tenant or regular user of the airport should have a copy of the Airport Emergency Plan incorporated into its own pre-accident plan. Here, paraphrased, are the general contents of an Airport Emergency Plan as listed in FAR Part 139.

AIRPORT EMERGENCY PLAN CONTENTS

1.   Instructions for response to:

  • Aircraft incidents and accidents.

  • Bomb incidents.

  • Structural fires.

  • Natural disasters.

  • Radiological incidents.

  • Sabotage and hijack incidents.

  • Power failure in movement area.

  • Water rescue situations.

2.   Available medical and rescue services including:

  • Ambulances and other transportation.

  • Hospitals and medical facilities.

  • Rescue squads.

  • Available surface vehicles and aircraft.

  • Hangars or buildings for injured or deceased.

3.   Crowd control.

4.   Removal of disabled aircraft.

5.   Alarm systems.

6. Coordination of airport and control tower functions.

7. Notification procedures.

8. Rescue from significant bodies of water.

9. Coordination with law enforcement, fire, and medical organizations.

10. Participation in plan development and review.

11. Training of airport personnel having emergency duties.

12. Review of plan every 12 months.

13. Full scale emergency plan exercise every 3 years.

14. Inclusion of appropriate FAA Advisory Circulars.

AIRPORT/HELIPORT CRITERIA

The rules and regulations on what standards the airport or heliport meet can be found in several places. The easiest to understand are found in ICAO publications and airport service manuals. If you operate internationally, it is worthwhile maintaining a set of these.

The ICAO manuals, of course, are not the definitive standards for any one country. In the United States, you would need to consult the Federal Aviation Regulations and the numerous Advisory Circulars in the 150 series dealing with airports and heliports. In the United States military, the Department of Defense has published airfield criteria used by all services. The differences between the DOD criteria and the FAR criteria are minor.

The problem is that few if any airports meet all aspects of the applicable criteria. Some airports were built before we had criteria and long before we had large jet aircraft. Some airports have been encroached on by civilization and they have no room for unrestricted approach paths and the like. Almost all airports operate under several deviations or exemptions of criteria. Some of the problems can be corrected, but some of them will never be corrected.

From an aviation safety point of view, we need to know what those deviations are. We should be pushing for the correction of those that can be corrected and we should be adjusting our flying operations to cope with those that can't be corrected.

Airport criteria is generally found under two major headings; airfield criteria and airspace criteria.

AIRFIELD CRITERIA

This refers to things that obstruct aircraft operations on the ground. Here is where you find information such as the minimum distance from a runway, taxiway, or parking ramp to an obstruction. You should also find a list of obstructions that we tolerate because we need them. These include radar reflectors, glide slope and localizer antennas, ceiling and visibility measuring equipment and so on. Even though these are "approved" obstructions, there are still rules on how they are to be constructed and cited to represent the least possible hazard to an aircraft.

AIRSPACE CRITERIA

This refers to things that obstruct airplanes or helicopters in flight. Here you will find information on clearance planes and height criteria that will allow you to determine whether something is an obstruction or not. That tree off the end of the runway keeps growing. When do we require it to be trimmed?

INSPECTIONS

Someone has to inspect the airport helipad at least once every day, and more often during severe weather or when something unusual has occurred. Things change. Lights fail. Parts fall off vehicles and airplanes. Airport maintenance is a full time job and it starts with a program of regular inspection to determine the need for maintenance.

Airfield inspections are part of the job of whichever line manager runs the airport. It is not an aviation safety job. The aviation safety manager should be interested in how the inspections are done and how well they are done, but the safety manager should not take on the burden of doing it. It is a line manager responsibility.

Ideally, the airport should be inspected by someone who is experienced in airport management. As a practical matter, the inspections can be done by anyone who can follow an inspection checklist and has been trained on inspection procedures. In some cases, the inspections are done very well by fire department or security personnel.

FOREIGN OBJECT (FOD) CONTROL

Foreign objects are a never-ending problem on airports and heliports. Some FOD is generated by the aircraft and by maintenance activities, but some is generated by the airport itself. Sealant between the cracks in the pavement deteriorates over time and this becomes FOD. In some cases, the pavement starts to deteriorate, possibly due to cold weather damage, and it creates FOD. Snowplows knock over taxiway lights which are now FOD.

High winds blow debris onto the airport from other locations. Jet blast sprays rocks from unpaved areas. There must be a method of identifying these problems and responding to them before they start damaging aircraft.

BIRD HAZARDS

Many airports have bird hazards. In some cases, the runways and taxiways are attractive to birds as they retain heat. In other cases, the airport is poorly located with respect to something the birds really like; a garbage dump or feeding area, for example. The problem is not completely hopeless. There are a lot of methods available for making the airport area unattractive to birds and some of them are very effective. In some cases, regular bird patrols and warnings to pilots are the best solutions. Additional information is available in the 150 series FAA Advisory Circulars.

SNOW AND ICE REMOVAL

While the snow and ice control plan is part of the Airport Certification Manual, it is sometimes published and distributed as a separate document. In general a good plan prioritizes the airport areas for snow removal; establishes timely commencement of removal operations; notifies tenants and air carriers of removal operations and specifies where snow is to be piled or dumped.

AIRPORT MAINTENANCE AND CONSTRUCTION

It is safe to say that at any given time, any airport has one or more ongoing maintenance or construction projects. In almost all cases, we attempt to continue flying operations in spite of the construction. We rarely close the airport.

The problem is that the people doing the work don't necessarily appreciate the hazard they may be creating to the aircraft. The contractor digging a new light vault near the runway may not know how far his dirt pile and equipment should be kept from the runway when he quits for the night. He may not appreciate that his normal method of marking an obstruction may be a hazard all by itself. Will the wing of your plane fit over a 55 gallon drum with a blinking light on it? Furthermore, the contractor has to get his equipment back and forth across the taxiway. This can make a mess of the taxiway with dirt and rocks. Keeping it clean has to be part of the contract.

Aviation safety managers can appreciate this very well. If possible, someone from the safety department should participate in the development of the project before the contract is even awarded. After it is awarded, someone has to examine it daily to make sure that nothing has happened that is hazardous to the aircraft.

FUEL HANDLING

There are some excellent publications on how to handle fuel safely in an airport environment. Most bulk fuel suppliers have this information available. One of the best sources is the FAA Advisory Circular on fuel handling and dispensing on an airport. This reflects National Fire Protection Association standards. Basically, your two concerns are contamination and safety.

CONTAMINATION

Fuel should be checked for quality at least twice. You should never permit fuel to be pumped into your bulk storage facility unless it is the correct type of fuel and free of contaminants. Next, you should check the fuel for quality on a daily basis as it comes from the truck; but before it goes into the aircraft. These tests are reasonably simple and are covered in the referenced Advisory Circular.

SAFETY

The tendency of a fuel to ignite is related to its flash point. Flash point is the minimum temperature at which the fuel will vaporize to form an ignitable mixture above the surface of the fuel. Avgas has a low flash point and is fairly volatile. JP-4, which has been widely used in military jets, also has a low flash point and is difficult to handle safely. At this writing, the United States Air Force has converted from JP-4 to JP-8, a much safer fuel to handle. Jet A, the commercial jet fuel, has characteristics comparable to JP-8 and is fairly safe to handle. This gives us problems as we have a tendency to mishandle it and take unnecessary risks.

As an example, static electricity is a common source of ignition in a fuel handling accident. We cannot stop static electricity from being created. The act of moving fuel through a hose creates it. The electrical potential created is somewhat related to temperature and humidity. The cold dry air of Alaska breeds a lot of static electricity, while it is not much of a problem in the damp heat of Florida. To do it right, we should ground both the fuel truck and the aircraft and we should bond them together. Finally, we should have good metal-to-metal contact (or a bonding device) between the nozzle and the tank filler neck. We are still going to create static electricity, but with everything at the same electrical potential, there should be no ignition.

If we are handling Jet A, we know from experience that we can skip some of these procedures and get away with it because of the high flash point of the fuel. This is an unnecessary risk, though, and one in which the penalty far outweighs the convenience. Our procedures for handling fuel should be the same ones we would use all the time any place in the world.

HELIPORTS

Because of the unique capabilities of the helicopter, the whole question of adequacy of heliports or helipads is one of controversy. There are plenty of standards available on what the minimum criteria for a helipad should be. The problem is that the helicopter in the hands of a good pilot is capable of operating from a pad that doesn't meet the standard criteria in any parameter.

Consider hospital EMS operations. Most hospitals were not built with a helipad in mind and many of the existing hospital helipads are, to put it kindly, at variance with the recommended criteria. Helicopter contractors, though, have a tendency to accept these pads because they want the contract. In the long run, this is not good business. It really goes back to some ideas mentioned in Chapter 21. The customer furnished landing area has to meet our standards. If it doesn't, we should not risk putting a helicopter worth several million dollars into it. The rebuttal to this argument is that we will lose the contract if we don't accept the helipad "as is." Perhaps. On the other hand, our insistence on adherence to our minimum helipad standards should be part of our total "safety" package. We are offering the hospital a safe operation because we have high standards and we are not going to bend them. If that is not satisfactory, maybe we are better off without that contract. We can't let the customer determine our level of safety.

AIRPORT AND HELIPORT SAFETY INSPECTIONS

The development of an inspection checklist for an airport or heliport is the same as described in Chapter 14. Listed here are three sets of guides for subjects that might be examined. The first could be used by the aviation safety manager to construct an overall airport inspection checklist. The second is an adjunct to this guide, but deals strictly with the way fuel is stored, handled and dispensed. This is provided as a separate guide because some organizations store and handle fuel; but do not have responsibility for the airport itself. The third guide could be used to develop a program where any pilot transiting the airport conducts a mini-inspection and notes current deficiencies and hazards. As stated earlier, this is a useful method of extending the reach of the aviation safety manager and obtaining pilot participation in the aviation safety program.

AIRPORT AND HELIPORT SAFETY INSPECTION SUBJECTS

1. AIRPORT MANAGEMENT AND SAFETY PROGRAM
   - Management organization
   - Staffing
   - Adequacy
   - Designated safety officer
   - Airport safety committee
     - Tenant participation
     - Effectiveness

2. AIRPORT CERTIFICATION MANUAL
   - Airport certification
   - Operating procedures
   - Responsibilities
   - Limitations
   - Obstructions
   - Maintenance
   - Lighting systems
   - Snow and ice control plan
   - ARFF Equipment and procedures
   - Hazardous materials plan
   - Traffic and wind direction indicators
   - Emergency plan
   - Self-inspection program
   - Control of ground vehicles
   - Obstruction marking
   - Navaid protection
   - Public protection
   - Wildlife hazard management
   - Airfield condition reporting

3. AIRFIELD INSPECTION AND FIELD CONDITION REPORTING
   - Inspection frequency
   - Qualifications

- Checklists
- Follow-up action
- Friction measurement method
- Condition determination
- Dissemination of information

4. AIRFIELD MAINTENANCE
   - Organization
   - Equipment
   - Responsiveness

5. PAVED AREAS
   - Condition
   - Rubber deposits on runway
   - Weed and vegetation control
   - FOD control
   - Painting/marking
   - Shoulder and overrun condition
   - Bird control
   - Directional signs
   - Drainage
   - Edges and drop offs

6. AIRFIELD/AIRSPACE CRITERIA
   - Runway/taxiway/ramp obstructions
   - Grading, gradients
   - Sight distance, runway humps
   - Condition of non-paved areas
   - Safety areas
   - Size (helipads)
   - Approach/departure obstructions
   - Landing area obstructions
   - Airport equipment (markers, antennas, VASI, etc.)
     - Citing
     - Frangible construction where appropriate
   - Waivers and exemptions to criteria

7. AIRFIELD EQUIPMENT
    - Lighting systems
        - Approach
        - Runway
        - Taxiway
        - Parking ramp
        - Lighting controls
    - Wind indicators
    - Traffic direction indicators
    - Directional signs
    - Distance markers
    - NAVAIDS
    - Landing aids
    - Emergency power supply
        - Coverage
        - Testing

8. AIRCRAFT PARKING AREA
    - Condition
    - Painting and marking
        - Lead-in lines
        - Stop marks
    - Tie-downs and chocks
    - Grounding points
    - Condition of fuel pits and covers
    - Condition of power receptacles
    - Ground support equipment parking
    - Control of vehicles
    - FOD control
    - Fire extinguishers
    - Fire department notification system

9. AIRFIELD EMERGENCY PLAN
    - Response
    - Aircraft accidents and incidents

- Bomb threats
- Structural fires
- Natural disasters
- Sabotage/hijacking
- Power failure
- Medical assistance
- Transportation
- Equipment
- Facilities
- Crowd control
- Removal of disabled aircraft
- Mutual support agreements
- Plan review (12 months)
- Airport emergency exercise (3 years)

10. AIRFIELD RESCUE AND FIRE FIGHTING
    - Airport category
    - Equipment required
    - Equipment available
    - ARFF rating
    - Fire department organization
    - Manning
    - Facilities
    - Condition of equipment
    - Training
    - Agents and supplies
    - Alarm system
    - Response times
    - Knowledge of hazardous materials on airport
    - Exercises

11. AIR TRAFFIC CONTROL FACILITIES
    - Control tower
    - Tracon

- Flight Service Station
- Weather support

12. PASSENGER HANDLING

- Equipment (boarding stairs, jetways)
- Control
- Emplaning/deplaning procedures

13. SECURITY

- Airport
  - Condition of fence
  - Control of access points
  - Fuel bulk storage security
- Security personnel organization/availability
- Aircraft security
- Cargo/baggage area security

FUEL STORAGE And SAFETY INSPECTION SUBJECTS

1. GENERAL

- Types of fuels used
- Major supplier
- Bulk delivery method
  - Truck
  - Tank car
  - Pipeline
- Transfer system
- Truck
  - Bottom fill
  - Top fill
- Hydrant
- Fuel pit/fill stand
- Fuel quality control
  - From supplier
  - To aircraft

- Contaminants
  - Solids
  - Water
  - Surfactants
  - Micro-organisms
  - Misc. contaminants
- Fuel identification
- Filtration
- Testing records
  - Training of fueling personnel
  - Contents
  - Frequency
  - Records
- Fueling safety program
- Procedures to prevent mis-fueling aircraft
- Procedures for segregation of contaminated fuel
- Written procedures for normal fueling
- Written procedures for defueling
- Fuel Spills
  - Procedures
  - Equipment
  - Disposal

2. BULK STORAGE
   - Fenced
   - Marked with warning signs
   - Fire extinguishers
   - Fire plan
   - Notification of fire department
   - General housekeeping
   - Safe distance from other structures
   - Emergency system shutoff
   - Grounding of fueling vehicles
   - Restriction of non-fueling vehicles

- Control of ignition sources
- Drop spout reaches bottom of tank
- Underground leak detection system
- Fuel spill containment

3. FUEL TRUCKS

- Loading
- Written procedures
- Top fill
  - Drop spout to bottom of tank
  - Deadman control
- Bottom fill
  - Loading hoses marked/coded
  - Coupler secure
  - Self-sealing truck valve
  - Deadman control
- Truck Markings
  - Type of fuel
  - Hazardous cargo markings
  - No smoking
- Two fire extinguishers on truck — 20-BC Rating
- Bonding and grounding wire connectors
- Emergency shutoff system
- Air filter and spark arrestor
- Fuel filter and filter separator
- Nozzle bonding device
- Nozzle dust cap
- Deadman control on nozzle
- Hose condition

4. FUELING OPERATIONS

- Fueling procedures/checklist
- Control of smoking
- Truck properly positioned
- Grounding points available

- Truck grounded

- Aircraft grounded

- Truck and aircraft bonded

- Nozzle bonded to receptacle

- Deadman control

- No other maintenance operations during fueling

- Fire extinguishers

AIRPORT AND HELIPORT SAFETY SUBJECTS FOR PILOTS

1. GENERAL

   - Current NOTAMs

   - Accuracy of airport documents

     - Approach plates

     - Departure plates

     - Airfield diagrams

     - Airport directory

     - Gate parking layout

2. CONDITION OF AIRPORT FACILITIES

   - Runways

   - Taxiways

   - Ramp

   - Approach/departure obstructions

   - NAVAIDS

   - Wind indicators

   - Runway/taxiway paint condition

   - Runway/taxiway identification

   - FOD control

   - Wildlife control

   - Airfield construction

3. AIR TRAFFIC CONTROL FACILITIES

   - Tracon

   - Control tower

- Flight service station
- National weather service

4. RAMP/GATE OPERATIONS
   - Lead-in lines
   - Stop marks
   - Marshalling
   - Gate numbers visible
   - Parking system
   - Ramp surface
   - Positioning of ground equipment
   - Communications with ramp personnel
   - Pushback/powerback procedures
   - Fueling procedures
   - Deicing procedures

5. DISPATCH/FLIGHT PLANNING AREA
   - Weather information
   - NOTAMs
   - Communications facilities
   - Planning facilities
   - Planning documents
   - Lounge

6. SECURITY
   - Aircraft security
   - Identification of personnel
   - Screening of passengers
   - Screening of baggage
   - Screening of cargo

7. LOADING OF AIRCRAFT
   - Passengers
   - Cargo

8. DEPARTURE

    • Communications with ramp personnel

    • Push back/power back procedures

    • Marshalling

    • Tower/ATC procedures

    • Noise abatement restrictions

9. OTHER SAFETY ITEMS NOT OTHERWISE COVERED

SUMMARY

Airports and heliports demand constant attention and the criteria can get a little complicated. Fortunately, there is plenty of reference material available. In addition to the references listed in the bibliography, the Federal Aviation Administration has other airport information including a video tape on airport self-inspection.

CHAPTER 25

ENVIRONMENTAL SAFETY

Airports, flight lines, and aircraft maintenance activities generate a certain amount of industrial waste. Some of this waste is classified as "hazardous." Almost all of it is hazardous to the environment in some way.

In the United States, the Environmental Protection Agency has considerable authority over how hazardous wastes will be managed. Many countries of the world are adopting similar guidelines and more countries will do so in the future. Aside from the potential hazards to the population, the safety of our planet is at stake.

Environmental safety may or may not be part of the overall safety program. This is only an introduction to the problem. For specific guidelines, consult the Bibliography.

TERMINOLOGY

Resource Conservation and Recovery Act (RCRA). This is the basic law enacted by the United States Congress. It directed the Environmental Protection Agency (EPA) to develop a program for protection of human health and the environment from improper management of hazardous wastes.

Hazardous Wastes. These are any solid, liquid, or contained gaseous material that is no longer needed or used and could cause injury or death or damage or pollution to land, air or water. There are two types of hazardous wastes; listed and characteristic.

- Listed Wastes. Any of the over 400 wastes listed in the RCRA Regulations.

- Characteristic Wastes. An unlisted waste which has any of the following characteristics:

- Ignitable. Examples are paint wastes and some degreasers and solvents.

- Corrosive. Examples are rust removers and alkaline cleaning fluids.

- Reactive. These are any unstable chemicals which react violently with water or other materials. Examples are cyanide plating wastes, bleaches, and waste oxidizers.

- Toxic. Chemicals that contain high concentrations of heavy metals (mercury, cadmium or lead) or specific pesticides.

TYPES OF HAZARDOUS WASTES FOUND IN AVIATION OPERATIONS

1. **CYANIDES**. Source: metal plating, steel hardening, rust prevention and stain removal operations.

2. **CHROMIUM COMPOUNDS AND TOXIC METALS**. Source: plating, stripping, and anodizing operations.

3. **ACIDS AND ALKALIES**. Source: pickling, cleaning, and washing operations.

4. **ORGANIC SOLVENTS AND PHENOLS**. Source: painting, cleaning, and washing operations.

5. **FUELS, OILS, GREASES AND DETERGENTS**. Source: spills, system leaks, washing of aircraft and vehicles.

6. **DEICING CHEMICALS**. Primarily glycol.

7. **AIRCRAFT BATTERIES**. Spent lead-acid, lithium, and nickel-cadmium batteries are considered hazardous waste.

MANAGEMENT OF HAZARDOUS WASTES

1. **SURVEY**. The first step is to conduct a hazardous waste survey of the airport, flight line, hangars and maintenance shops. The survey should include flow measurements, sampling, analysis, and calculation of the amount of waste generated by type.

2. **CONTROLS**. Listed below in order of desirability are methods of dealing with hazardous wastes.

- Reduction. The most desirable way of managing hazardous waste is to produce less of it, either by using less of the chemical involved or by substituting a non-hazardous chemical.

- Recovery and Reuse. Much of the waste generated by aircraft cleaning and washing operations can be recovered and reused.

- Recycling. Most petroleum products and glycol can be recycled into usable products. This is usually less expensive than treatment or disposal.

- Treatment. This is the process of chemically treating or neutralizing a waste so that it is no longer hazardous and it can be disposed of in ordinary sewage systems.

- Disposal. This is the last choice. It involves packaging the waste and transporting it to an authorized hazardous waste disposal site.

TRAINING

In the United States, regulations require that generators of hazardous waste establish personnel training programs designed to reduce the potential for errors that might threaten human health or the environment. The program must include training to ensure compliance with all applicable regulations. See Title 40 CFR Section 262.34.

In addition, hazardous waste generators are required to maintain preparedness and prevention programs (40 CFR ß 265) and contingency plans and emergency procedures (Subpart D of 40 CFR Section 265).

SUMMARY

Environmental safety is a subject that will always be with us. In the United States, the regulations are very specific and the penalties for noncompliance are severe. There is a strong incentive to reduce hazardous waste generation, as the status of a waste generator is determined by the amount of waste generated per month. Achieving "Exempt" status or even "Small Quantity Generator" status is highly desirable.

SUMMARY

Here's what we've done.

We've covered some basic philosophy and theory about aviation safety and briefly discussed some human factors aspects.

We've discussed how to organize and build an aviation safety program, and covered the elements that commonly make up an aviation safety program.

You now have:

• Program development worksheet (Chapter 20.)

• Sample aviation safety program (Chapter 20.)

• Flight operations safety inspection subjects (Chapter 14.)

• Aircraft maintenance safety inspection subjects (Chapter 22.)

• Airport and heliport safety inspection subjects (Chapter 24.)

• Fuel storage and handling safety inspection subjects (Chapter 24.)

• Pre-accident planning guide (Chapter 17.)

• Environmental guidelines (Chapter 25.)

• Suggested additional reading (Bibliography.)

Think about this. You are in an industry that has a remarkable safety record developed through the efforts of a lot of dedicated people. There is no lack of interest in aviation safety or lack of enthusiasm for it. Maintaining the record takes constant effort. Improving it will take even more effort, but there is no one in aviation who thinks the record is as good as it can be. There is plenty to be done. Good luck!

RHW

BIBLIOGRAPHY

This bibliography lists references consulted during the writing of this book and additional sources of information potentially useful to an aviation safety manager. It is by no means exhaustive. Safety information is found in more places than can be listed here.

Because the computer and access to the Internet is rapidly becoming the premier research tool, availability of data on CD-ROM and aviation safety Internet Web Sites are listed where known. These are no doubt already out of date, but they are a starting point.

We start with basic information on the Federal Aviation Administration, National Transportation Safety Board, National Technical Information Service and the International Civil Aviation Organization. The remainder of the bibliography is organized by major topic and generally follows the Chapter titles of the book.

FEDERAL AVIATION ADMINISTRATION

Federal Aviation Administration
800 Independence Avenue, S.W.
Washington, DC 20591

The FAA is responsible for Federal Aviation Regulations, Advisory Circulars, and numerous manuals and pamphlets. Publications can be ordered directly from the FAA and many are free. One easy and fairly inexpensive way to maintain and update a complete set of FAA publications is to purchase them on CD-ROM. One source is:

Summit Aviation
Computerized Aviation Reference Library
PO Box 759
Golden, CO 80402
(1-800-328-6280)

The FAA also has an Internet Web Site, www.faa.gov. Specific FAA publications are referenced throughout this bibliography.

NATIONAL TRANSPORTATION SAFETY BOARD

National Transportation Safety Board

490 L'Enfant Plaza East, S.W.

Washington, DC 20594

The NTSB is responsible for regulations dealing with reporting and investigation of aircraft accidents and incidents. They publish accident reports and special studies. All of their publications are available through the National Technical Information Services (NTIS). Regulations pertinent to aviation are also on the CD-ROM from Summit Aviation listed above. The NTSB Web Site is www.ntsb.gov.

NATIONAL TECHNICAL INFORMATION SERVICE

National Technical Information Service

Technology Administration

U. S. Department of Commerce

Springfield, VA 22161

(703-487-4650)

NTIS is the resource for government-sponsored and worldwide scientific, technical, engineering, and business-related information. They index nearly three million documents. The NTIS Web Site is www.ntis.gov.

INTERNATIONAL CIVIL AVIATION ORGANIZATION

International Civil Aviation Organization

999 University Street

Montreal, Quebec

Canada H3C 5H7

ICAO was organized independently of (and slightly before) the United Nations, but now operates in harmony with the UN. It offers several publications relevant to aviation safety which are listed in this bibliography under the appropriate heading. The ICAO Web Site is www.cam.org/~icao.

SAFETY MANAGEMENT

- *Accident Prevention Manual.* ICAO. (Doc 9422-AN/923) Montreal, Canada. 1984. Although somewhat out of date, this is still an excellent source of ideas on aircraft accident prevention,

- _Accident Prevention Manual for Business and Industry._ 10th Ed., 2 vols.Chicago, Illinois: National Safety Council. 1992. This is the basic reference for industrial safety in the United States. It is not specific to aviation.

- Allison, William W. _Profitable Risk Control._ Des Plaines, Illinois: American Society of Safety Engineers. 1988.

- Hammer, Willie. _Occupational Safety Management and Engineering._ Englewood Cliffs, New Jersey: Prentice Hall, Inc. 1976.

- Heinrich, H. W., D. Petersen, and N. Roos. _Industrial Accident Prevention._ New York: McGraw-Hill Book Company. 1980. This is the 5th edition of Heinrich's book originally published in 1931. Heinrich is considered a pioneer in the safety field and many of his ideas are still valid today. Dan Petersen and Nestor Roos have revised and updated the original text.

- Lowrance, William W. _Of Acceptable Risk._ Los Altos, California: William Kaufmann, Inc. 1976.

- Petersen, Dan. _Safety Management. 2nd Ed._ Goshen, New York: Aloray, Inc. 1988.

- Peterson, Dan. _Techniques of Safety Management._ 2nd Ed. New York: McGraw-Hill Book Company. 1978

- ISO 9000 and ISO 14000. Information on these standards is available from American National Standards Institute, 11 W. 42nd St., New York, NY 10036. (212-642-4900.)

HUMAN FACTORS

- _Aeronautical Decision Making._ The FAA has published a series of manuals on this subject as described in FAA Advisory Circulars 60-21 and 60-22. The manuals are available through NTIS.

- Alkov, Robert A. _Aviation Safety—The Human Factor._ Casper, Wyoming: Endeavor Books. 1996.

- Green, R. C., H. Muir, M. James, D. Gradwell and R. L. Green. _Human Factors for Pilots._ Brookfield, Vermont: Ashgate. 1991.

- Hawkins, Frank H. _Human Factors in Flight. 2 Ed._ Edited by H. W. Orlady. Brookfield, Vermont: Ashgate. 1993.

- *Human Behavior: The No. 1 Cause of Accidents.* FAA Pamphlet P-8740-38. 1982. This pamphlet quotes the study by Shaw and Sichel on accident risks mentioned in Chapter 7.

- *Human Factors Guide for Aviation Maintenance.* 1996. This is an extensive collection of studies and research developed by the FAA Office of Aviation Medicine. It is available on CD-ROM from Galaxy Scientific Corporation (770-491-1100) and in hard copy from the U. S. Government Printing Office (202-512-1800.) Stock Number for the hard copy is 050-007-01098-2. The CD-ROM version contains video clips and includes summaries of meeting proceedings on the subject.

- Maslow, A. H. *Motivation and Personality.* New York: Harper. 1954.

- Poliafico, Frank J. *Emergency First Care.* Upper Saddle River, New Jersey: Prentice-Hall. 1996. This is an excellent text for people involved in setting up emergency first aid and CPR programs.

REPORTING

National Transportation Safety Board, *Notification and Reporting of Aircraft Accidents or Incidents and Overdue Aircraft, and Preservation of Aircraft Wreckage, Mail, Cargo, and Records* (49 CFR 830. Washington, DC. 1996. These regulations are also available on CD-ROM from Summit Aviation *Computerized Aviation Reference Library.* (1-800-328-6280.)

- *Aviation Safety Reporting System.* Federal Aviation Administration Advisory Circular 00-46C. Also on CD-ROM as listed above.

- *Callback* is a free monthly safety bulletin from The Office of the NASA Aviation Safety Reporting System, P.O. Box 189, Moffett Field, CA 94035-0189.

AIRCRAFT ACCIDENT INVESTIGATION

- *Aircraft Accident and Incident Investigation.* 8th Ed. Annex 13 to the Convention on International Civil Aviation. Montreal: ICAO. 1994. This contains the rules for the conduct of international investigations.

- *Manual of Aircraft Accident Investigation.* 4th Ed. Doc 6920-AN/855/4. Montreal: ICAO. Amended to 1986. This has not been technically revised in over 20 years, but it is still an excellent reference.

- National Transportation Safety Board Regulations, 49 CFR 800 et seq. Washington, DC: Government Printing Office. 1996. The regulations pertinent to aircraft are on the Summit Aviation CD-ROM referenced above.

- Wood, Richard H. and Robert W. Sweginnis. *Aircraft Accident Investigation*. Casper, Wyoming: Endeavor Books. 1996.

ANALYSIS

- Roland. H.E. and B. Moriarty. *System Safety Engineering and Management*. New York: John Wiley and Sons. 1983.

- United States Congress, Office of Technology Assessment. *Safe Skies for Tomorrow; Aviation Safety in a Competitive Environment*. (OTA-SET-381.) Washington, DC: Government Printing Office. 1988.

- Vincoli, Jeffrey W. *Basic Guide to System Safety*. New York: Van Nostrand Reinhold. 1993.

AIRPORTS

- *Aviation Ground Operation; Safety Handbook*. 4th Ed. Chicago, Illinois: National Safety Council. 1988. This is a fairly broad overview of safety in aircraft ground operations including terminals, flight lines, hangars and maintenance facilities.

- Federal Aviation Administration. *Back to Basics; Airport Self-Inspection*. Video Tape. Order FAA Film Catalog from Public Inquiry Center, APA-230, Federal Aviation Administration, Washington, DC 20591. See also Advisory Circular 150/5200-18B, *Airport Safety Self-Inspection*.

- Federal Aviation Administration. Numerous FARs and Advisory Circulars in the 150 series deal with airports. FAR Part 139 is particularly important.

- International Civil Aviation Organization publishes Annex 14 (Aerodromes) to the Civil Aviation Convention along with an Airport Services Manual (Parts 1-9) and an Aerodrome Design Manual (Parts 1-5.) Contact ICAO at the address listed above for their catalog.

- National Fire Protection Association. NFPA establishes the National Fire and Electrical Codes and publishes many other useful documents. The codes in the 400 series are applicable to airport operations. Contact NFPA for a catalog.

National Fire Protection Association
11 Tracy Drive
Avon, MA 02322-9908
(1-800-344-3555)

HAZARDOUS MATERIALS AND ENVIRONMENTAL PROTECTION

The training requirements and procedures for hazardous materials in aircraft are found in:

- Department of Transportation Regulations 49 CFR Parts 171-175.
- Annex 18 to the Convention on Civil Aviation (ICAO)
- FAA Advisory Circular 121-21B.

There are numerous Environmental Protection Agency (EPA) publications dealing with hazardous waste. FAA Advisory Circular 150/5320-15 is titled, *Management of Airport Industrial Waste*.

ASSOCIATIONS

Anyone involved professionally in aviation safety should consider individual or corporate membership in these organizations.

AMERICAN SOCIETY OF SAFETY ENGINEERS (ASSE).

This is the key safety society in the United States. It has around 40,000 members and chapters in most major cities. It publishes a monthly journal, *Professional Safety*. While the articles seldom deal directly with aviation safety, many of them have direct application to aviation. ASSE is also an excellent resource for technical publications in the safety field.

American Society of Safety Engineers
1800 E. Oakton St.
Des Plaines, Illinois 60018-2187

FLIGHT SAFETY FOUNDATION (FSF). Flight Safety

Foundation is a non-profit organization supported by its membership. It holds seminars throughout the world and specializes in publications of current aviation safety interest.

Flight Safety Foundation
601 Madison St., Suite 300
Alexandria, VA 22314

INTERNATIONAL SOCIETY OF AIR SAFETY INVESTIGATORS (ISASI). This society is the only one in the world that deals specifically with aircraft accidents. It has about 1500 members internationally and publishes a quarterly journal, *Forum*. It hosts an annual seminar devoted to subjects of interest to aircraft accident investigators.

International Society of Air Safety Investigators
Technology Trading Park
Five Export Drive
Sterling VA 22170-4421

INTERNET ADDRESSES

As already mentioned, listing Internet Addresses in a book is a little risky. These, however, seem fairly stable. All use the http:// protocol.

1. The Air Safety Home Page. <airsafe.com>. This is managed by a professional aviation safety analyst and deals primarily with airline accidents organized by date or type of aircraft.

2. Aviation Safety Reporting System (ASRS). <www.afo.arc.nasa..gov/ASRS/ASRS.html>.

3. Aviation Week Group. <www.awgnet.com>. This is a very useful site for research. Their _Safety Oasis_ section contains links to a number of other data bases.

4. Canadian Transportation Safety Board (CTSB). <bst-tsb.gc.ca>.

5. Federal Aviation Administration (FAA). <www.faa.gov>.

6. Flight Safety Foundation. <rhytech.com1~fsf>.

7. International Civil Aviation Organization (ICAO). <www.cam.org/~icao>.

8. Investigation Research Roundtable. <www.mnsinc.com/benner/index.html>.

9. National Technical Information Service. <www.ntis.gov>.

10. National Transportation Safety Board (NTSB). <www.ntsb.gov>.

11. Southern California Safety Institute (SCSI). <www.scsi-int.com>. The leader in aviation safety training and host of the International Aircraft Cabin Safety Symposium.

12. U. S. Government Library. <www.fedworld.gov>. Indexes publications from other government agencies.

INDEX

INDEX

I